D1368809

# GONE ARE THE DAYS

PATRICIA SLOANE
FOR ST LOUIS.

AN ILLUSTRATED HISTORY OF THE OLD SOUTH

# GONE ARE THE DAYS

HARNETT T. KANE

BONANZA BOOKS
New York

This 1989 edition is published by Bonanza Books,
distributed by Crown Publishers, Inc.,
225 Park Avenue South, New York, New York 10003,
by arrangement with E.P. Dutton,
a division of NAL Penguin, Inc.

Printed and Bound in the United States of America

Library of Congress Cataloging-in-Publication Data

Kane, Harnett Thomas, 1910-
Gone are the days: an illustrated history of the Old South / Harnett T. Kane.
p. cm.
Reprint. Originally published: New York: Dutton, 1960.
Includes index.
ISBN 0-517-03885-4
1. Southern States—History—Colonial period, ca. 1600-1775.
2. Southern States—History—1775-1865. I. Title.
F209.K3 1989
975'.02—dc19 89-948
CIP

h g f e d c b

# CONTENTS

# INTRODUCTION

THE SOUTH was the first America, older than any of the other areas that would make up the United States, predating Puritan New England or Dutch New York or the Pennsylvania of the Quakers. It was the meeting place of three great cultures—Anglo-Saxon, Spanish, and French; and several of their clashes within its borders shaped the course of New World development.

For generations this South had a major role in determining the direction of American life. Washington, Jefferson, and other early national leaders were men whose careers the new United States shared as a heritage. But from its start the South possessed a character, a setting, and an outlook that set it apart from the rest of the country.

Here was an opulent land, with towering forests and ripe vegetation that approached the tropical. Much of it had a climate of burning sun and violent rain that nurtured a great potential agricultural wealth, with a crop season that lasted through eight or nine months of the year.

The locale fostered a somnolent mood. Under warm skies, across a fragrant, humid earth, men moved slowly, riding casually and living most of their days in the open—in the afternoon shadow when possible, on a wide porch by preference. From its beginning to its end, the Old South had largely a rural cast.

It was never a single, unchanging area, but a collection of contrasting subregions: the Atlantic coastal colonies of Tidewater Virginia and Maryland and North Carolina; the warmer (and warmer-tempered) Carolina of Charleston and the Low Country; the rolling Piedmont and the back country toward the original West; then Kentucky and Tennessee, and the drowsing Gulf South in a crescent curve beginning with the sandy edges of Florida and extending to the no less sandy borders of Mexico. There were also the wide alluvial spread of the Mississippi, from New Orleans to the southern stretches of Missouri and beyond that belt other areas, extending to Arkansas and down to the world of Texas, parts of which had the look and manner of the South. And always, too, the mountains, the Alleghenies, the Smokies, the Ozarks, with a people left behind by shifting population, to carry on a half-submerged existence among the coves and high valleys.

Endless green plains, the rolling Bluegrass Country of Kentucky, the clay hills of Georgia and Mississippi, dreaming Louisiana bayous, high river bluffs at Natchez and Vicksburg . . . the Old South encompassed them all.

In Florida and Texas, Spanish elements contributed to the richness of the region, and in the Mississippi Valley the French left tangible evidences of their presence in style and spirit. But in general the South received much the same settlers, in much the same classes, as did other parts of the future United States:

Englishmen and Irish, Scots and Welshmen, Germans and Swiss and North Europeans. The "cavalier" myth, which claimed that Southerners were of a different and more gentlemanly breed than other newcomers, has died a hard death.

At an early date, however, the South obtained the major element that, with its climate and its rural expanses, set it apart from the rest of the nation—its slave population, seized across the sea and transported by force. In every development that followed, the Negro would be there, unheard from, perhaps hardly seen. Nevertheless he would influence the white man in a hundred ways.

By then the South had produced the first of the great staple crops that would enrich it, and in yet another fashion cast a shadow over its future. Tobacco, then rice and cotton and sugar, were to bring multiplying wealth but also a swarm of assorted problems. Land was available at fairly cheap rates, and the pressures increased for the lowest-paid labor, that of the slave. Black men and big crops . . . the design was fixed, dominating all economics, all attitudes, all thought. And the land was so exuberant in its production that growers wasted it, depleting thousands of acres, leaving gullied wastes as they moved on to fresh areas in the distance.

To be sure, the Old South had more small farmers than great ones—men of meager holdings or a middle class of yeomen who worked their properties with their families, perhaps a slave or two; who lived in simple houses at a riverside or in the uplands. But the plantation with its increasingly large-scaled residence—eventually a pillared white one—came to rule the scene. While the South witnessed repeated clashes between privileged planter and lesser resident, it was the former who fixed the direction of affairs.

On his estate the Southerner carried on a life largely isolated from town or country, acquiring an assurance, a sense of command, and an individuality that might range from the sturdy in character to the blithely eccentric. Although he had a heavy responsibility, he also possessed an unlimited power. He worked hard, yet he also exercised many of the prerogatives of a feudal lord.

For such plantation people, a bountiful land fostered a bountiful manner of existence: a wide-handed welcome to friend, genial hospitality for strangers, hours of casual enjoyment. Some have argued that this capacity to appreciate leisure might be counted among the Old South's major accomplishments. With it went a related ability, the art of good talk.

This was a conservative regime that resisted change, and stressed continuity, tradition, the established way. The matter of family appeared more important than in most other areas of America, with Southerners ready to trace a connection at a moment's notice, down to a remote cousin many miles away. And the Southern civilization had a sense of "place," of warm association with a land, a valley, a county.

The Old South was full of paradoxes: the most relaxed, the most easygoing part of America, and at the same time the touchiest, the most sensitive. With a somewhat marked emphasis on outward elegance, it had an underlying robustness, a lusty vigor; during most of its existence the Old South remained close to a shifting frontier. In spite of the feeling of family and kinship, many times its leadership came from individuals who rose from lesser rank. Although outwardly more "aristocratic" than most other parts of America, its social system was open to entry from below.

The South produced many of the best known of America's aristocrats, such as the Randolphs, the Lees, and the Carrolls, and it also gave the country the most rampant of democrats, Andrew Jackson. And with Thomas Jefferson the region contributed the man whose words of freedom would sound around the world.

With the passing of the first decades of the 1800's, the Old South became more and more convinced that it occupied a unique niche in the country, with special requirements, and it claimed clear assurances that it would be allowed to maintain its position. At the same time it watched the North enlarge in prosperity and influence. The South's rural basis, its background of great crops and slavery, discouraged voluntary workers from other countries; they went instead to the North. For much the same reasons, new industry and manufacturing did not enter the region. Improved roads, canals and railroads . . . each crisscrossed the other area, and slowly the South fell behind.

To a large degree, nevertheless, Southerners trained in political affairs still dominated American public life, in Congress and in the courts. But the slavery issue asserted itself with increasing fervor, and one region faced the other in a complex of tightening emotions. Thus the stage was prepared for a conflict either unnecessary or unavoidable, according to the view of the individual observer.

On the outcome of the terrible hostilities the Old South staked its future. Perhaps inevitably, it lost, and the trend of the American experiment was settled for generations to follow. For the South there remained old hurts and new dilemmas, hard and gnawing ones, with years of dissension, decades of adjustment.

Yet there continue survivals that are inheritances of the earlier day: an ability to savor an hour of pleasant relaxation, a feeling of undiminished identification with the land, an affection for a slumbrous locale with a haze of warm, dim beauty over a valley or a distant plain; the enjoyment of casual and easy fellowship, happy conversation. . . . In a swiftly changing world might these not be values worth cherishing?

HARNETT T. KANE

Florida and Cuba Were There, Approximately.

"Terra florida" made up most of the South, with an inflated Cuba nearby and "India" and "Cathay" not so far away, in this map in Münster's edition of Ptolemy, 1540. The New World outlines are surprisingly good.

# 1

# THE CLANK OF ARMOR, THE SCREAMS OF VICTIMS

"Drive them out by whatever means you see fit."
—KING PHILIP II of Spain.

IT WAS in the South that the story of the United States had its beginning, and it was not an Anglo-Saxon one. Many decades before the first Englishmen put foot on Southern soil, Spain's powerful, high-decked galleons rode the waters to and from the shores of the Gulf of Mexico and the South Atlantic. For a long time it appeared that this South, perhaps all of North America, would have a Latin rather than a North European cast. Only accidents of fortune at several points prevented Spanish settlements at, say, the site of Charleston or Williamsburg, or French ones at Annapolis and Savannah, and, eventually, Richmond and Washington.

Well in advance of Columbus, ancient maps indicate that unknown voyagers had set down the rough shape of the Atlantic coast; but Europeans approached the New World by slow degrees. Men had speculated repeatedly over shorter ways to reach the splendors of the Orient. Scholars insisted that, the world being round rather than flat, a vessel could find the fabled East by sailing steadily westward. And one by one explorers sailed forth despite frightening tales of seas that would boil and smoke beneath them and snake-like monsters that would coil out of the ocean.

Touching the New World, Columbus seemingly believed to his death that he had arrived close to India itself. After him, voyagers who held much the same opinion turned the West Indies into swarming plantations worked by Indian and some Negro slaves.

In time the Spaniards' eyes glistened as they heard the red men's tales of shining metals and emeralds scattered over the area that was to become the American South. The Indians reported some places that could be visited only at night because their daytime dazzle would blind the newcomers.

In 1513 the first known European to explore the mainland approached what he considered a wondrous island called Bimini. Juan Ponce de León (Juan of the Lion's Paunch), who had sailed with Columbus, now reached for the prize of his

Dyſe figur anzaigt vns das volck vnd inſel die gefunden iſt durch den chriſtenlichen künig zů Portigal oder von ſeinen vnderthonen. Die leüt ſind alſo nacket hübſch. braun wolgeſtalt von leib. ir heübter. halß. arm. ſcham. füß. frawen vnd mann ain wenig mit federn bedeckt. Auch haben die mann in iren angeſichten vnd bruſt vil edel geſtain. Es hat auch nyemantz nichts ſunder ſind alle ding gemain. Vnnd die mann habendt weyber welche in gefallen. es ſey můtter. ſchweſter oder freüide. darjnn haben ſy kain vnderſchayd. Sy ſtreyten auch mit einander. Sy eſſen auch ainander ſelbs die erſchlagen werden. vnd hencken das ſelbig fleiſch in den rauch. Sy werden alt hundert vnd fünfzig iar. Vnd haben kain regiment.

career. According to one of the first North American myths, Indians had told him of a magic fountain that would restore a man to youth and virility. Research makes it evident that Juan, a vigorous fellow in his early fifties, sought far more than a trickle of water reputed to perform a service he did not need, and yet the tale will always be connected with his memory.

The season of Ponce de León's landing was Easter, the place a point between the future St. Augustine and the St. Johns River. Gazing across the pounding water and sandy coast, molded by wave and wind, the pioneers studied the grasses, thick vines, and stilt-like mangrove trees. "And . . . they named it 'La Florida' because they discovered it in the time of the Feast of Flowers." For months Ponce de León and his followers moved about the scented beaches, the twisted Florida Keys.

These Southern trail makers met successive bands of Indians, but the natives had seen them first. By word from the islands the red men had learned of the Spaniards' well-merited repute as enslavers, cripplers, and torturers. The Indians fought back, and Ponce de León left. A few years later the ambitious Spaniard returned, to find the Floridians even less friendly. Attacking fiercely, the natives sent the invaders staggering. The Spaniards retreated to Cuba, where Ponce died of his injuries.

But on came the procession of conquistadors. While most of the other large European countries were split by dissensions, Spain had established a centralized government, and she had no rival as the most swiftly advancing empire of her day. Mexico, Peru, many islands, thousands of miles of plain and coast—from everywhere poured a wealth that loaded Spanish ships with the greatest cargoes on earth. And, asked the explorers, why not a similar return from the area above the Gulf of Mexico?

To the Old World, the New meant Cannibals. A German artist of 1505 presented this version of Indian domestic life across the Atlantic, basing it on travelers' accounts. He was one of the first, if not the first, to portray the strange people of these strange lands.

She Began a Long Tradition.

The chief's daughter who pleaded with her father for the life of Juan Ortiz was to have many successors in Southern—and American—stories. The chief gave in to her, as did the other fathers who followed.

Many men tried to answer the question. In 1528 Pánfilo de Narváez sighted the Tampa Bay area, and began a saga. Marching along the coast, the party saw earth of a kind that a later Englishman called "rich as dung itself." The Spaniards, however, sought gold rather than dung. Month after month they hunted, suffered deprivations, and ultimately ate their horses to survive. They built crude rafts in which to escape, using the animals' hair for ropes, their own spurs for crude spikes. Most of the remaining group drowned in the blue-green waters; four, one a Negro slave, wandered across the South and Southwest until after eight incredible years they appeared before unbelieving fellow Spaniards in the California vicinity.

A compatriot of Narváez had a particularly bizarre adventure. The handsome young Juan Ortiz was one of those persons who lead charmed existences. Sent out to hunt the missing explorer, he was lured ashore by red men who took him to their chief, Ucita. Throwing Juan to the ground, they stripped him, pounded four posts into the earth, and tied him to them. He was to be cooked alive over a slow fire. As the low flames rose and Juan writhed, he became aware that a lovely girl, the chief's daughter, was begging for his life.

Chief Ucita relented, and Juan, his flesh seared, was taken from the rack. The Spaniard's troubles continued, for he had to serve as a menial among the hermaphrodites, half-man, half-woman creatures of the tribe. When a child died, Juan was assigned to guard the body in the night. Dozing, he woke to realize that an animal had just seized it. In desperation he tossed a spear into the dark. In the morning a wolf was found with the weapon in its throat.

This feat improved Juan's reputation. He took his place as a warrior in the tribe, learned to hunt, and to enjoy Indian foods and habits. His skin sun-bronzed and tattooed, he looked almost like one of the braves. Did he love, or at least make love to, the girl who saved him? On that interesting point the story is uncertain. . . . Again Juan Ortiz' luck left him. A rival tribe dispersed his, and the surviving members muttered that the accursed Spaniard had brought on their losses. The chief's daughter darted into his tent with the news that he was to be sacrificed the next day.

Juan fled to the other tribe, and the girl accompanied him; but, alas for romance, she went only a short distance as a guide and then disappeared from his life. The new band accepted the Spaniard with a promise that if white men appeared, he would be allowed to join them. For years Juan stayed with the Indians, until a new expedition approached—His Hispanic Majesty's most awesome expedition to the continent.

Hernando de Soto had arrived with the grand title of *Adelantado,* ruler of all Cuba and all Florida, the latter stretching far to the west and north. Six hundred foot soldiers, two hundred cavalrymen, heavy cannon, horses and hogs, thousands of pounds of clattering equipment—all this and a tale to impress the Indians, to wit, that de Soto was a god, "Child of the Sun." But the red men had met too many Spaniards, experienced too much of their cruelty. Landing near Tampa Bay, the explorers met the first of many hard rebuffs. One "Indian," however, ran gladly up to them—Juan Ortiz.

By one account, Juan blurted out a quick explanation. By another, his long years as a red man had made him forget most of his Spanish, and only with difficulty could he manage a few words. In any event, the *Adelantado* welcomed the remarkable Ortiz, and he proved a rare adviser as he donned armor to resume his life as a Spaniard. Eagerly de Soto asked: Where were the precious metals? Juan shook his head. This vicinity had none, and yet, he said, the Indians spoke of places that gleamed with rich things. (Señor Ortiz remained a Spanish gold-lover at heart.)

He helped direct the party as it moved slowly out of the present Florida, into Georgia and Alabama, the edges of South Carolina, Tennessee, far down into Alabama, up again through Mississippi. The Indians answered always in much the same fashion: No one had gold here, but farther on . . . The great party declined; in one battle two hundred and fifty men suffered injuries and in another nearly sixty of the precious horses succumbed. On an April day in 1541, after two years of struggle, de Soto beheld an Indian settlement on the east bank of the *Mechacebe*, or Great River, and he and his men became the first Europeans to set eyes on the Mississippi.

With improvised barges, the explorers made a difficult crossing. Staggering on, they continued month after month through Arkansas until, exhausted and fever-ridden, they sank to the ground. Their clothes were animal skins or the tattered remnants of original garments, and most of them looked like skeletons. After they stumbled back, they reached Louisiana and the Mississippi again, and here the *Adelantado* "fell sick and died." To hide his fate from the Indians, his aides dropped the body into the waters de Soto had discovered.

Their spirit shattered, the Spaniards tried to find their way to Mexico, moving about what is now Texas, only to be met with torch and arrow. The South had become a place of horror to the conquistadors. Riding down the Mississippi, they fought storms and treacherous currents until they reached the Gulf and, at last, Mexico. Only a fraction survived, and among the missing was Juan Ortiz. When he sought to ford a river, his Spanish armor carried him under. Had he stayed an Indian, Juan might have lived longer.

Although the expedition failed, it did learn more of the size and nature of the North American interior than any party before it. Yet another century and a half would pass before Europeans again risked the Mississippi. Spain made other attempts to find profit in the South, including an ambitious scheme that involved the South Carolina coast and the Pensacola vicinity. All collapsed, and the Spaniards turned away from the region.

For several generations France, the other major power of Europe, had speculated about the possibilities of North America. Let Spain claim title as much as it wished; the French monarchs looked on the continent as open to all nations. In 1562 the French made their first serious effort to colonize it. On a bleak winter day several vessels left Le Havre under the command of Jean Ribault, able navigator and Huguenot, or French Protestant. Most of the would-be settlers professed the same faith; in a day when religious differences racked the kingdom, they sought a new life in the New World. At the St. Johns River in Florida,

His Was a Saga. Hernando de Soto of Spain.

Below: The Start Was Magnificent. Hernando de Soto's landing at Tampa Bay had glory and glitter and massive size.

Right: The Great River, the Great Hour. De Soto and his men reached a peak of achievement when they found the Mississippi, in the heart of the present South. From then on, the way was down. . . .

Below: No One Had Seen So Much. De Soto and his dwindling forces went on and on, in an incredible, hazardous march over much of the South.

The End Was Muted. De Soto's body was lowered into the Mississippi, the stream he had discovered, as disaster closed in.

Ribault erected a stone column with the insignia of his government. Impressed by the beauties and the promise of the scene, he and his men continued on to Port Royal Sound on the South Carolina coast, where they erected a fort as the nucleus of a future France across the sea. Here Ribault left twenty-eight men, with assurance that he would be back with reinforcements.

In France again, the navigator was alarmed to discover the flames of religious war rising about him, and escaped to London. There he spoke so vigorously of the glories of the Southern coast that he gained Queen Elizabeth's interest, until political crosscurrents trapped him and sent him to the Tower of London for two years. This luckless man was to know nearly every kind of mishap.

By then the little French band at the South Carolina fort had become desperate. Rising in mutiny, rebels killed the officer left in charge and built a rickety vessel for a trip across the Atlantic. Tossed about on the water, they came close to starvation, and one of the party proposed a solution. Let them draw lots and eat the man who lost. They did, and *he* lost. His flesh kept the rest alive until a vessel picked them up.

In France, religious disputes simmered down and a new, larger Huguenot party of three hundred persons, minus the unhappy Ribault, sailed across the Atlantic. In Florida they found the tall column left by the original group. The Indians had mistaken it for a symbol of male fertility, and ornamented it for worship! Five miles inland from the mouth of the St. Johns, the Frenchmen put up a triangular fortification, partly moated, with ten-foot walls and palm-thatched huts inside and out—Fort Caroline, the only European settlement north of Mexico.

What of Spain? To her this was Spanish land, and the strangers were not only French but, what was worse, Protestants, and also intruders at a dangerous spot. Spain's gold-filled galleons followed the Gulf Stream along the Florida coast before striking out for the Azores. Adding fuel to the fire, several bands of men at Fort Caroline grew restless and engaged in piratical adventures. Spain decided to blast at this Gallic beachhead against her New World empire, and the stage was set for the first international clash for control of the continent.

The last brief peace left to Fort Caroline enriched future generations. A settler, Jacques Le Moyne de Morgues, became the first European to portray the

Opposite page: Cypress Knees, Herons, Crawling Things. To the Spanish and French, the Southeastern swamps were beautiful, and also accursed, places.

Right: The French Claim Asserted. Jean Ribault arrived quietly to stake out his nation's claim to the Southeast.

life of the original Southerners. He pictured the tattooed chief and tribesmen, Indians in the fields, on alligator hunts, scalping victims. While Le Moyne's sometimes naïve drawings gave the red men an oddly European look, they offered a provocative panorama.

Although Le Moyne worked, many of those around him did not. Rather than plant crops, they demanded food from the Indians, and eventually had to live off acorns and rattlesnakes. Famine threatened when Jack Hawkins, English slave trader and sometime corsair, put in for water. In return for guns and powder,

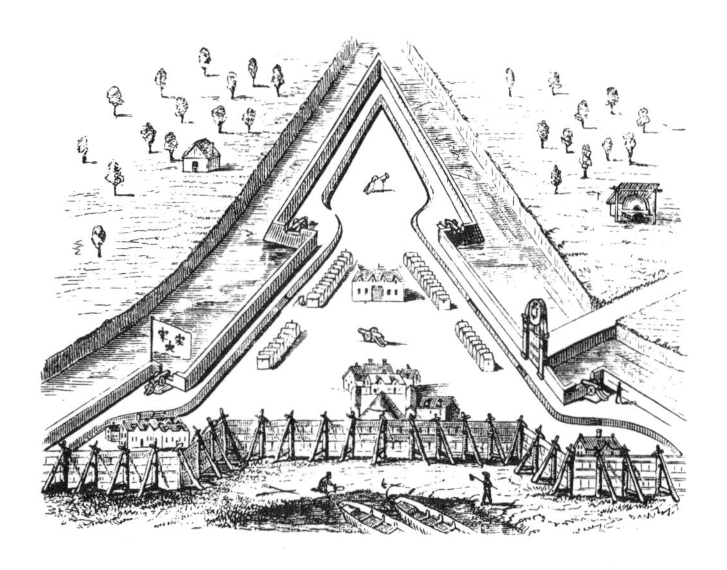

Stout Defense Against Indians—and Spaniards. Fort Caroline was France's outpost on what is today the South Carolina coast.

The Red Men Worshiped It. Returning to the Southern coast after several years, the French learned that Indians regarded this French column as a male symbol.

Hunting Alligators in Florida. The artist Le Moyne de Morgues became the first European to draw American natives from life in rich and vivid detail.

To the "Publicke Granarie." Twice annually the Indians filled canoes with produce and rowed them to large buildings. And, the Europeans found, they never cheated one another.

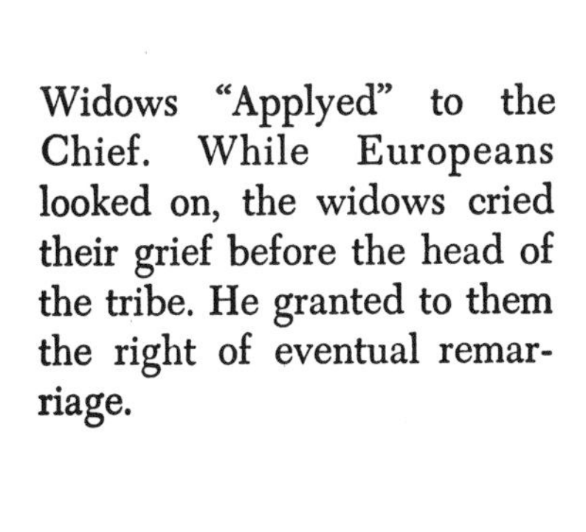

Widows "Applyed" to the Chief. While Europeans looked on, the widows cried their grief before the head of the tribe. He granted to them the right of eventual remarriage.

he gave rations to the stranded Frenchmen. Feeling pity, Hawkins then offered to take them back across the sea. After considerable thought they declined—a decision, as matters turned out, that they were to regret.

At that moment two fleets with widely varying intentions were sailing toward Fort Caroline. In the first rode Jean Ribault, doughty founder of the earlier

Pomp and Slaughter. Pedro Menéndez de Avilés ably represented his king as he rode toward the South, death in his thoughts.

French settlement, on his way to save the fort with a highly impressive collection of six hundred soldiers, workers, gentlemen of rank and their families. In the other stood Pedro Menéndez de Avilés, Spain's leading admiral—his purpose, annihilation. Menéndez' king had decided to occupy Florida after all, and if the admiral encountered colonists or "pirates" of any other nation, he was to "drive them out by whatever means you see fit."

Unaware of the forces gathering upon them, the hungry French colonists had finally made up their minds to start for home. Fashioning crude ships, they were about to depart when Jean Ribault arrived, to be greeted with surprise and relief. Overnight the situation at the fort showed a happy improvement. At the same time Admiral Menéndez plowed the waters a short way off, hunting Frenchmen. Not quite a week later, the men and women at Fort Caroline stared in another kind of surprise as five Spanish vessels bore down upon them.

Though the Spaniards were outnumbered, they had nevertheless caught the French ships' crews by surprise. Menéndez' forces tried to board the French craft, but the crews cut anchor cables and sailed off. Menéndez and his men, seeing the size of the French settlement, also rode away, thirty-five miles southward to a good harbor which they had christened St. Augustine. The French, they surmised, might soon be seeking them out, and now, in September of 1565, they went swiftly to work to fortify the point.

Ribault and his men moved much as Menéndez had expected. Worse for the Spaniards, Menéndez found his ships becalmed inside their harbor when the enemy arrived at St. Augustine, and the French had victory in their hands. What followed demonstrates the role of simple accident in men's fate. The hurricane season had come and the skies had been blackening. Suddenly a northeaster roared over the coast, driving the French far down the shore. Menéndez guessed that the winds would hold off the enemy for some time, and he guessed further that they had left their fort without strong defense. Here was his chance.

With several hundred men the Spanish admiral started on foot from St. Augustine to Fort Caroline. Heads lowered against the pounding rain, the Spaniards felt their way across sand and swamp, swam rivers, and pressed steadily onward. After nearly three days they crept toward the fort and the two hundred and forty people inside it. Because of the wind and rain French officers had permitted sentries to return to quarters. In the dawn the Spaniards slashed out in an attack that was a complete surprise. Their powder wet, they used pikes and swords, and most of the Frenchmen died in or near their beds. After a few women and children were killed, the rest were spared, as were musicians, because Menéndez liked sweet sounds, even when made by French lips and hands. A little later the determined admiral hanged certain victims and nailed a sign above them: "I do this, not as to Frenchmen, but as to Lutherans." (To Spaniards of that day all Protestants were Lutherans.)

A number of men managed to escape, and Menéndez' followers hunted them down like game, shooting them with confiscated French firearms. Among those who ran off was the artist Le Moyne. Hiding, he watched as an elderly companion, exhausted, crept to the fort, sank to his knees, and cried out in surrender. At

that the Spaniards "hacked him to bits" and held up the pieces on their spears. Along with a few others the artist reached a vessel, and escaped.

But this was only a prelude. After a short rest Menéndez and his troops headed back to St. Augustine. Where was the French fleet? The Indians brought an answer: The winds had smashed it, and nearly five hundred survivors wandered miserably along the sands, where the red men were picking them off with arrows. Going out eagerly with part of his force, Menéndez came upon a large band of bedraggled victims. Although they outnumbered the Spaniards, they were hungry, and many were sick from exposure.

Desperately, the Frenchmen begged help, offering all the money they had. Menéndez shook his head. They appealed for a vessel in which to return to France. Coldly Menéndez answered: He might give one if he had it to spare—and if they were Catholics. Now they could only surrender.

He explained further: Any Romanists among them he would befriend. Others must place themselves at his mercy and he would "act toward you as Our Lord may command me." After debate among themselves, the French gave up. Producing small vessels, Menéndez instructed them to send their pistols and swords to him in the boats, and they complied. Then twenty Spanish sailors rowed back and took ten Frenchmen into the vessel. This process continued, ten men each trip. As the successive groups touched shore, Menéndez fed them, and then explained: he had only a comparatively few followers with him, and the French must accompany him with their arms tied behind their backs. When the French agreed, they were trussed with matchcords from their own arquebuses.

The march began. Leading his prisoners around a cluster of sand dunes, Menéndez drew a line in the ground. As each file of Frenchmen reached the line, out of sight of their fellows, the Spaniards seized them by the neck or hair or shoulders and thrust swords into them. Some died quickly, the weapons in their chests or throats; with others, who struggled wildly, considerable hacking was needed. A few, who cried out that they were not Protestants, were spared.

Returning to St. Augustine, Menéndez waited for further prey, the Frenchmen still at large. Indians reappeared with tidings. Scores of other shipwrecked men were nearby, unable to escape. Hastening to them, Menéndez discovered a special prize—the commander, Jean Ribault himself. Sadly the Frenchmen inquired: Would Menéndez lend them a boat to get to their fort? The Spaniard replied that their fort had been taken and their companions wiped out. To prove what he said, Menéndez let them see the bodies on the sands.

The shocked Ribault made other pleas: their two kings were at peace; would Menéndez not allow them to make their way back to France? Those with him offered Menéndez 100,000 ducats if he let them live. To this the Spaniard made an ambiguous reply: He had real need of such a sum, and it would "grieve him" considerably not to take it, but he would not commit himself. After a night of argument among themselves, a large part of the group, about one hundred and fifty,

Opposite page: Death at Fort Caroline. In the wet and early morning the Spaniards struck out against the surprised, unorganized Huguenots.

America's Oldest Settlement. As part of their duel with the French, the Spaniards laid out and fortified their St. Augustine.

Death at Fort Caroline. Le Moyne de Morgues, who saw part of the killings, drew this re-enactment of the tragedy.

surrendered with Ribault. Once more the Spaniards sent over a boat, and once more they took over ten Frenchmen at a time. Again hands were tied and again, methodically, the men were slashed to death. Ribault himself was speared like a pig as he writhed on the ground.

In Spain, Philip II gave his approval. In the "great success that has attended your enterprise, we have had the most entire satisfaction . . . we believe you did it with every justification and propriety." In all, about three hundred had been murdered, and the king indicated that he wished the survivors to be made galley slaves. Although Spain maintained a long official silence, rumors of the bloody exercises trickled out bit by bit until the whole ghastly story was known. Weeping in outrage, Queen Catherine of France told the Spanish envoy that neither Turks nor Moors had ever practiced such cruelty. And yet no break resulted, for, as the French victims had said, the two nations were "at peace."

A few defenders of Menéndez have noted that his forces were smaller than those of the Frenchmen and that he would have had trouble in feeding his prisoners. It has been argued, too, that his behavior was not greatly at variance with the standards of his time. Above all, his approach worked; for nearly two hundred years Spain controlled the southeastern United States. More than that, by massacring the French, Spain became the potential ruler of all of North America. Had she managed her affairs in another way, the continent might still have a Hispanic flavoring.

Hands Bound, Throats Cut. Harshest of the Spanish acts were these murders of helpless men, first bound with their own ropes.

But the event would not be forgotten. A name was eventually fixed upon the point, Matanzas, meaning "Slaughter." And blood drew blood. Two years later a Frenchman set out to avenge his countrymen. Dominique de Gourgues sailed to Fort Caroline, now called San Mateo by the Spaniards, and slew all he encountered there. Remembering Menéndez, he hanged some to the same trees the Spaniard had used, with a message: "Not as to Spaniards, but as to Traitors, Robbers and Murderers."

The squalid happenings in Florida gave the South and the future United States the oldest permanent settlement within their borders. St. Augustine never became a large city; for most of its history it has had a sleepy Latin aspect—a town of galleries with wooden or ironwork ornamentation, of slow movement along narrow streets. Nevertheless it was Spain's capital of its far-spread Florida, and its chief stronghold north of Mexico. A line of military posts rose from Tampa Bay to the present Port Royal in South Carolina, while earnest priests labored to accomplish what Spain's armored men failed to do, win the Indians of the South.

Below the Gulf of Mexico the Spaniards achieved a saga unparalleled in man's experience. Within the span of a lifetime they took more land than had Rome in five hundred years, planting their name from jungle to icy mountain passes. While they dealt barbarously with civilizations such as those of the Mayans and the Incas, they nevertheless brought the printing press to the New World, created universities and cathedrals, and contributed a distinctive Hispanic culture that has never been lost.

But in the area that was to be the South, the Spaniards never sank firm roots into the waiting soil. Through their long stay the Spaniards did not realize the true wealth that lay within reach, greater than the gold and silver for which they searched: the agricultural plenty.

At St. Augustine as at other points, the Spanish arrivals remained largely soldiers at a far outpost. Twenty years after Menéndez' exploit, Sir Francis Drake made a raid on St. Augustine and burned it to the ground. In 1665 another English freebooter looted it. This time the court ordered a stronger fort, and for decades men worked to erect thirty-foot walls, twelve feet across at the base, of coquina or shellstone. Examining the costs, the king said wryly that its bastions must have been made of silver. Still, the Castillo de San Marco was an impressive example of power and grace. Several times the people fled to it, to survive while their community was razed.

Today the fort still remains, and so does something of older St. Augustine. The city gates, several times rebuilt, stand where they did when they bordered the early moat, as tall rectangles topped with Moorish designs. A part of St. Augustine lingers as the Southeast's most tangible relic of the Spaniards' bid for power. Stuccoed walls show the stains of strong sun and driving rain, and palm trees rise in half-hidden patios with the ripe flowering of hibiscus, coral vine, and bougainvillaea.

But for the most part the Spaniards came here in small numbers, leaving the wide lands nearly empty. And meanwhile, along the Southern shores above St. Augustine, the English had begun their defiance of the Spanish kings.

Above: St. Mark's of St. Augustine. Castillo de San Marcos, built at vast cost, defended Florida through the centuries. Inset: Somnolence and Balconies. Some of the streets of St. Augustine, capital of Spain in the South, long retained their air of other generations.

The Antique Gates. Like a scene in southern Europe, this entranceway to St. Augustine changed only slowly with the years.

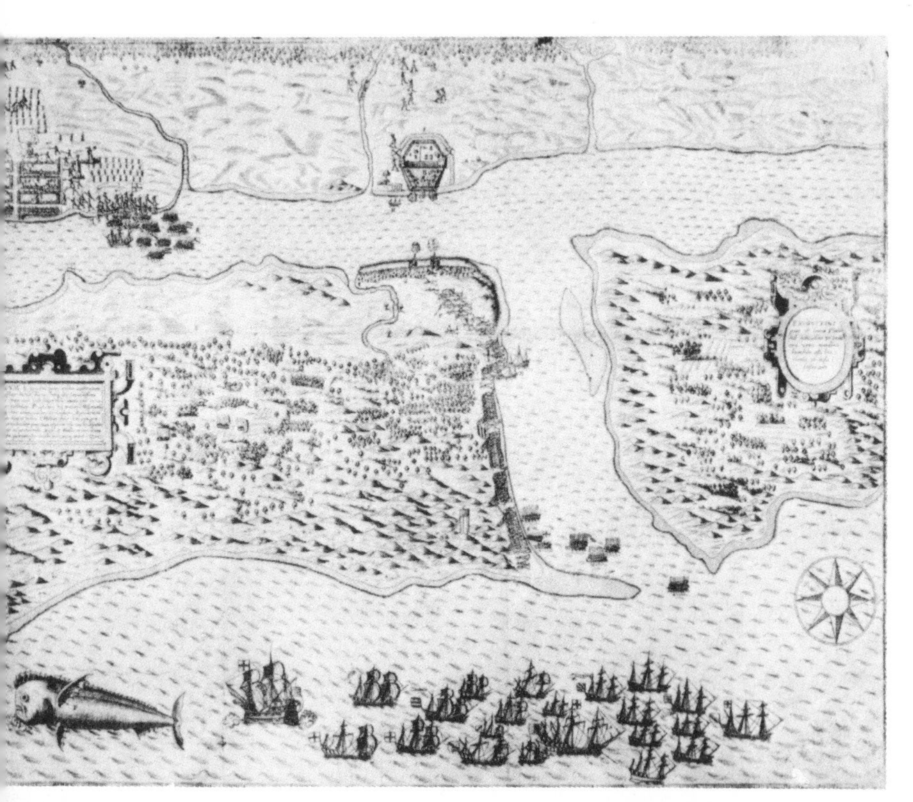

Left: Everyone Fought Over St. Augustine. A British map shows the Spanish town and environs in a battle won by the English. They burned the place, but the fort and people survived.

Above: "Rivière d'Appalachicola." A French artist was strongly impressed with the foliage, animal, and bird life of the Appalachicola.

Below: Most Southerly of All. Key West, at Florida's tip, survived many vicissitudes as a "foreign"-flavored edge of the South.

Top of page: Roanoke Landing. Despite the English efforts to show friendliness, some of the Indians were not quite impressed.

# 2
# A LITTLE GIRL NAMED VIRGINIA

"Near this place was born on the 18th of August, 1587, Virginia Dare, the first child of English parents born in America. . . ."

TODAY there stands at Roanoke Island, North Carolina, a plain stone marker honoring the site of Britain's original colony in the New World, and the first she planted anywhere on earth. Through much of their history Americans have speculated about Virginia Dare and the pathetic episode she symbolizes. It is a tale of failure and loss, perhaps of death in torment. But in failure there lay a seed of later success, the eventual achievement of Anglo-Saxon civilization in the hemisphere.

Only a few Englishmen ever saw Virginia. No one knows just how she looked or how long she lived or under what conditions. Still, she became the South's first heroine, a token of the determination of her people. Out of Roanoke Island there came the accomplishment of the generation that followed.

England was late in joining the competition for the New World. For a long time she had lived in the shadow of Spain, the great naval power of the day. She had problems enough to occupy her with nearby France and Scotland and Ireland. But under the Tudor monarchs, and Queen Elizabeth in particular, there began a new era, a Golden Age that was partly material, partly of the spirit, a time of soaring opportunity and mounting excitement for many of the British. The country had a new national consciousness, an enlarging pride. It was an age of renaissance, when a man like Walter Raleigh could be a fighter, courtier, poet, financier; a period of great naval figures such as Drake, Hawkins, Frobisher, Cavendish. With rare courage the virile "sea dogs" set out on voyages of far-ranging discovery. Sweeping down on Spanish galleons, they returned with gold and jewels hung around their throats. In the late 1500's England and her rival operated in a state that was neither peace nor war, and "singeing the Spaniard's beard" had become a happy pastime.

While Spain fumed, the time for open hostilities had not yet arrived when in 1584 the self-made Walter Raleigh took a patent from his queen and friend, Elizabeth, granting him the right to occupy any "remote heathen and barbarous lands" not held by another Christian ruler. Previously Raleigh's daring half-brother, Sir Humphrey Gilbert, had reached Newfoundland, claimed it for his country, then drowned on his way home. And now Raleigh sent out an inspection party that sailed until it anchored on a warm summer day off a long stretch of shifting sands that would later be part of North Carolina.

Here, as one of the pioneers reported to his sponsor, they caught "so sweet and so strong a smel, as if we had bene in the midst of some delicate garden abounding with all kinds of odoriferous flowers." Grapes or scuppernongs hung on hills and plains, "climbing towards the tops of high Cedars, that I thinke in all the world the like abundance is not to be found." At Roanoke Island they met an Indian chief who smiled and struck his head and breast and their heads and breasts, "to show wee were all one."

After two months of trading and surveying the locality, the Englishmen left with, among other things, a pearl bracelet for Raleigh and two voluntary guests, "lustie men" named Manteo and Wanchese, who quickly became London celebrities. As a result of his achievement Raleigh won a knighthood, and the land received a name, "Virginia," after the Virgin Queen.

Months later a party of seven ships, organized by Raleigh, sailed for the South with Richard Grenville in command. Just why had Carolina been chosen? Its comparatively easy climate had advantages; it lay close enough to St. Augustine to offer a potential threat to Spain's Florida, and also to Spain's treasure ships. Never-

"Father" of English America. Walter Raleigh, man of enterprise, courage, and ill-luck, contributed more than any other to the founding of the Anglo-Saxon colonies.

theless several kinds of trouble would dog the British at the Fort Raleigh they promptly set up. The Carolina coast lacked a good harbor; Roanoke was low, swampy, a poor choice. And, as in the case of the French settlers in Florida, there arose a succession of mishaps.

For a time, like others before them, the Englishmen searched hard for gold, hunted the elusive water passage to the East that men still believed lay within reach, and neglected to till the ground. In a quarrel over a small theft the newcomers foolishly burned an Indian village, and relations with the natives became far from idyllic. At least one colonist attended to his tasks; he was John White, destined to give the world a series of superb illustrations of Indian life. Yet even the artist White grew hungry as supplies diminished. Reinforcements were due from England, but when would they come?

Overnight a fleet stood off from shore—not the expected one, but that of the sea rover, Francis Drake, fresh from rewarding assaults on the West Indies and Florida. Confused, close to starvation, the Englishmen ashore hesitated, then accepted an offer to take them back to their homes. But their decision turned out to be a hasty one. Only two weeks later there appeared three of Raleigh's ships, ready to reinforce the colony. After careful search for the missing settlers, the new vessels also sailed off, leaving only a token party of fifteen to maintain England's claim to the spot. Its supplies were enough for two years.

The First Colony. "Arrival of the English in Virginia" read the Latin title of John White's map showing Roanoke and the shoal-strewn North Carolina vicinity. "Hatorasck," lower left, was Hatteras.

Did Virginia Dare Grow Up Like This? A latter-day artist visualized Virginia, glowingly, as a maiden reared by the Indians.

B
A
C

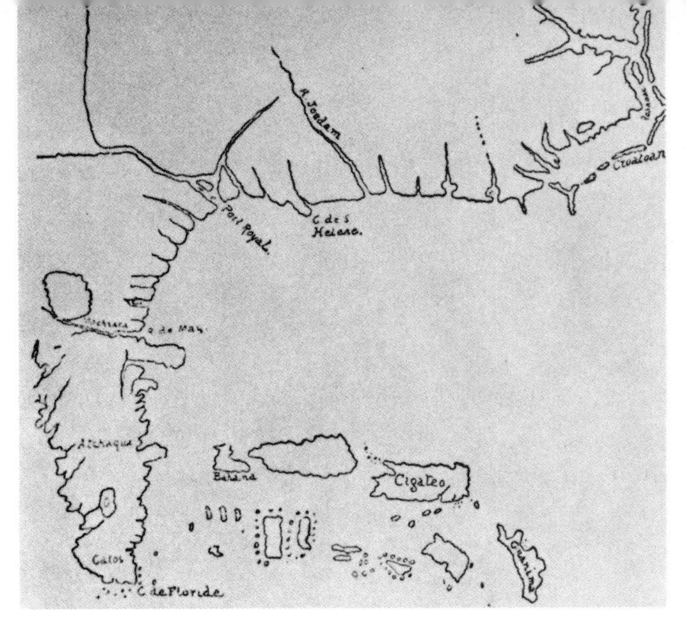

Left: The South of 1585. John White, governor-to-be of Virginia, offered his country this version of the Southern coasts as he saw them.

Right: London Was Fascinated. To show England what Indians looked like, Governor White, grandfather of Virginia Dare, took samples with him.

Opposite page: Town of Chief and Nobles. John White portrayed the "Towne of Pomeiock . . . Compassed Abowt with Poles." *A* was the temple, *B* the chief's residence, *C* an artificial pond. Houses of poles had mats that could be lifted for air.

In London, Sir Walter and his friends, though sore in spirit, did not give up hope for another England in America. John White produced seventy-five drawings of New World scenes and characters that fascinated the home country: Indian villages with oddly shaped houses, temples, tribesmen hollowing tree trunks for their "boates." The returning band also brought samples of new oddities: white potatoes, Indian corn or maize and tobacco from which they strangely "drank" smoke into their lungs. "Irish" potatoes and tobacco . . . each product was to have tremendous repercussions.

Within the year Walter Raleigh gathered three ships with a group of about a hundred, including seventeen women and nine children—a party whose purpose was steady and permanent settlement. The appointed governor was the artist John White. Instructions called for settlement farther north in the Chesapeake Bay area, considered a more promising location than the Carolina one. The vessels headed first to Roanoke Island to pick up the little band that had been left there. Governor White and his followers found the fort torn down, houses "standing unhurt," the whole overgrown with "Melons of divers sortes, and Deere within"—and a single skeleton. What had happened to the abundant supplies? The mystery was a prelude to a larger one to follow.

For some reason—a clash of wills among officials or perhaps the lateness of the season—the colonists stayed on at Roanoke. Within two weeks they watched a ceremony that should have been an augury of good things to follow. Manteo, the Indian who had once been taken to London as an item of display, left his nearby Island of Croatan to become the first red man to receive Protestant baptism in the New World. As a reward for friendship, the English named him "Lord of Roanoke."

Harvest Feasts. John White pictured a great feast with ornamental heads on the posts, three of the "fayrest Virgins" in the center, and men and women in dance, holding gourds and plants.

"Very Wonderfull" Way of "Makinge Their Boates." Tree roots were burned, upper right; boughs burned off, upper center; and trunks, foreground, burned and dug out with shells.

For the colonists there followed a still more stirring incident, the birth of Virginia Dare. Eleanor, daughter of Governor White, and Ananias Dare, the governor's assistant, were the parents. There must have been a feeling of drama in the air when the men and women clustered together for the christening. The small form within its blankets was an embodiment of so many dreams, so many hopes—a new life for this land that was to be a new Britain across the sea. For none did the occasion have a greater meaning than it had for John White, for this granddaughter gave the governor a still larger stake in the venture.

During the first few weeks, difficulties grew and flourished. Having arrived too late to plant crops, the colonists faced a diminishing food supply. Already Indian hostility had shown itself. As Governor White told of this period, the settlers asked him "with one voice" to return for help, so that he felt "constrayned" to agree.

Just before he departed, the colonists devised a plan to be used if they found it advisable to move inland. They would leave a sign giving the new location; were trouble indicated, they would carve a cross over the letters. With this understanding, the governor bade an uneasy goodbye to his relatives and to the others.

He reached England at a crucial hour. Hostilities with Spain had broken out at last, and the Spanish fleet, the largest in the world, was about to launch its attack on the island. The mother country needed every available vessel to fight the Armada. Anxiously White visited all the influential men he knew, without success. Walter Raleigh and those around him had been called upon to save England, and could do nothing.

Even now John White's colony, his daughter, and granddaughter might be in bleak distress. But England itself faced catastrophe. Sir Richard Grenville had hoped to send a sizable party to Virginia; his ships were held back. White managed to obtain two small, inadequate vessels, and set sail. Then, to his chagrin, the men themselves kept him from going beyond the Caribbean, for they preferred to hunt Spanish treasure vessels, and did. So close to Carolina and his family there, and still so far. What was happening to the colony?

The Armada launched its attack, only to go down in defeat. White's hopes rose, only to fall again. Walter Raleigh gave over his part in the Carolina venture to others; he fell from the queen's favor and his finances were temporarily, at least, very much limited. As for other possible financiers, the interest of the court and merchants had been deflected to India and the Mideast, and the Carolina coast faded as a point of interest.

But John White's interest did not fade. He kept up his desperate efforts until, in the spring of 1590, three years after he left the colony, he managed to start again for the Atlantic Coast. He had hoped to take more settlers; all he could get was permission to accompany a fleet of privateers, as little more than a passenger. As before, the men preferred to go after Spanish game. "Regarding very small, the good of their countrymen in Virginia," they "determined nothing less than to touch at those places." Eventually, however, when the privateering season ended, the crews agreed to proceed to North Carolina.

And then this small fleet with John White anchored at the Island of Croatan, where Manteo, "Lord of Roanoke," had been friendly to the English. As the vessels approached the island, a spiral of smoke lifted in the distance, and the men went out in boats. Were the colonists alive, after all? They could find no one, Indian or white. Rowing away, they made out a light in the dark, called, but received no reply.

A day or so later John White and the men pushed their way to the old fortifications at Roanoke, built in the shape of a star with huts outside. The fort had been abandoned, and weeds and grasses thickened around it. The houses had been

A Black Bird Above One Ear. The sorcerers were "verye familiar with Devils," and their enchantments often went "contrary to nature."

A Victory Observed. Back from "the Warr," the tribe sang, and prayed with "rattels" to mark a success.

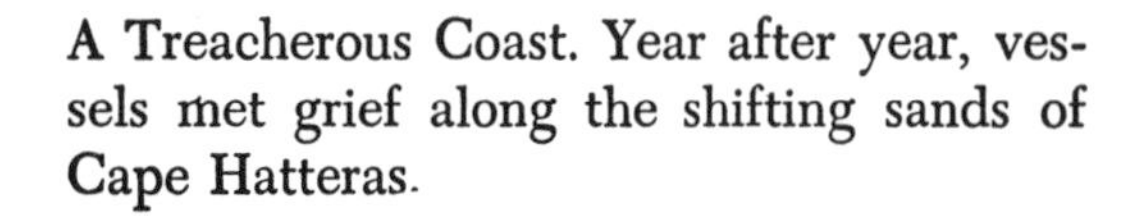

A Treacherous Coast. Year after year, vessels met grief along the shifting sands of Cape Hatteras.

torn down and the area surrounded by a new palisade of tree trunks built "very Fort-like." From one of the tree trunks the settlers had peeled the bark and carved the word CROATAN. On another tree atop a nearby hill John White read the letters CRO—and no more.

As White later declared, these discoveries gave him fresh encouragement. The Indians of Croatan Island had generally maintained good relations with the colonists. And there was no cross marked above the word to tell of impending trouble. White and the men would trace their way back to Croatan Island for a closer search.

Nets and Spears. Lacking steel and iron, the Virginia Indians attached sharp fishtails to rods. They also used traps narrowing at the end, as at upper left.

But further ill fortune intervened. The weather turned threatening, and the landing party hurried back to the ships. The next day, perhaps . . . Then, as the storm worsened, a cable on White's ship snapped, and they could not land. The long trip to reach there, and now this! The other men insisted that they must press on to the West Indies, and promised to come back later. They did not.

John White never returned to Carolina. A few years later his final recorded words were sad ones: "And wanting my wishes, I leave off from prosecuting that whereunto I would to God my wealth were answerable to my will." Within the next few years other parties made efforts to find the colony at Roanoke; the weather or other difficulties always prevented a complete search.

Later English settlers heard varying stories. The whole band had been wiped out, or so some Indians claimed. No, said others, vaguely, the Spanish had done it. Still others maintained that most of the colonists had been killed by a hostile tribe, but a number had escaped to Indians who protected them. Tales filtered through of red men with highly un-Indian beards. Among the Croatans of succeeding generations, certain individuals with an Anglo-Saxon look supposedly had the names of members of the lost colony. And a settler of twenty or so years later encountered a "Savage Boy about the age of ten yeeres" who had "a head of haire of a perfect yellow and a reasonable white skinne, which is a Miracle amongst all Savages."

Were the three Dares, Virginia, her mother and father, killed before the child could walk; or did she live with the Indians and leave descendants among them? The riddle remains unsolved.

Chiefs of Virginia. They wore their hair long, with a coxcomb style down to the neck; bird feathers in their hair, perhaps in their ears, and bodies painted for battle. Others hunted deer in the background.

NOVA BRITANNIA.

# OFFERING MOST

Excellent fruites by Planting in
VIRGINIA.

Exciting all ſuch as be well affected
to further the ſame.

LONDON
Printed for SAMVEL MACHAM, and are to be ſold at
his Shop in Pauls Church-yard, at the
Signe of the Bul-head.
1609.

Old-Time Promotion. Many were drawn by such promises, often far from fulfilled.

Roanoke Landing. Despite the English efforts to show friendliness, some of the Indians were not quite impressed.

# 3

# CAPTAIN JACK AND THE "BEWITCHING VEGETABLE"

"I shall yet live to see it an Inglische Nation. . . ."

IN SPITE of everything, Sir Walter Raleigh retained his confidence in the future of the Atlantic settlements. In December of 1606, two decades after his early efforts in that direction, the weary courtier might have beheld a stirring sight. He was a prisoner in the Tower, having offended Queen Elizabeth and later her successor, James I, son of Mary of Scotland. A lusty male, Raleigh had played a dangerous game with his monarch, and when she learned of his dalliance with one of her maids his ultimate fate was settled.

A winter morning witnessed the sailing of three vessels that brought the first enduring English colony in America at Jamestown, Virginia: the *Susan Constant*, the *Godspeed*, the *Discovery*. Before many months, most of the passengers would be dead, and some of the survivors were to wish they could join their companions in the grave. Nevertheless those who hung on were to fit their ways to the peculiar new land, and in so doing determine the future of the South—and also, in a fashion, that of Great Britain.

It was high time for action by the English. Spain still drew fantastic wealth from her American colonies. Soon the French would fortify Quebec, launching a great venture of their own, and then reach down the Mississippi, eventually, to New Orleans. And the Dutch were about to turn New York into a thriving little empire of their own. England found herself in the midst of a transformation from feudalism to a day of trade and industry. She had to grow, to succeed in this New World, or go down before her rivals. At home the many changes meant disloca-

Tiny, Red-Bearded, and Prickly-Tempered. The one-time poor boy, John Smith, infuriated "gentlemen" by making them work—and saved Virginia.

How they tooke him prisoner
in the Oaze 1607.
C. Smith bindeth a saluage to his arme
fighteth with the King of Pamaunkee and
all his company, and slew 3 of them.

C. Smith taketh the King of Pamavnkee prisoner. 1608.

tion, loss of farms and estates, loss of work for thousands in the cities. Debtors' prisons were filling up, and hungry men crept about London's streets, foraging for food. It was at this time that a group of merchants and public men formed the Virginia Company to launch a venture vital for them and for their country.

As the three ships of the company went forth, a light appeared—a comet, a good omen or a bad? Many felt certain it was the latter. The future settlers were very much of a mixed bag. The larger part classed themselves as "gentlemen," a term indicating ties to families of some property or minor rank. (One gentleman expired on the way, when his "fat melted within him.") A single member could claim nobility—George Percy, eighth son of the Earl of Northumberland, and he did not remain long in the colony. About a quarter were workers and artisans, including goldsmiths, jewelers, and refiners. The old delusions about New World gold and rubies died hard. Sealed orders of the company, a joint-stock enterprise, held the names of seven who were to form a governing council, but instructions were not to be opened until the ships reached the other side.

In that curious situation quarrels flared up. Center of much raging dispute was a prickly character about whom every colonist soon had an opinion, for or against. He was the short, well-muscled, red-bearded Captain John Smith, at twenty-seven an individual of roaring temper and a high estimate of himself. A tenant farmer's son, a self-made, overdefensive professional soldier, "Little Jack" has been termed an inflated liar, a contagion-carrier of dissension, and many other things. Yet in time it developed that John Smith was the ablest man of the lot.

He might also be considered the vainest. Telling of the way he fought for the Austrians against the Turks, the captain described himself as a "subjugator of nine and thirty kings." In trial by combat, he asserted, he slashed off the heads of three Turkish opponents. Captured, he served as a slave until a panting, highborn lady helped him escape. (Females, it seemed, often collapsed happily before the highly masculine Jack.) Although his critics looked on such stories as romantic imaginings, recent inquiries tend to bear out many of Smith's claims.

John almost did not reach Virginia. Shipboard enemies charged him with attempted mutiny and sentenced him to death. On an island shore, he said, he watched his gallows rise, but his opponents could not "persuade him to use them"! He lay in chains when, as one of the party wrote on April 26, 1607, "About foure a clock in the morning we descried the Land of Virginia." Along Chesapeake Bay they encountered Indians, "creeping upon all foure from the Hills, like Beares, with their bowes in their mouthes." Arrows flew, the newcomers fired, and the red men retired "with a great noise." Up a wide river, which the Englishmen named the James for their king, they stopped at a promontory with deep water, the site of their future capital.

Opening their secret orders, the settlers learned that John Smith, of all people, was one of the seven councilmen. For a time he continued in ostracism while other, and inadequate, individuals took charge. Early reports were good: straw-

Opposite page: The Saga of Smith. John Smith, in his *General History*, began these incidents in the colonists' complicated relations with the Indians.

Left: Important Day for Virginia. In 1619 the solemn colonists held America's historic first representative assembly.

Chesapeake in Some Detail. John Smith lived on as an excellent mapmaker, a historian (illustration from his book) and, said detractors, a chronic liar.

Below: Happier Hours for Virginians. About 1620, life broadened when the government sent a goodly supply of ladies to "make wyfes."

berries "four times bigger and better than ours in England," oysters "as thicke as stones." The settlers erected James Fort, a triangle with semicircular bulwarks, and meager houses against the wall, a guardhouse and church. Seeking treasure and that ever-elusive water passage to the Orient, the colonists had varying experiences with the Indians—amicable gatherings around a fire, fights over apparent thefts of English knives—and then settled down to real trouble.

Food supplies declined, and what they had in the storehouse had "as many worms as grains." Like Roanoke Island, Jamestown proved a bad location. Chosen primarily as a point of defense, it lay in low, flat terrain upon which the heat poured down; river water sickened the men and malaria cut them off. Dysentery took hold, then typhoid, and every day or so a body was pulled from a cabin for hasty burial. Settlers died of "the swelling," "the bloudie Fluxe," "a wound given by the Savages," but in most cases "meere famine." "There were never Englishmen left," wrote one man, "in such miserie as wee."

John Smith could not be kept down. Moving about busily, he bargained with the wily Indians and approached the enigmatic Chief Powhatan. This led the bearded Jack into the most controversial incident of his career, the Pocahontas episode. After several clashes the captain found himself before the chief, who sat in dignity on a couch covered with raccoon skins, surrounded by braves and squaws.

Tribesmen brought up stones, thrust Smith's head upon them, and an executioner raised his club. A moment later a handsome girl of twelve or thirteen darted out, "got his head in her arms and laid her own upon his." To save John, Pocahontas risked "the beating out of her own braines." Powhatan gave in to the wishes of his favorite, and John went free. In later years the captain disclosed that she "much exceeded" the other Indians for "feature, countenance and proportion," and he termed her "the only Nonpariel" of the region. Others remembered her in her earliest years as, wearing only a brief loin ornament, she did cartwheels about the settlement. "Little Wanton," she was called, the term implying a sprightly spirit. As time went by, John Smith's enemies said he might have married Pocahontas and "made himself a king among the Savages."

Returning to Jamestown, John Smith met a second threat of death. His opponents, blaming him for the loss of several companions, called for his execution. Again sheer luck, this time without sex, preserved the captain. A long-awaited relief ship came in, and he was spared. In the following months Smith himself became governor—actually dictator, the enemy faction charged. "He who will not work shall not eat," he ruled, and forced even the most gentlemanly of gentlemen to labor. He registered many complaints: "This country is long on land and short on men." The company insisted on exporting more gentlemen, and also tailors, perfumers, and similar individuals, leading Smith to dispatch a "rude" message: "When you send again I intreat you rather send but thirty carpenters, husbandmen, gardiners, blacksmiths, masons and diggers up of trees, roots, well provided, than a thousand of such as we have. . . ." To halt the cursing of unwilling workmen, he ordered a can of cold water poured up the sleeve after each oath!

Left: How To Grow Silkworms. Hoping to encourage Englishmen to settle in Virginia and become producers of needed silk, Edwin Williams explained the process in his "*Virginia . . . Richly and Truly Valued*" of 1650. Worms were to grow and spin between racks.

Above: Liberal Spirit Over the South. The enlightenment of the influential Sir Edwin Sandys helped give the colony greater freedom, wider rights.

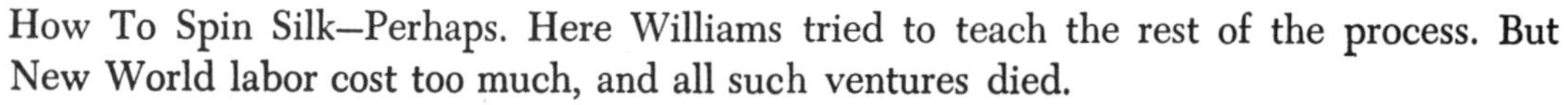

How To Spin Silk—Perhaps. Here Williams tried to teach the rest of the process. But New World labor cost too much, and all such ventures died.

Jamestown suffered repeatedly, first a fire that gutted the fort, then planting disappointments, and a winter so frigid that fish froze in the river. The generous, handsome Pocahontas now appeared "every once in four or five days," bringing "so much provision that saved many of their lives, that else for all this had starved with hunger." Again, when her father prepared a great feast, the girl slipped in with a warning that Powhatan meant to kill Captain Jack, and Smith remained on guard.

Later, John Smith told how Pocahontas diverted him with an "anticke" in which "thirtie young women came naked out of the woods, onely covered behind and before with a few greene leaves, their bodies all painted . . . singing and dauncing with most excellent ill varietie, oft falling into their infernall passions, and solemnly again to sing and daunce . . . solemnly invited him to their lodgings." Inside, "all these Nymphes more tormented him than ever, with crowding, pressing, and hanging about him, most tediously crying, Love you not me? love you not me?" Captain Jack, in any case, called it all tedious.

John Smith's Virginia days ended. Injured in an explosion, he left for England and, it was said, Pocahontas' friends told her he died. In any event the girl

Above: Halfway House to Wealth. From colonial wharves went the fragrant tobacco leaves. At left stood Negro workmen, as slavery made its appearance.

Left: Virginia and Tobacco, Tobacco and Virginia. For most Britons, the two words were all but synonymous.

went less often to Jamestown. Then followed the "Starving Time," when settlers ate horses and any other animals they could find, "dogges, Catts, Ratts and myce." Gaunt sufferers crawled out to lick the ground for "the blood which had fallen from their weak fellowes." A few dug bodies from graves and made stews with wild roots. One man went mad, killed his wife, salted her, and stored her away for his continued nourishment. Between fall and spring, the population fell from a high of five hundred to only sixty, who looked like "anatomies," with dulled eyes staring from their sockets.

On the horizon rose two vessels bearing a band who, on their trip to Virginia, had been shipwrecked in rather romantic circumstances. Their first ship had been caught in a storm, and wedged among rocks in the Bermudas. The passengers and crew made their way ashore and lived a pleasant and pastoral life until they were able to build new craft. The episode is said to have inspired Shakespeare to write *The Tempest.*

At their first sight of Jamestown the new arrivals gave up hope for the place and forthwith returned to their ships, it being their intention to abandon the colony. The Virginia experiment seemed doomed. Suddenly, fortune shifted. The Bermuda vessels lay becalmed in the James when the Englishmen beheld a group of imposing new ships entering the stream with fresh settlers and fresh supplies! They would all stay.

To office came Sir Thomas Dale, a new governor, and settlers complained that he made John Smith appear a gentle philosopher. Dale's rules established a wide range of capital offenses, including disrespect for authorities, blasphemy, even the killing of a chicken without the governor's permission. Wearying of

Tobacco Moved in Many Ways. (A) It rolled by hogsheads with wooden hoops. (B) It rocked by wagon. (C) It rode the waters. Steps in Tobacco Culture: (D) Carrying by means of a double canoe. (E) Inspection. (F) Tobacco house for smoking and hanging of leaves. (G) Pressing of leaves. (H) Placing in barrels in warehouse. (J) Hanging for curing purposes.

such life, some "digged holes in the earth and there hidd themselves" until they were famished. Those who "filched for their bellies," it was claimed, had bodkins thrust through their tongues or were chained to trees until they supposedly starved. Several who tried escape, complainants charged, were hanged or broken upon the wheel. But other testimony supported Governor Dale and his methods, and under his regime Jamestown improved and strengthened.

Relations with the Indians were still poor, however. Then one of the colonists hatched a plan. Knowing that Pocahontas remained her father's delight, the colonists by means of bribes persuaded other Indians to lure the girl aboard a vessel. The boat rode away, and the girl continued a captive for months. When Powhatan agreed to the settlers' first demands, the latter stiffened their terms, and the matter dragged on. "Exceeding pensive," Pocahontas slowly accepted her situation. She was taken to live in the minister's house at Jamestown and learned sewing. Odd as it sounds, the stern Governor Dale himself helped instruct her in religion. And now Pocahontas' story merged with that of a major development for the South.

For years the men of Jamestown had struggled to produce timber, tar and pitch, glass and soap, as export commodities that the home government desired at low rates. The company dispatched Poles and Hollanders to teach special skills. But with scant manpower and lack of experience, such projects did not prosper. An important source of income evaded the colonials until 1612, when a recent arrival named John Rolfe began to evolve the first great crop of the South—tobacco, the golden leaf.

Columbus had noticed the strange growth and the Indians' custom of smoking. Spanish and Portuguese seamen learned to puff on the "bewitching vegetable," but it remained for Sir Walter Raleigh to make the habit a court fad in England. While the less fashionable gaped, London fops did elaborate tricks with smoke under the names of the "Retention," the "Gulpe," and the "Cuban Ebolition."

King James I, a dour Scotsman, detested the custom as one "Lothsome to the eye, hatefull to the Nose, harmefull to the brain, daungerous to the Lungs, and in the blacke stinking fume thereof, nearest resembling the horrible Stigian smoke of the pit that is bottomless." Yet ironically it was in the settlement bearing James' name that tobacco made it possible for England to survive in the South.

Young John Rolfe, member of a family of some substance in Norfolk, had been a passenger on that vessel trapped in the Bermudas, and there he and his wife had a child. The infant girl died on the distant shore; eventually the couple arrived in Jamestown, and here the wife followed her baby in death. In Virginia the widower Rolfe watched the Indians caring for patches of tobacco. He had become a seasoned smoker, enjoying the mild Spanish island leaf favored by most English users of the weed. When he put the Virginia variety in his pipe, he found the flavor harsh, and for months he experimented with the growing and curing processes. In 1613 a first tentative shipment was made, yet England continued to take her tobacco from Spanish sources. More efforts would be needed in Virginia.

By then Mr. Rolfe had acquired an additional interest. The captive Pocahontas, ever more absorbed in the white man's religion, "openly confessed her Christian faith." With Governor Dale giving consent, the chief's daughter was baptized with the biblical name of Rebecca.

Soon the girl was converted also to the person of John Rolfe, widower. Thus far no Englishman had stood before the altar with an Indian. As affection increased between the pair, John sent Governor Dale a remarkable letter. After much prayer, Rolfe offered "these passions of my troubled soule." He thought he understood the "heavier displeasure which almightie God conceived against the sonnes of Levi and Israel for marrying strange wives." He had asked himself what provoked him to love one "whose education hath bin rude, her manners barbarous, her generations accursed."

John knew he would be taunted by "the vulgar sort, who square all men's action by the base rule of their own filthiness," and he insisted it was "not any hungry appetite, to gorge my selfe with incontinency." The righteous Rolfe concluded that the "spirit of God" had led him "for the good of this Plantation [Virginia], for the honour of our countrie, for the glory of God, for my owne salvation, and for the converting to the true knowledge . . . an unbeleeving creature, Pokahuntas."

No one failed to note how much the union would help the colony in its Indian relations. In the background waited the gentle girl, far less gruesome to behold than her suitor admitted, and much less "unbeleeving." Governor Dale approved, and in April of 1614 the couple were joined. The father-in-law, Powhatan, sent a brother and two sons as his representatives. Much impressed, Governor

Dale conceived a similar project for himself. Powhatan had another daughter, not quite twelve. Sir Thomas asked for her as "neerest companion, wife and bedfellow," and for emphasis offered hatchets, copper and baubles. The union, said the governor, would be a "pledge of perpetuall friendship." Powhatan said No; after all, he noted, in Pocahontas the English already had such a pledge. (And Sir Thomas also had a white-skinned wife waiting across the sea.)

The Rolfes' marriage inaugurated a long period of English-Indian amity. During that period John Rolfe's tobacco growing, and that of his neighbors, increased so swiftly that British imports of Virginia leaves equaled, then exceeded those of the Spanish type. London learned more about the colony when John and Pocahontas Rolfe went there on a visit with their young son. Officials and populace joined in hailing Mrs. Rolfe, or "the Indian Princess" or "Lady Rebecca." The nobility invited her to its palaces; the Lord Bishop of London outdid himself, and at Whitehall she caused considerable comment as she watched a masque by Ben Jonson. As part of a growing Indian-princess vogue, taverns were named after her.

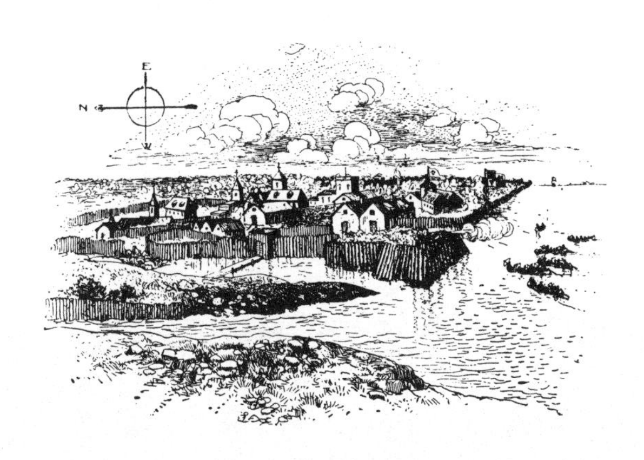

Jamestown, 1622. The year of the Indian rising.

The king, receiving Pocahontas at court, drew her into conversation about Christianity. As a result the monarch instructed his bishops to raise funds to educate children of "those Barbarians in Virginia." John Rolfe was completely overshadowed, and some said seriously that steps should have been taken against him for aspiring to a princess without court approval! Pocahontas, and also England, had come a long way. . . . For the Indian party the London damp proved treacherous. Several died, and Pocahontas, taken ill, was moved up the Thames.

One who visited her there was her old friend John Smith. At first sight, he said, she turned and obscured her face, as "not seeming well contented." He went away for several hours, but when he came back she "began to talke," reproaching him gently and remarking that others had assured her of his death. There is undeniable pathos in the scene. But now Pocahontas left life before John, dying suddenly to the sorrow of many thousands. When Rolfe returned to Jamestown, he left his son, also ailing, to be brought up in England, and after a time took a third wife (not Indian) in Virginia. Young Rolfe eventually went also to America, to become a planter of the crop his father made possible. As generations passed, the Bollings, Randolphs, and other reigning Virginia clans proudly traced descent from the Indian girl whose husband had apologized for loving her.

Thus the colony found its crop, and the "bewitching vegetable" was the new stamp of England's domain in the South. By 1616 the crop totaled 20,000 pounds; in three years the amount tripled, and five years after that, reached 500,000

Above: Pocahontas Baptized. After John Smith went to England, Pocahontas was captured and became a Christian, in this idealized scene.

Left: The Great Pocahontas Episode. In this often-debated episode Smith told how, under the eyes of Powhatan, the Indians prepared to beat out his brains. Then the maiden intervened.

Below: Christian to Wife. As many eyes watched at Jamestown, Pocahontas changed her name to Mrs. John Rolfe.

Indian Hut to English Court. Hailed in London, Pocahontas Rolfe drew the interest and conversation of the king. Soon afterward, she met death in the uncongenial English climate.

pounds. Growers dropped seeds in every available corner, including market places and streets. A law was passed forbidding carpenters and similar artisans from turning to tobacco planting. Ministers of the Church of England, who needed cash like anyone around them, turned their own bits of land to the cultivation. In the absence of hard money, tobacco became the medium of exchange, and ministers, like others, were paid in it, so that parishes with fine types of growth were especially sought after by men of the cloth.

With tobacco the demand for laborers increased sharply. Impoverished Englishmen, learning of the opportunity, longed to emigrate. Yet transportation cost far more than they had, or could earn in a year, and this situation encouraged the system of indentured service. It was not slavery; a man of a certain means provided passage for a poorer one, and in return the newcomer committed himself to work for a set period, usually four years.

The plan brought occasional injustices and disputes, with charges of mistreatment and exploitation. Now and then, too, young men and even children were kidnaped by "crimps." The latter, or their agents, sometimes passed the victims on to "soul drivers" who took them through Virginia and other colonies, "selling" them for higher rates than they had paid. But the law gave protection to the indentured servant, and he could go to court against an employer. Before him, too, lay the certainty that within a stated period he would be his own master.

The new settlers arrived in Virginia in a mounting flood—as many as two thousand a year, the first great bands to fill the American acres. In a number of cases former "indented" servants rose to rank and wealth in the colony, while others formed part of a large element, the yeomen or small farmer class. In later years there rose a myth of far-flung tobacco plantations that sprang up overnight. Virginia would have large estates, but not for many years. As late as 1702, the governor's records indicate that 90 per cent of the people were small farmers, and that holdings seldom aggregated more than six hundred acres. Such men worked in the fields with members of their families, perhaps a servant or two, and that was all.

Before that date, however, there had begun a movement that would cast an ever-lengthening shadow over the South. In the year 1619, John Rolfe wrote, a Dutch "man of warre" came to Jamestown and sold "twenty Negars," a group that was Virginia's first. These early Negroes were termed "Christian servants," and it was expected that they would eventually be freed. Instead, those who followed in slow trickles fell into complete bondage as the years passed. For many decades, however, white labor dominated Virginia.

By contrast the same year of 1619 witnessed a vital episode in the progress of world liberty. In the choir of Jamestown's church, during six days of raging August heat, settlers gathered for the first representative assembly held in the New World. According to the colony's original charter, Virginians were to have "all the privileges of free Denizens, and persons native of England." In earlier England men had died to give their fellows the rights that the Virginians received. During following years there would be flare-ups over encroachments on these liberties by crown and governor, but a principle of representative government was established.

Soon afterward came another advance—fuller ownership of lands. At first the company had hesitated to grant land outright, and men failed to develop property that was not their own. Slowly small distributions had been made; now the governor gave a hundred "headright" acres to all "freemen," men who provided their own passage to Virginia, and indentured workers would get similar lands on finishing their service. Later colonists would receive fifty acres each, and fifty for each grown child and servant. Other grants went to company stockholders and individuals who would bring over large groups of settlers. The "headright" plan of land ownership, basis of property in the colonies, had been created. About the same time, after long delays, the company acted to assure another kind of fuller life for the colonists when it sent over a first sizable band of girls to "make wifes" for the area. A male who won the approval of a new arrival was to pay the cost of her transportation. Hardly a miss, we are informed, failed to find a taker.

The year of 1620 marked the sailing of a London expedition that the company planned to settle in southern Virginia. Driven off course, the group stopped, instead, off a rocky point in what was then the northern part of the vast colony. Its members were the stalwart Pilgrims who were to make the history of New England. Once again accident ruled events.

For eighteen years after Pocahontas' marriage, peace with the Indians permitted the Jamestown settlers to extend plantings up the river. So well did the average Virginian get along with the red men that the natives often visited, had meals, borrowed implements, exchanged gifts. As the Virginians planned a university at a new "Henricropolis" settlement, they talked also of a school to educate natives.

Peace with the Red Men. A European drawing of 1707, reflecting the friendly relations which lasted for years following Pocahontas' marriage.

But under the surface the Indians were uneasy and dissatisfied. Powhatan had died, to be succeeded by Opechancanough, chief of the Indian Confederacy. Already twelve hundred Virginians lived along the James, and as their holdings increased they would inevitably push back the red men. For the original Americans it was not a happy prospect.

To the Virginians, Opechancanough talked reasonably: "Sooner should the sky fall than the peace be dissolved." Then, on a spring morning of 1622, the sky

Left: Suddenly, New Menace. The era of Indian peace ended one day when the red men rose in crafty war against the Virginians.

Below: Defense at the Borders. Through the years thousands of colonists used guns and any other weapons against assault.

collapsed. Moving about their fields, the colonists found nothing strange when Indians appeared here and there. As usual, many growers had guns propped together against fences, with hatchets and knives standing at the side. Now, at almost the same moment over a 140-mile front, the red men seized any weapons at hand, drew out their own, and ran toward the settlers.

Men, women, and children were felled, scalped, heads and arms chopped off. The assailants destroyed houses, slaughtered cattle, laid waste to fields. Whole families died, although occasional women lived on to tell in horror how they saw their babies disemboweled, their husbands cut to pieces.

Many Virginians barricaded their doors and otherwise escaped death. Jamestown suffered less than it might have, as the result of an earlier act of goodness by one of the colonists. A young Indian had been deeply stirred when the settler Richard Pace treated him as he might a white son. On the night before the uprising, the Indian's brother informed him that his assignment was to murder Pace. For hours the boy sat awake. To whom did he owe responsibility: his people, or the man who had been generous to him?

Before dawn the Indian went to Richard Pace to cry a warning. The planter managed to reach Jamestown, and the fort prepared itself. . . . As word of the killings spread, the infuriated Virginians armed themselves and marched out to murder and burn as had their enemies. Among the casualties of the sorry warfare were ironworks at Falling Creek, wrecked by the Indians. Large funds, intended for the establishment of the first North American university, had been invested there. The project collapsed, and with it plans for the education of red men. And the victims of the massacres included John Rolfe, whose union with Pocahontas had initiated the long years of good will. In all, 345 died—a third of Virginia's population.

The bloody episode helped bring a crisis in the affairs of the company, and before long the king took over Virginia as a crown colony. Had the Indian attack come only a few years earlier, it might have ended Virginia. But now this new America was too well rooted; surviving, it would encourage the extension of English settlements in the South. Among them would be another place of hope for the mother country, nearby Maryland.

# 4

# GROWING PAINS FOR THE CHESAPEAKE

"Noe person or persons whatsoever . . . professing to believe in Jesus Christ, shall from henceforth bee any waies troubled, Molested or discountenanced for or in respect of his or her religion. . . ."
—Maryland Toleration Act.

An impressive but not quite welcome visitor paid his respects at Jamestown in 1629. Receiving him politely, Virginia officials nevertheless encouraged him to leave. Before long, however, his family returned to the vicinity to establish a neighboring colony and become early molders of Southern life. He was the Catholic, George Calvert, first Lord Baltimore; in the Maryland it founded, the Calvert family was to introduce the principle of religious liberty with the first colonial act granting Christians freedom of worship.

Virginia and Maryland in the early years of the seventeenth century made up all of the South, and during those years settlement expanded, daily life was slowly enriched—and disputes sharpened. Then, for both colonies the mid 1600's became a time of growing pains as power shifted along the banks of Chesapeake Bay, which they shared. This period saw fuming argument over land, government and, not least, faith in God.

Conformity ruled the England of that era. As one observer has declared, a Catholic in England then enjoyed the same popularity as did a Communist in the United States of the 1950's and 1960's. Catholics could not go to universities or practice law, had to pay fines if they did not attend services of the official Church of England, and might be executed for certain offenses. Now George Calvert, a convert to the Church, well educated, ambitious, a friend of King James, looked across the sea with colonial plans in his mind.

The king gave the Calverts a wide, unfilled area lying between the Chesapeake and Delaware bays, an area once part of Virginia. When the Virginia Company faded away, the region reverted to the crown. And now, early in 1634, Leonard, one of Lord Baltimore's sons, led several hundred people aboard two ships, the *Ark* and the *Dove*. Benefiting by English experience at Roanoke Island and Jamestown, the family planned skillfully, equipping their settlers adequately and choosing them with greater care than had their predecessors.

Sailing up Chesapeake Bay in the spring, the vessels stopped at a handsome bluff, which became the pioneer Maryland settlement of St. Mary's. Baltimore urged the settlers to make friends with the Indians. They did, and in a highly unusual transaction these pioneers bought a ready-made village site. In the new colony no one ate rats or salted away the body of a wife against days of famine.

Peace was urged in another direction. A letter of instruction counseled the first colonists to avoid arguments of faith; in relations with others they must be "very carefull to do justice to every man." Disputes did arise, even on the trip overseas, but for the time being they remained minor. In creating Maryland the Calverts had a double motive. The first was practical, that of getting a good return on a large investment; the second, that of helping their co-religionists. Curiously, the family's efforts for tolerance encouraged so many Protestants of the dissenting sects that from the moment of the first sailing, the colony's Catholics were outnumbered by those of other faiths.

On paper, Maryland's government was a throwback to earlier stages of English history. The crown granted feudal privileges, making the Calverts "True and Absolute Lords and Proprietors" with the power to create large manors and hold the lands with the average colonist as a mere tenant. But in such a large region, which cried for settlement, the newcomers had a bargaining position. The Calverts gave way bit by bit until the Marylanders had much the same ownership rights as other Southern colonials.

Opposite page: Mulberry at St. Mary's Point. It saw turmoil, civil wars, invasions, counterinvasions. Yet it lived, and so did Maryland.

In the same way, the lord proprietors felt that they had unlimited authority in government; yet English law required them to permit popular assemblies. Perhaps shockingly to some of their rulers, the colonists asserted themselves. As Englishmen accustomed to speaking their minds, they turned down Lord Baltimore's first code of laws; in retaliation he vetoed bills adopted by the assemblies. During this tug of war the proprietors also gave in, step by step.

From the start life for the Marylanders was far from dull. An influential Virginian, William Claiborne, conducted what amounted to his own private war

Above: They Built a Dynasty. George, first Lord Baltimore, and his son Cecilius gave the South its first broad measures of religious liberty, and perpetuated a name.

They Bought a Village. Maryland began peacefully when the Calverts purchased a ready-made Indian site at St. Mary's.

on the colony. Previously Claiborne, with one hundred followers, had set up a plantation and Indian trading post on Kent Island in the bay. The island lay within the new Maryland line, and Governor Calvert offered to recognize Claiborne and the post—under Maryland law.

Furiously Claiborne refused, and Maryland accused him of stirring up the Indians and arming them against the new colony. Each side went at the other with boats and guns, and two small pitched battles were fought. Maryland defeated Claiborne, but the latter nursed his grudge and bided his time until the next chance arose. It was not long in coming.

In England the ominous Civil War—King against Parliament—was building up, with repercussions in every colony, but nowhere more violent than in Maryland. More and more Puritans fled to the New World for safety or at least ease of mind, settling both in Virginia and in Maryland. The determined planter Claiborne went among the new settlers, rousing them against the Calvert regime, arraying Protestant against Catholic with growing success. By 1644 the Puritans in England raised the flag of revolution, and gave the William Claiborne party the signal for which it waited.

An angry New World civil war broke over the colony. From Virginia, Claiborne led his partisans in a bold invasion of the neighboring colony. When he captured the Maryland capital at St. Mary's, Governor Leonard Calvert escaped to Virginia. Claiborne and the Puritans took over Maryland, seizing Catholic properties and holding them for two years.

But Virginia's governor, no lover of Puritans *or* of the angry Mr. Claiborne, assisted the Maryland leader in gathering followers on Virginia soil. With them Calvert stormed his own colony and won it back. (For noncommitted Marylanders the period must have been a confusing one.) Working now to satisfy the powerful Protestant element, Leonard Calvert placed one of their group in the governor's chair and in 1649 introduced the famous Toleration Act.

The measure declared that no Marylander "professing to believe in Jesus Christ" would thereafter "bee any waies troubled, Molested or discountenanced." The act, a milestone in American history, tried to forbid religious name calling—"Papists," "Puritans," and the like. Only a few years later, however, the Protestants revolted against the Calverts and modified the Toleration Act, making it apply to all except Catholics! They deposed the Protestant governor and chose two commissioners, to rule in his stead—one of them the familiar William Claiborne. The new regime took over Catholic holdings, exiled some Catholics, sentenced ten to death, and hanged four of them.

Affairs seesawed in an uncertain balance. In due time the Calverts appealed directly to Oliver Cromwell, now in full command in England, and much to the surprise of the New World Puritans, he recognized the family's privileges. Returning to power, the Calverts scored a marked victory when the Toleration Act was readopted. Nevertheless another reaction followed, and the Catholics of Maryland lost even the freedom to vote, were made to pay double taxes, and not allowed to worship publicly.

Despite all this the Romanists of Maryland held to their beliefs, maintained

a place in the region, and some years later gave America its first Catholic bishop, and also one of the revered signers of the Declaration of Independence, Charles Carroll of Carrollton. For the rights they ultimately achieved, they had struggled hard.

Across Chesapeake Bay Virginians engaged in other battles, usually with royal governors, sometimes among themselves. Hardly fifteen years after their first representative assembly, they revealed how seriously they held their rights. The governor, Sir John Harvey, acted to degrade the council, ordering property confiscated, "reviling" members, and adding emphasis to his views by snatching up a cudgel to knock out the teeth of a man who did not agree with him.

Responding, council members shoved Sir John into a chair, read him a list of grievances, and packed him off to England. The king, not to be intimidated, sent his governor right back again, and Sir John set out in earnest to wreck his enemies. One of the main ones, Sir John promised, would not be worth even a "cow tail." Uncowed, the council put the arrogant governor on trial and convicted him of a string of offenses. At that point the king gave in, naming a new executive, and matters simmered down.

In Virginia and in Maryland other forces crystallized to fix the course of Southern development. For years yeomen farmers managed to hold their own against the gradual growth of larger planters. But when the civil wars ended in England and the Stuart kings returned, Parliament adopted an act in 1660 de-

Above right: The Convivial Touch. Gentlemen at the old Maryland Club enjoyed their hours of repose.

Above left: Annapolis Had Style, Elegance. Ranking colonials, against paneled walls and fireplace at the Brice House.

Opposite page: A Settled Capital for the Colony. Serene-looking heart of a prosperous Maryland was the old statehouse at Annapolis.

claring that colonists could deal with foreign nations only through the mother country and its ships. Freight costs rose, prices dropped, and tobacco rotted unshipped at the Chesapeake landings.

All elements in the two colonies suffered, but the small farmer was the

Everyone Stopped at Waterloo. From Baltimore went a heavily traveled stage route, with a stop at the well-known Waterloo Inn.

The Port City Outstripped All Rivals. Sailing vessels carried flour, tobacco, a hundred other products from Baltimore.

main victim. Sadly or angrily growers told one another that a full year's labors netted hardly enough for food. Many of the yeomen farmers faced a hard prospect: they must become tenants or laborers, or try to make a new start by moving to the hillier soil to the west. Reluctantly hundreds took the latter course, and tobacco cultivation reached the backlands. The Southerners were on a historic westward march that would lead them, area by area, across the continent.

Another threat arose. For decades after the arrival of the first band of Negroes at Jamestown, the number of Africans continued small. By 1650 Virginia counted only about 300; twenty years later, out of a population of 40,000 Virginians, the blacks totaled little more than 2,000. For years the colonists hesitated, more or less uneasily, over the status of the "Negro servants." Did the dark men have the same rights as indentured white servants? Could they be held as slaves when they became Christians, as many did?

Self-interest won over conscience, and by degrees the chains tightened. The Virginia Legislature declared that, in spite of his Christianity, the Negro was a slave. Another ruling: a child "got by any Englishman upon a negro woman" would be bound by the status of the mother. For years the English had had little part in slave trading, until 1672 when King Charles granted a monopoly charter to the Royal African Company. (The king's family had money in the firm.) The rush for Negro flesh was on, and during the next two decades the company gave various colonies, including Caribbean ones, more than 40,000 slaves.

Other English groups clamored to be let in on this good thing; the monopoly ended and many men, many elements entered the trade in "black gold." The slave traffic, cruel and inhumane, brought a grim harvest of death in Africa and on the seas—a harsh chapter in the long history of man's inhumanity to man. In the colonies the great source of labor became the black man, for he was much cheaper than the indentured servant, and, of course, there was no ending of his term of work. He served until death, and his children and grandchildren served with him and after him. Tobacco farming grew in scale, especially in the old seaboard area, and the slave trade provided the base of the changing civilization.

Some of the self-reliant small farmers remained, and now and then they acquired a slave or two of their own, but others moved slowly westward. To the north, in New England, Pennsylvania, and other colonies the soil did not encourage slavery. In Virginia and Maryland and colonies which appeared to the south of them, staple crops called for large-scale cultivation. But as human bondage became ever more profitable, a kind of time bomb was set to ticking in the region's economy.

Already, uneasy new times were in the making for the Virginians. By the mid-1670's returns from tobacco had dwindled, taxes increased, and men of the steadily growing hinterland complained that the coastal areas denied them a fair chance. Here was an issue—frontier against the Atlantic counties—that would break out angrily again on many an occasion in the South.

In the governor's chair sat the emphatic Sir William Berkeley, who served for twenty-five years, with interruptions, as one of the most disputed figures of the colonial day. The first part of his rule proved popular. A strong Royalist,

Eminent Marylander, Charles Carroll of Carrollton. For their right of worship, his fellow religionists fought over a long period.

Governor Berkeley offered King Charles refuge in Virginia as Cromwell's Puritans reached power. When the Puritans assumed control of the colony, Berkeley retired to his estate for eight disapproving years. The Stuarts' return meant restoration also for Berkeley, and he took over with an iron hand. Never a vigorous democrat, Sir William once thanked God that Virginia had no printing presses and no public schools.

His opponents charged that he called no elections for the House of Burgesses; that he gave nothing to the western sections and kept everything in the Tidewater. Until then all freemen had the ballot in Virginia, but under the new Berkeley regime only property holders could vote—a clear step backward. New factors entered with Indian troubles and the rise of a figure of protest in the person of a young planter, Nathaniel Bacon.

No gaunt-cheeked agitator, Bacon belonged to a well-placed English family, had been to college, and had enjoyed leisurely European travel. Two years after arriving in Virginia, he served as a member of the Governor's Council, the upper governing house. The Indians were being thrust steadily backward, and at times the whites wrote a harsh record of violation of agreements. When the red men struck, settlers in the outer areas became inflamed and called for an expedition. The governor did little, and according to some, the explanation was that he had too big an interest in the Indian beaver trade, and also that he feared armed colonists might turn their guns on him.

In 1676 red men killed Nathaniel Bacon's overseer; promptly the excitable young man gathered recruits for an expedition of his own. The disturbed gover-

Jekyll-Hyde of Colonial Virginia. Sir William Berkeley was widely popular for years, then was thoroughly hated as a tyrant. Lady Berkeley had her own colorful career. From her first husband (a governor of Albemarle, N.C.) and Sir William she received vast properties. Then she married Philip Ludwell, who became Governor of North Carolina. Rich and ambitious, she became perhaps the most powerful woman in the colony, and intervened in government.

William Claiborne. A Virginia thorn in Maryland's side.

The Colonials Pushed Westward. "Plan of an American New Cleared Farm" showed a typical pattern of settlement as men sought fresh lands.

nor called upon them to put down their arms and threatened to hang Bacon as a "rebel." When these announcements had no effect, Sir William tried another approach, summoning an assembly to placate the settlers by returning the vote to the freemen. Indian affairs simmered for a time. Accepting the governor's lead, the colonists chose members of the new body—including Bacon himself.

The governor hesitated, changing tactics several times. When Bacon went to Jamestown, Berkeley set off a blast of guns and had him seized. Then the governor released him and sat by as the new burgesses adopted strong reforms, and ordered an official expedition against the Indians. Then came a disquieting report. Bacon's followers heard that Berkeley had decided on still another approach, namely, Bacon's murder.

Bacon, demanding that he be commissioned to head the Indian foray, led his followers to Jamestown with a threat to "pull it down." What ensued had the flavor of an operetta. The crusty governor strode forth to bare his breast and cry: Let his enemies aim at the heart! Then Berkeley offered to meet his rival in single combat, in true feudal style. With the flourish of a leading man, Bacon shouted that he would not touch a hair of the grizzled head. But, "God damne my blood, I came for a commission, and a commission I will have. . . ."

He got his commission and struck at the Indians, only to halt with fresh news. Making another of his revolving turns, Sir William Berkeley branded Bacon a dangerous rebel against his king. Infuriated, Bacon and his men charged back to Jamestown and burned it to the ground. They destroyed the property of wavering individuals and killed a few as the embryo civil war took a widening toll. But then, seemingly worn down after months of summer fighting, Bacon sickened and died. Certain sources insisted he was poisoned; his followers buried him secretly, and his remains were never found.

Their focal figure gone, Bacon's men scattered. Some later observers have judged Nathaniel Bacon merely an erratic young man who nursed an irrational

The Governor Did Little or Nothing. When Indians attacked in western Virginia, settlers complained that Governor Berkeley ignored the situation.

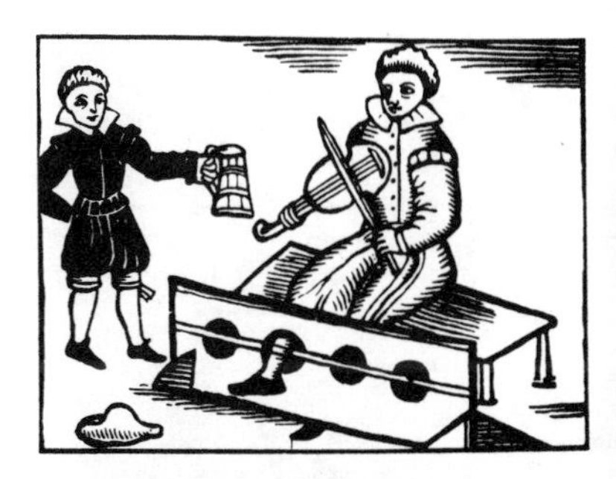

Life Could Be Cruel. "Dangerous," "difficult," or at least nonconforming Southern colonials, like others, faced the prospect of ducking stool, pillory, stocks.

Charles Calvert as a Boy. A portrait by John Hesselius, 1761.

hatred of all Indians. Yet Bacon's Rebellion had some roots in the demands of colonials for greater rights, demands that culminated exactly a century later in the American Revolution.

With the collapse of Bacon's Rebellion, the victorious Berkeley supervised a reign of terror, confiscating property, banishing men, hanging nearly twenty-five others. Hundreds of harried border-country farmers escaped to other areas, and Berkeley's followers proceeded to repeal most of the Baconians' reforms, turning the clock back again. When the royal government investigated the unhappy events, its commissioners ruled against Sir William, and Charles II declared that "the old fool has put more people to death in that naked country than I did for the murder of my father."

In comparative peace the 1660's approached their end, and Virginia's greatest century was at hand.

The Governor Bared His Breast. Melodramatically, Sir William exposed himself to the hated rebels of Nathaniel Bacon's army.

Household Objects Used by the Southern Colonials. Writing chair, Chippendale table, and tea urn.

Right: Weaving Was a Necessity of Existence. Especially in more remote areas, a colonial suffered if he could not weave.

Home of the Lees. Stratford, in Westmoreland, was an essay in sturdiness and grace.

# 5
# GOLDEN DAYS IN THE OLD DOMINION

"*Ben* is in a wonderful *Fluster* lest he shall have no company . . . —But, blow high, blow low, he need not be afraid. . . . *Virginians* are of genuine Blood—They will dance or die!"
—PHILIP VICKERS FITHIAN, 1774

THE FIRST century of struggle had ended, and as the 1700's advanced, Virginia neared its peak, an era when life at higher levels had a sheen that became proverbial—a grace and elegance that provided America's closest facsimile of the county aristocracy of England.

In a sense this element was hardly "typical." The large growers, totaling only

Above: Biggest and Mightiest of the Colonies. Virginia's seal symbolized her rank in this England of the New World.

"Busiest Hands on the Plantation." Traditionally, none worked harder than the Virginia housekeeper. Kitchen supervision was a major responsibility.

a few hundred, made up a minute band as compared with the army of plainer farmers and simple yeomen. Nevertheless the planters stamped their identity on the region in a way that would not be lost. Many a visitor from overseas was amazed at the scale of things. "In most articles of life," said one, "a great Virginia planter makes a greater show and lives more luxuriously than a country gentleman in England, on an estate of three or four thousand pounds a year." Their properties were veritable small towns, the center of several thousand acres with hundreds of field slaves, with overseers and occasional white tenants as well.

As a matter of fact, the Virginia pattern had not worked out as English officials proposed. The latter had wished the colony to supply the raw materials that they had to import from other nations. Instead tobacco provided a cash crop so lucrative that it crowded out everything else. London had visualized villages and cities with craftsmen, artisans, and professional men. But the major crop dictated a rural regime, and farms or plantations stretched in unbroken lines along the waterways.

A hungry master, tobacco depleted the soil; every seven years or less, new ground was required, and for decades no town of any size was to appear. As the tobacco farms grew up, most of them fronted on waters leading to the deep "interior sea" of Chesapeake Bay, the arm of the ocean that spread from North to South like a vast highway. At one end the Chesapeake reached close to Pennsylvania, on the other to what became North Carolina. In the words of an earlier American, dependable highways were "like angel's visits, few and far-between." For this area the waters served as the roads.

Along the Potomac, York, James, Roanoke, and Rappahannock settlers built wharves, and English vessels sailed regularly from one to another, then back to the mother country. The ships were the colonists' major contact with the outer world, taking tobacco and leaving clothes, furnishings, and a hundred other sup-

Publick Notice.
To be SOLD for ready money,
(Pursuant to the Will of ALEXANDER SPOTSWOOD, Esq; deceas'd)
Several Thousand Acres of valuable Land, lying in Culpepper County, in such Quantities as shall be agreed on. Attendance will be given at the Court House of the said County from the 10th to the 20th of June next.
J. Spotswood

Public Notice: "all Sorts of Locks . . ."

The Elegant Westover. Imposing, ornamental, the Byrd family home retained its dignity even in later, difficult days.

plies that the growers had ordered through their British agents. The region needed few shops or stores, for each planter had his representative over the Atlantic, who bought what was necessary.

Although it was an aristocracy, it was largely a self-made one. A single nobleman, Thomas Lord Fairfax, became a permanent resident, arriving to look after a magnificent property of 5,000,000 acres. (His family bought out several other recipients of a grant so large that many protests resulted. Fairfax reportedly came to America because his fiancée turned to another man, and although he gave many an entertainment, he never invited women!) And a number of colonists were younger sons of the gentry, youths with meager prospects because of laws that gave nearly everything to the first-born.

Yet there is scant support for the theory maintained by certain later Americans that by and large the Virginians came of a class different from those who went to New England or Pennsylvania or other colonies. Students conclude that most Virginians were not "cavaliers" but average Britons of all elements, all groups. In England itself classes had long been in flux. The nation maintained no such rigid caste distinctions as, for instance, did Spain, and between classes there was considerable shifting. Tradesmen in Liverpool or Bristol might point, if they wished, to grandparents who had been of high rank. At the same time rising businessmen went steadily into the nobility, buying country properties and receiving appointments from the crown.

Now, in any case, the Virginians were creating a rough replica of the rural England that they admired. For a century or more such Virginians would think of their region as, in the words of the poet-divine John Donne, "a suburb of England." Land and slaves, slaves and land—they provided a double base for the spreading new estates. These men had a lust for acreage, often more than they could possibly use, like the plain American farmer who insisted he did not want much land, "only what joins mine."

Right: Unchanged Through the Years. The slave cabin was one of many that made a separate village of an estate.

Below: No Party Without the Fiddler. They were ready to dance for hours and he was prepared to play for the same long time.

A Sorrow for All. Whites and Negroes attended the last rites for a family servant.

The common Planters leading eaſy Lives don't much admire Labour, or any manly Exerciſe, except Horſe-Racing, nor Diverſion, except Cock-Fighting, in which ſome greatly delight. This eaſy Way of Living, and the Heat of the Summer makes ſome very lazy, who are then ſaid to be Climate-ſtruck.

The Saddle-Horſes, though not very large, are hardy, ſtrong, and fleet; and will pace naturally and pleaſantly at a prodigious Rate.

They are ſuch Lovers of Riding, that almoſt every ordinary Perſon keeps a Horſe; and I have known ſome ſpend the Morning in ranging ſeveral Miles in the Woods to find and catch their Horſes only to ride two or three Miles to Church, to the Court-Houſe, or to a Horſe-Race, where they generally appoint to meet upon Buſineſs; and are more certain of finding thoſe that they want to ſpeak or deal with, than at their Home.

"Except Horse-Racing" and Cockfighting. In 1724 Hugh Jones' *Present State of Virginia* testified to certain colonials' dislike for "Labour," except for riding, games, and the like.

To the Public

Ladies may be furniſhed with all Sorts of Locks, and Tetes de mouton: and Gentlemen may have falſe Hair, &c. And Ladies and Gentlemen may have their Hair cut in the neweſt and moſt faſhionable Manner, by

Their Humble Servant,
Benjamin Catton

Just imported from LONDON,
A choice parcel of stay
With which Ladies, and others may depend on being faithfully and ſpeedily ſerved, after the neateſt manner at moderate Prices by

Their Humble Servt.
John Clark

Public Notice: "Their Humble Servant. . . ."

"Publick Notice" . . . "Pursuant to the Will . . ."

One would cut a road to fortune by tying his interests to the governor's, gaining position and property favors. Another speculated in areas to the west, while a third turned to trade of several kinds. Although eventual descendants would look down on commerce, many of the early Virginians went wholeheartedly into practically any available form of business, not excluding the slave trade. And frequently young men saw a ready path to success and fortune through the nuptial chamber. Anyone of intelligence, the saying went, should find it as easy to love a lady with wealth as one without it.

In times when death could come swiftly from many directions—disease, accidents, exposure, Indians—marital relicts were everywhere. Colonial females had traditionally been in short supply. Since women had fewer legal rights and usually knew little about the handling of their financial affairs, a man might be a necessity in more ways than one. Women, even then the more durable sex, married three or four times, now and then using up as many as six mates. Both George Washington and Thomas Jefferson took well-to-do widows.

Journalists and memoirists reported frankly regarding some weddings. When

Slowly It Grew. By degrees Norfolk became colonial Virginia's best harbor point.

Symmetry in Brick. The Capitol at Williamsburg dominated perhaps the most beautiful public buildings of all the colonies.

Official Grandeur for the Colony at Williamsburg. The "Bodleian plate," about 1740, shows William and Mary, left page, and Capitol and Governor's Palace, right page, of impressive size and stateliness.

Beverly Randolph won Betty Lightfoot in 1737, the *Virginia Gazette* informed the world that she was an "agreeable young Lady, with a Fortune of upwards of 5000£." Another source commented with warm interest on the union of William Carter, twenty-three, and Sarah Ellyson, eighty-five, "a sprightly old Tit, with three thousands pounds fortune."

At an early date Virginia women drew many an interested eye. In the New World climate the girls expanded in several directions, and one father wrote that ". . . because Maypoles are not the fashion here, our daughters grow enough to serve in their stead." An enthusiastic newcomer fancied them the shapeliest females in the universe. Other strangers noted the comparative absence of old maids; according to one source spinsters (and also bachelors) were "as scarce among us and reckoned as ominous as a blazing star." Girls often married before sixteen, and a father referred to one of his daughters of nineteen as an "antic [antique] virgin."

In at least one case a frugal widow served some of the meats left from her husband's funeral at the supper following her second marriage. The story went that most such widows returned from the graveyard to discover a petitioner in the parlor. In earlier Virginia's most famous breach-of-promise suit, Samuel Jordan's bereaved Cicely found the Reverend Greville Pooley calling on her two days after the final services. A reticent type, Cicely seemingly said Yes, but added that the ceremony would have to wait until she was "delivered"—of the late Samuel's child, that is. By the time the baby arrived, William Farrar, administrator of Samuel's estate, persuaded her to marry him instead. Promptly Minister Pooley went to court, and the matter of the popular lady's favor ended up in England. Officials ruled that they could not pass on the matter, and Mr. Pooley gave up. As a commentator said, in a related reference, "In short, this was a paradise in Earth for women."

No matter how languid a life some thought he led, the planter in those days had to be several things in one: a farmer, an organizer, and an administrator. Out of the water-edge wilderness he constructed a sleepy-looking yet teeming enterprise. In the center stood the main house, of a size and finish that increased with the years. The small, single-storied wooden structures of the 1600's had been replaced by two-storied buildings that might have several wings, and additions constructed as family and fortune spread.

Nearby clustered subordinate units—stable, dairy, icehouse, storage quarters, office, school building, kitchen, this latter kept separate for protection against fire and, as one source declared, for "sweetness" of atmosphere. At one or two

sides were flower or "pleasure" gardens, as well as vegetable plots for the family and slaves, and always the rows of Negro huts. In this setting the master had a variety of matters to concern him: London market prices for tobacco, his items of equipment, drainage and fences, the slaves' health, decisions as to the size of crops and new plantings, pending land purchases. His wife had a simple, all-encompassing assignment, that of attending to the human needs of the establishment from sick children to pregnant slaves to the operator of workshops among the aged.

While a squire might live serenely across the sea, the colonial planter survived only if he labored at his tasks, and failed if he loafed over them. A bad season or two, an unexpected blow of nature, a year of too general overplanting—a man might be ruined before he realized it. Slave labor called for considerable capital; the investment in acres and Negroes was far from liquid, and repeatedly Virginia planters complained of a lack of cash, and watched without hope of remedy as charges mounted against them by the season.

They were dependent on English merchants for the marketing of their produce, for management of their affairs in Europe, for buying and selling. Frequently Virginians accused their London factors of sharp practices in the handling of their money, and of sending shoddy, much-handled goods in place of materials for which high prices were assessed. John Custis complained that of thirteen pieces of plaid, "there is but two or three that looks anything like new." The rest were "sullied and eaten by the moth and worm as full of holes as they can be." To prove that the damage had not happened on shipboard, he noted that someone had tried to patch the rotten items. But this was the system, and most planters had to accept it.

Nevertheless the life of the Virginia planters had many rewards. While they were vigilant to protect their political rights from usurpation by officials across the sea, they kept those rights largely to themselves. Their small group held most of the places in government, most of the honors and profits. Here was rule by gentlemen, and mainly for gentlemen. The same individuals or members of the same families held rank as vestrymen of the Anglican Church, performing some duties of a public nature; as justices of county courts, military officers, revenue officials, as burgesses and, highest honor of all, as appointed members of the Governor's Council.

Frequently such posts passed from father to son; in other cases the planters were voted into office by an enfranchised minority. Not only were voters small in number; they were also easily swayed.

To win election as burgesses, for instance, members of the gentry resorted to such devices as drinks and entertainment for the voters. Even George Washington himself was known to have paid for "treats."

The system had abuses, with some favoritisms and occasional frauds and scandals in land dealings. And yet many of these Virginians developed strong feelings of public responsibility, of duty to their place and their heritage. It was expected of a plantation man that he take an active interest in public affairs; otherwise he would be held to have shirked his obligation. He acquired an aptitude for debate and a skill in argument that were not dependent on the inflated oratory of later years, but were addressed more directly to reason. Though the use of classical references and a certain amount of ornamentation were popular, mainly they tried to win agreement by appeal to logic. A New England observer, attending a Virginia legislative session, expressed the opinion that the exchange was the finest example of public persuasion he had ever heard.

But no matter how hard he worked in the daylight hours, the Virginia planter was ready for pleasure and relaxation in the evening. The climate, a caller theorized, "seems to create rather than check pleasures." The rural atmosphere, he added, made the Virginians "just such planters" as fox hunting in England made farmers. (The fox was imported and his pursuit made part of the seasonal life of the Tidewater.) Several times a year the plantation man gave large balls and regularly visited friends and neighbors for similar festivities. He used weddings and engagements, anniversaries and christenings as pegs for other gatherings. And Sunday church assemblies were not the austere meetings that Puritans favored. Strangers were surprised when planters embraced the chance for social visits as they gathered on the lawn before the service and afterward as well, and "stopped in" for calls on the way to and from church. Sermons had to be short; the Tidewater folk made it clear they disliked windy ministers, meaning any who talked beyond fifteen minutes.

At certain seasons the visitor found himself in the middle of endless successions of great meals, "fish feasts," barbecues, evening games, balls and visitings between families. Calls could last two days or two weeks. Sons were constantly courting, daughters being courted, while the fathers played cards and older women looked on behind their fans. A ball might go on for days at a time, with intermissions. Richard Lee of Westmoreland County gave one that drew seventy-five guests—for three days and nights.

An outsider would hear more conversation than he had in years. The Virginians, and eventually other Southerners, made an art of language; in the words of an observer, they were "eminently endowed with a Knack of talking." In their parlors, their gardens, about their tables, the tobacco people delighted in long sessions: argument, exposition, reminiscence, all in a casual, polished style.

Between exchanges everyone took to the ballroom floor. One of the colonial governors boasted: "Not a bad dancer in my government!" Versatility was required. According to one account, "About Seven the Ladies & Gentlemen begun to dance in the Ballroom—first Minuets one Round; Second Giggs; third Reels; And last of all Country-Dances; tho' they struck several marches occasionally—The Music was a French-Horn and two Violins—The Ladies were Dressed Gay, and splendid, & when dancing, their Silks & Brocades rustled and trailed behind them!"

The jigs, or "giggs," sometimes came last, as an added frivolity. As another visitor declared: "These dances are without method or regularity: a gentleman and lady stand up, and dance about the room, one of them retiring, the other pursuing, then perhaps meeting, in an irregular fantastical manner. After some time, another lady gets up, and then the first lady must sit down, she being, as

Its Spire Soared Over Virginia. "The Court Church," Old Bruton, drew the gentry in carriages and on horseback.

they term it, cut out; the second lady acts the same part which the first did, till somebody cuts her out. . . ."

For special events the plantation people dressed elaborately, as they thought the English squires might do. At least one outsider thought they wore costumes "too good for their circumstances." Even in plainer farmhouses a wife sometimes appeared in dress that dazzled the European. Women wore their hair high, donned chintzes and silks, bright coats, striking pumps, and many petticoats, while men chose broadcloth or linen, richly buttoned and ornamented.

Strangers found the Virginians consuming great quantities of meats, many hot breads, fowl, and a wide choice of vegetables. At large establishments breakfast was at 8:30 or 9:00 A.M., with hash, fricassee, or other meat dishes, ham, coffee or tea or chocolate. The main meal came between noon and 3:00 P.M., usually the latter hour, with warm meats, game, chicken, fish and Chesapeake oysters, supplemented with items such as greens boiled with bacon. Supper after dark would be a light one, but Sunday brought extra places at the table and additional dishes, roast pig, fresh game, sweets, cakes, and cheeses. With it all went ale, persimmon beer, port, rum, and imported claret.

Almost any presentable passer-by saw doors opened to him, the table spread, a bed provided. Many have thought this hospitality arose from simple yearning for outside company in isolated areas. In one case a Virginian supposedly sent his manservant to a tavern to invite any gentlemanly individual to his house. (To prevent hard feelings, the tobacco man privately reimbursed the landlord for his loss.) After all, the stranger might have news of London or at least of other planters! Frequently a master would go out to a landing place or road, bid someone to stop, and then, a few days later, accompany him to his departure point. On an especially festive day, one gentleman brought along a Negro fiddler and a bowl of spirits to speed the guest on his way. A Swiss traveler declared: "Even if one is willing to pay, they do not accept anything, but are rather angry. . . ."

Visitors and natives also enjoyed horse racing. A number of men imported fine British horses, and through the years great names developed among the Virginia breeders. An occasional guest reported that the tobacco people talked as much about the bloodlines of the mounts as they did about their own. Planters had their private tracks, with subscription events to which people thronged. Yet racing remained the prerogative of the gentry. Newspapers tell of laborers, artisans, and others who were fined for taking part, this "being a sport only for gentlemen."

In death as in life the Virginia clan continued together. Since churches were usually far distant, family cemeteries were the rule. With funerals went the firing of guns, large gatherings of relatives and friends, heavy meals and no less heavy imbibing. The will of Edmund Watts of York insisted that he had seen so much "debauched drinking used at burials, tending to the dishonor of God and religion," that he had determined "no strong drink be provided or spent at my burial."

All was far from ordered or genteel. New arrivals were astonished at times by the combination of splendor and gross carelessness, cluttered halls used as catchalls, unmade upstairs bedchambers. Slothful servants went unchecked; farm implements rusted away in the grasses. At country inns or "ordinaries" foreigners stared at crude manners, the grossness of men at the tables and in the grog rooms, to say nothing of bedbugs, belching, and murderous brawling.

Even the biggest planters argued insultingly before friends and snarled publicly at their wives. One or two ministers were dismissed from teaching posts for continued drunkenness, while the consort of an elevated colonial church official

The Raleigh Tavern. In the long white building, with eighteen dormers, Virginians danced and exchanged toasts. In the Apollo Room, right, they were also to plan insurrection against their king.

appeared frequently in her cups, and, as the historian Louis Wright pointed out, was almost dragged from her pew by a marriage connection of Martha Washington, because of her trenchant gossip.

Virginians spoke openly of John Custis of Arlington and his refusal to hide his hate for Mrs. Custis. Infuriated, this man of high estate once drove their carriage into the Chesapeake. When she asked their destination, he cried, "To hell, Madame!" Coolly she replied: "Drive on. Any place is better than Arlington." Before he died Custis wrote an epitaph and ordered his son to have it carved on his headstone or risk disinheritance. It read:

> Beneath this Marble Tomb lies the Body
> of the Hon. John Custis, Esq.
> Age 71 years, and yet lived but seven years,
> which was the space of time he kept
> a bachelor's home at Arlington
> on the Eastern Shore of Virginia.

At its worst the system bred a certain tempestuousness and arrogance. Often quoted is a passage in the diary of Sally Cary, expressing her opinion of a newly arrived bondsman who had killed a cat that clawed him: "A vile wretch of new negrows, if he was mind I would cut him to pieces, a son of a gun, a nice negrow, he should be kilt himself by rites." Sally was then twelve. . . . And there was point in the remark of Governor Gooch that the gentry looked not altogether happily on an imported teacher, considering him "both too dear and too Proud, for they don't like those Qualities in any but themselves."

The outstanding example of such pride was Robert "King" Carter of Coromantan, who had at times the manner of a grandee. Carter left 300,000 acres and 1,000 slaves, and his countrymen said he never passed up an opportunity to add to either holding. At "his" church the other parishioners and the minister as well awaited his arrival before starting service, or even going inside. On occasion the "King" gave an order to the man of God: Pray for rain, and the minister prayed.

Yet the man's records reveal him as a hard-working business administrator, a

Guardhouse and Magazine. The latter was built about 1715 for storage of "all Arms, Gun-Powder and Ammunition . . . belonging to the King."

William and Mary College of Williamsburg. Except for Harvard, it is America's oldest college, and a landmark in the architecture of the South.

A Steady Division. To the east, quiet settlement; to the west, an enlarging frontier.

Quilting Party in Western Virginia. Life was much plainer in the outlying areas.

realist who never deluded himself with romantic ideas about New World "nobility." Like other Virginians who sent sons to London for education, Carter urged them to drop notions of fashionable aristocracy and get on with their labors. Through the years various planters entered their sons at Oxford, Cambridge, Edinburgh, and arranged for their English agents to exercise general supervision over them. A few girls (including, strangely, one of only four years) were also sent abroad for their schooling. But as time passed so did the custom; too many Virginians complained that the young men learned "dissipation" and all-too-elegant tastes, spoiling them for the New World.

The Virginians still wrote to England for Chippendale tables, French chests, ornate clocks, and tapestries, for oil paintings and wines and books. Nevertheless realists among them did not delude themselves that they were true English squires. With all their faults, these were practical men, men of strength and will, who labored hard for themselves and their children.

A shining light of the tobacco regime, if not a completely typical one, was William Byrd II, whose diaries portray a rare mind and lusty personality. Grandson of an English goldsmith, William II had his seat at the handsome plantation of Westover. When his father prospered greatly in Virginia, the youth went to London for his education, enjoyed association with fellow wits and tavern habitués, made warm friends with the writer Congreve, with highborn (and generous) ladies, and equally warm friends with lowborn (and no less generous) ones. He wrote for the Royal Society; for years he corresponded with the Duke of Argyll and other Englishmen of rank. His collection of more than three thousand books was one of America's finest of the period.

Between his many other activities William Byrd chased practically any skirt that swished within reach, often successfully. Following a card game with Mrs. Chiswell of Williamsburg, Byrd "kissed her on the bed till she was angry and my wife also was uneasy about it and cried as soon as the company was gone." Again, arriving at a friend's house, he dallied joyously with a servant girl; when the friend's wife came in, he dallied no less joyously with her. On another occasion a maid at an inn briskly turned him down; on still another he asked a Negro girl to kiss him. . . . Here was a man of parts.

Five years after his father died, Byrd wrote that he had the older man's grave opened "to see him but he was so wasted there was not anything to be distinguished. I ate fish for dinner." And for years he carried on a peppery semifeud with his wife. Once he punished her by refusing to let her borrow a book from his library. On another night, "After we were in bed my wife and I had a terrible battle about nothing, so that we both got out of bed and were above an hour before we could persuade one another to go to bed again." Then they had a spat because Mrs. Byrd planned to pluck her eyebrows. "She threatened she would not go to Williamsburg if she might not pull them; I refused, however, and got the better of her, and maintained my authority." They brought their slaves into the quarrels. "My wife caused Prue to be whipped violently notwithstanding I desired not, which provoked me to have Anaka whipped likewise who had deserved it much more"!

But William Byrd had other moments, as his diary (none of it intended for others) reveals:

I rose at 5 o'clock and read two chapters in Hebrew and some Greek in Josephus. I said my prayers and ate milk for breakfast. I danced my dance. [Apparently a kind of calisthenics.] I wrote a letter to England. George began to plaster the house. I read some Latin. I ate boiled pork for dinner. In the afternoon I wrote more letters to England and read more Latin and some Greek in Homer. Then I took a walk about the plantation. I said my prayers and had good health, good thoughts and good humor, thanks be to God Almighty.

Year in, year out, William Byrd II struggled at the manifold problems of plantation management. He conferred with overseers, directed the running of a sawmill, traded with Indians. He tried to bring in Swiss settlers, and became a prospector for iron and coal. He was responsible for the establishment of two famous Virginia points of settlement—the first at Petersburg, the other at an obscure spot to be known as Richmond. He accumulated an estate of 180,000 acres.

Through the 1700's, the Byrds and their fellow planters built a procession of brick Georgian mansions which have served as their monuments. These houses had an English air, with differences; the perfect balance and symmetry of the general style, the delicate ornamentations were enriched with new roof styles, new methods of placing windows. The colonials did their own planning, choosing a doorway from a design book, devising a chimney to fit their needs. Out of these efforts rose structures that survived many generations: Westover, Stratford, Brandon, and others.

Twice annually, at "publick times," most Virginia paths led to Williamsburg, the colonial capital after 1699, when Jamestown burned down for the second time. Here, six years earlier at the old Middle Plantation, Virginians had begun the College of William and Mary—after Harvard, the oldest in America. The seriously concerned church officials had gone to London to urge the Treasury to help establish an institution to look after the colonists' souls. Hearing this, one official snapped: "Damn your souls. Make tobacco." But the Virginians did not intend to live by tobacco alone, and the college went up.

During most of the year, Williamsburg was a drowsing village, with rows of neat weatherboard houses with broad brick chimneys; craftsmen's shops and quiet inns, and the air of an English village as modified by the Chesapeake. Then regularly the town awoke as the center of the colony's business, of legal proceedings, private transactions, taproom conviviality and, above all else, the pomp of the governor's court. All who could, pressed into the capital—bewigged burgesses to attend formal sessions and dance afterward at candlelighted balls; growers small and large, there to fight over lands and leases; tanned woodsmen with coonskin caps, country women carrying chickens for sale; nondescript men hurrying to the races; Indians in dusty blankets, William and Mary students missing lectures for the sake of the more interesting show on the streets.

Carriages rocked into town, a few carrying outriders at back and front. Cows and hogs moved slowly out of the stream of traffic as whiskery farmers, on their first visit, gawked at the powdered women with their beauty spots and wide, flowered dresses of a sort that country folk had never seen. At such times few went to bed early; men stayed up to dance and sing, argue politics in drawing room or tavern. A French visitor of 1765 summed it up: "In the Day time people hurrying back and forwards from the Capitoll to the Taverns, and at night, Carousing."

Through the town extended the wide central thoroughfare, Duke of Gloucester Street, which an authority was later to term "the most historical avenue in all America." At one end stood the imposing central structure of William and Mary College, designed by Sir Christopher Wren (or at least in his office), at the other, the impressive brick symmetry of the Capitol, and between them the governor's home, an elegant establishment with the proud name of Palace. Here, many agreed, were the most stately public buildings in the colonies.

The *H*-shaped Capitol had an ornamental cupola, high, delicate, graceful, carrying the arms of Queen Anne, and a wide yard enclosed by a brick wall. The governor's mansion rose at the end of a double drive, with a steep hip roof and many dormer windows, a balustrade and cupola—a place of handsomely appointed rooms, a ballroom wing, flanking buildings, and tall iron-grilled gate.

In the early evening guests strolled in the several gardens of the Governor's Palace: the ball garden, the fruit and vine garden, a "falling garden" that led to a canal. Formal lines of boxwood made geometric patterns with a background of bright plantings. Inside, dancers advanced and retreated to the steady rhythm of the music, and women took note of the newest costumes, the manners of the court. Whatever Williamsburg did, others would follow.

A short way off stood Raleigh Tavern, scene of dances, auctions, and general good times. Historic in another fashion was Bruton Church, the "Court Church," tall-towered, with the governor's canopied box pew. Larger buildings and smaller ones seemed to grow out of a setting of trees and gardens, and among the most talked about was Ludwell House, home of the remarkable widow Lucy Paradise.

Disturbed by a talkative man in London, the lady once caused a stir when she calmly doused him with hot water from her tea urn. In her Williamsburg hallway, Lucy occasionally greeted guests as she sat in her coach (she had had it taken apart and reassembled inside) and had herself rolled up and down. This, of course, provided all the joys of a ride without drafts or dust. . . . And Williamsburg could claim that it gave America its first theater, far back in 1716, and kept it alive through many years. Here was a whole colonial world in miniature, and one to be imitated and adapted as Virginians began to move through the rest of the expanding South.

Proud, Self-Contained, Sophisticated. Facing its famous promenade, the Battery, Charleston became a shining city-state.

# 6

# GLITTER IN THE LOW COUNTRY

"Carolina is in the spring a paradise, in the summer a hell, and in the autumn a hospital." —DR. JOHANN DAVID SCHOEPF

A NEW SOPHISTICATION, a fresh gloss, and with them a whole new set of influences came to the South when a band of eight lordly followers of the Merry Monarch Charles II fixed eyes and hands upon a spreading area below Virginia. Eventually an observer was to declare that in all the region, only the

South Carolinians did not feel a secret envy of the Virginians. The Carolinians, according to critics, cheerfully admitted their own superiority.

Practically everything about Charleston, center of this coastal civilization, was at variance with the atmosphere of other places in the South. It brought to America a look and air of the tropics, with an early population and manner clearly of British West Indian origin. It drew Europeans of five or six derivations, to provide a many-accented flavor: French, Dutch, Scots-Irish, Swiss, German. Charleston became the first city to develop in the South, and the only city below Philadelphia. It enjoyed a position as the richest metropolis in all the colonies, one whose bright cosmopolitanism shocked the prim-minded.

At the start nearly everything seemed set against success for South Carolina. Its low, mosquito-infested coast suffered the periodic ravages of disease, flood, and hurricane, while the hostile Spanish waited to pounce from nearby St. Augustine. And Carolina's founders launched the colony with a fantastic hodgepodge scheme calling for great ready-made baronies, ranks of New World "nobility" with high-flown plans to keep separate "orders" of men in their places, and white-skinned serfs fixed forever to the masters' lands. The fact that Carolina survived at all is a tribute to the basic durability of its people.

In the British Barbados of the mid-1600's sugar had brought sudden wealth—and too many settlers. Great holdings absorbed smaller ones, and as times grew worse Sir John Colleton saw an advantage to himself and England as well in guiding the excess population to empty land along the Atlantic shores. In London he interested others, including the shrewd Sir Anthony Ashley, who fathered the peculiar plan for a feudal America.

The "Grand Model," these sponsors proudly called their blueprint. It was designed to avoid a "too numerous democracy," and prepared, strangely, by John Locke, the philosopher who later was to write stirring essays on freedom. But the Locke of this period disapproved even of the gathering of youths in schools; such education (as opposed to private tutoring) made them forward and mischievous! The project, which flew in the face of all English experience in America, provided for vast baronies of twelve thousand or so acres for a selected few, the nobles to carry titles such as "landgraves" and "caciques." These derived from the Germans and the Indians respectively, since the sponsors were forbidden to use English titles.

Each "order" was to have a role in the venture, but since the clock could not be turned too far back, settlers were promised the same legislative rights as Englishmen at home, and to draw as many as possible, freedom of religion was assured. A propaganda campaign got under way, with brochures rich in praise of glorious Carolina. Appeals even went out to old maids, with assurances that if they were only "civil and under 50," honest males would make wives of them. For good measure, men received a pledge that Carolina bears had fat that prevented baldness!

In early 1670 the first party of 150 settlers, including a number from the West Indies, arrived at a rare harbor formed by the union of the rivers Ashley and Cooper. (According to the ancient Southern saw, the streams met here "to form

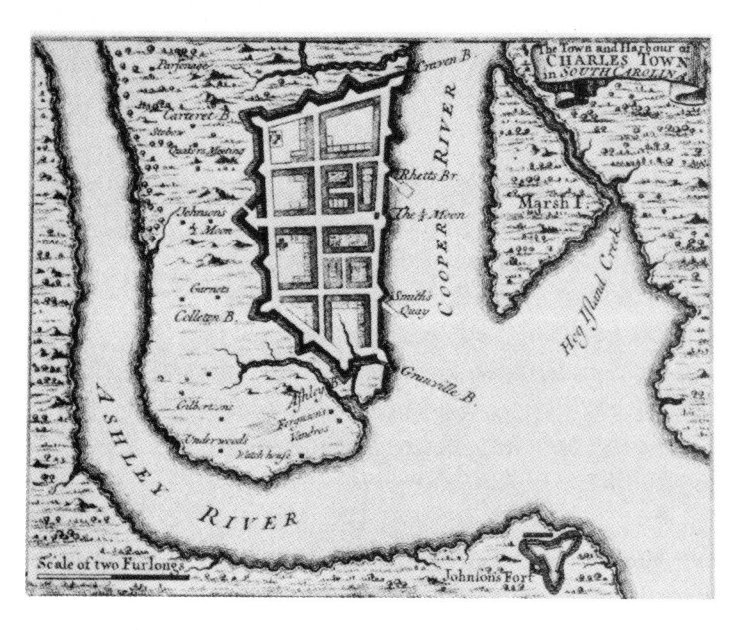


They Met "To Form the Atlantic Ocean." Sixty years after its establishment, Charleston dominated the point where its two rivers joined the Atlantic.

"To Avoid a Too Numerous Democracy." Edward Hyde, Earl of Clarendon, joined other proprietors in envisioning a highly select Carolina.

Busy Landings, Busy Sails. Before 1739, this "Exact Prospect" of Charleston gave a foretaste of the town's future.

The Charlestonians Worshiped in High Style. In 1836 Thomas Middleton painted this interior of St. Philip's. Its hot-tempered rector once challenged another churchman to a duel.

the Atlantic Ocean." In the words of a modern Charlestonian, "I think Grandpapa really believed that.") At first the newcomers located themselves some miles inland, then moved toward the shore.

They discovered a rich land of deep, somnolent swamps, long stretches of sand and moss-hung forests splashed by climbing vines. For many miles along the shore lay the remarkable sea islands, their sounds and inlets forming an intricate pattern.

The first Carolinians went to work to fell trees, make tar and resin products, and begin a trade with the West Indies, combining agriculture and trade in a union that lasted for centuries. Behind the coast lay Indian territory, and the busy settlers found money in animal skins, establishing trading posts reaching far inland toward the Mississippi. Colonists from the islands, knowing the swift returns to be made from slavery, introduced African captives, and Carolina was on its way as a colony grounded in human bondage.

As had never happened in Virginia, all business moved through a central point, Charles Town. The streams veining the area were not deep Tidewater passageways but shallow inlets that large vessels could not penetrate. Barges and boats slipped in and out, stopping always at the capital town.

Soon the early colonists were followed by Scotsmen, by English dissenters who welcomed the liberty of conscience permitted them; by Congregationalists, Quakers, a few Jews and, as an especially important element, a large band of Huguenots. Oppression across the sea had led these French Protestants to migrate. They brought with them energy, ambition, and skill, and from them came some of Charleston's leading names: Manigault, Legaré, Poinsett, Laurens.

As for the original, grandiose plan of managing Carolina, most of it fell away of its own weight. "Landgraves" and "caciques" hung on for a time, but the colony never had serfs and the other feudal classes, and "disrespectfully" the settlers shrugged it all away. Bit by bit, they obtained a good measure of self-rule, and the colony was managed by a new, home-grown aristocracy.

In the early years of the settlement, tradition goes, a New England captain dropped off a parcel of rice seeds from Madagascar. A Charlestonian planted them, and Carolina discovered its destiny, giving the South its second great crop. Nature had endowed Carolina superbly for rice culture. Its soils, built up by many waters, sprouted rice shoots rapidly under the warming sun; when the Carolinians evolved effective methods of handling the crop the road to riches lay open.

The best lands for rice, the Carolinians decided, were level areas lying slightly inland along fresh streams that lifted and fell with outer tides. Banking their fields, ditching them for drainage, the growers used sluices to flood the earth. Such methods required capital; embankments needed frequent inspection,and care had to be taken against invasion by briny water. Carolina rice had little room for the small man; merely to survive, a planter had to operate on a large scale, and South Carolina was to become a colony of widening acres and lengthening lines of slaves who worked in the water under a burning sun and swarms of busy mosquitoes.

The West Indies welcomed Carolina rice, and England asked for it. Sailing

A RICE FIELD

vessels thickened about the harbor, and still Charleston merchants complained that they could not get enough ships to handle their produce. There evolved an unusual pattern of business, with planting and commerce combined, growers serving also as Charleston merchants, with isolated country homes at the swamp edge and town houses and warehouses in the city.

Many Carolina fortunes were founded by men who grubbed at a variety of tasks. Judith Giton, progenitor of a major clan, had escaped persecution as a Huguenot by going from France to Holland to England. In South Carolina she took a husband, Noé Royer, a weaver and also a refugee. In later years she described how they worked the land together, operating whipsaws and cutting trees. For six months at a time Judith did not see bread. On the death of her first husband she married Pierre Manigault, who had similarly fled mistreatment in Europe. Pierre acquired a little boardinghouse, which Judith ran, then put up a cooperage and distillery, added warehouses, stores, and slaves, and grew wealthy.

The Manigaults' son, Gilbert, expanded further in trade, plantations, slave dealing, and moneylending. In time Gilbert was described as one of the three richest men in the colonies, with nearly 500 slaves and 48,000 acres. Gilbert's son Charles went to the Europe the grandfather had quit, but as the scion of a fortune. Following the usual continental Grand Tour, Charles took law at the Temple Bar. Later a family connection, Nathaniel Heyward, counted fourteen estates with a reported 2,100 slaves—an enormous holding even by Charleston's generous standards.

Dozens of other Carolinians rode about Paris and London, Geneva and Rome, among them the Grimkés, Rutledges, Moultries, Izards. They brought home a new certainty of their own command and a new gloss of manner. It was of such groups that the French traveler Crèvecœur wrote: ". . . the inhabitants are the gayest in America; it is called the center of our beau monde, and it is always filled with the richest planters of the province, who resort hither in quest of health and pleasure." Remembering the riches of Peru, he grew enthusiastic: "Charles-Town is, in the north, what Lima is in the south; both are Capitals of the richest provinces of their respective hemispheres."

For all its increasing savoir-faire, the town remained only a short distance from a jungle area, and on the edge of a frontier. Large and powerful planters oc-

Right: The Flow Must Be Watched. The rice fields depended on many floodgates.

Opposite page, top: A Crop for the Wet and Steaming Lowlands. Rice demanded large-scale holdings, large-scale operations.

Opposite page, bottom: Manigault of Goose Creek. The ranking planter, Gabriel Manigault, presided over his rice estate. Water color, about 1800, by Charles Fraser.

cupied the coast, and smaller, struggling growers went to the backlands, while crafty traders with the Indians followed trails long distances into the wilderness. By 1715 swaggering white traders had become so dishonest, and relations so involved, that the red men decided on revenge. Capturing one agent, the Indians, as the historian Louis Wright reported, broiled him alive "for several days in a slow fire," and swept down on plantation after plantation until much of South Carolina lay in ashes. Hundreds died, while others managed to escape to Charleston. The whites retaliated, and ultimately, under harrowing conditions, peace returned.

A few years afterward another menace, that of predatory sea traders, became insupportable. For years the colonial shores had been a happy hunting ground for individuals who operated at times as heroes against Spanish shipping, and again as outright pirates preying on craft of all nations. Merchants to a large extent tolerated these enterprises. English shipping duties were annoying, and many a colonial welcomed smuggling as a sensible help to a trader, while certain governors along the Atlantic had cozy deals with the sea rovers.

In the Italian Manner. Against a background of Rome, Ferdinando Cavalleri painted Charles and Elizabeth Heyward Manigault and their children during a grand tour.

"Mr. Peter Manigault and His Friends," About 1754. Manigault, lower left, hand on bottle, was a graduate of London's Inner Temple. A dialogue accompanied the picture:

PETER MANIGAULT: "Your toast, Howarth." TAYLOR, an officer: "Hey to the Midnight! Hark a-way! Hark a-way!" DEMARE, an officer: "Success to Caroline. G—d damn!" CAPTAIN MASSEY: "This one bumper, dear Isaac?" MR. ISAAC CODIN: "I shall be drunk, I tell you, Massey." COYTMORE, an officer: "Whose toast is it?" COLONEL HOWARTH: "Squire Isaac, your wig, you dog." MR. GEORGE ROUPELL: "Pray less noise, Gentlemen."

Gradually, however, the businessmen found pirates interfering a bit too much with their own shipments. The Charlestonians learned of one Edward Lowe, who sliced off a victim's ears, cooked them, and made the wretch chew and swallow them. They heard, too, more and more about "Blackbeard," or Edward Teach, a gentleman whose dark hair burst all over his face like a "frightful meteor." Very much the actor, Blackbeard wore red silk sashes, three pistols, and often appeared with a two-foot knife clenched between his teeth. He burned brimstone around him and, further to enhance his air of menace, stuck lighted matches of the long hemp variety beneath his hat. (Blackbeard was said to have enjoyed fourteen wives, perhaps the most phenomenal of all his feats.)

In 1718 Blackbeard Teach captured a vessel carrying a Charleston council member and his four-year-old son. To town officials he dispatched a message: Send medicine for several of his sick pirate-crew members or he would forward them the heads of the man and son. Not doubting that the rascal would do it, the Charlestonians complied, and arrived just as Blackbeard prepared to do in the pair. Not yet satisfied, Blackbeard blockaded the port for days, seized vessels coming out and made others pay for going in.

At the same time, another frightening report: near Charleston waited a second major pirate, Stede Bonnet. A Barbadian like so many other Carolinians, Stede had been a British major and a well-educated, well-to-do property owner. Apologists said that Bonnet's "Humour of going a-pyrating proceeded from a Disorder in his Mind . . . occasioned by some Discomforts he found in a married State"—in a word, a nagging wife. As a pirate, Stede was distinguished by the particular joy he took in drowning his victims.

But by now Charlestonians were in no mood to be understanding. They sent out two vessels, under command of William Rhett, after the wife-hating pirate. Rhett's ships swept down, were stranded, and after a time the pirate vessel was also grounded. The ships, within firing range of each other, exchanged blasts for five hours, and half the Charlestonians died. Then the tide shifted, the first of the Charleston vessels floated free, and the pirates surrendered.

Captured, the gifted buccaneer Bonnet managed to slip away in women's clothes but was recaught. Overnight still more pirate crews ranged about the port. More than annoyed, the men of Charleston impressed the best available ships and, after further adventures, brought in a netful of twenty-four bandits. On a day that Carolinians considered a happy holiday, the lot were hanged. At the end Bonnet, that enemy of wives, wept pathetically and asked that he be spared. The Charlestonians said No, and the era of piracy ended.

Another kind of victory for Carolina was wrought by a quiet figure, one of the South's first important women—Eliza Lucas, who as a teen-age girl changed part of the story of the region's agriculture. Eliza, daughter of the British governor of the island of Antigua, arrived in 1738 in South Carolina with her family, including a sick mother. When troubles in Antigua forced her father to leave his three Carolina plantations, the seventeen-year-old girl assumed their management. At the main estate, Wappoo, Eliza tried to plant cotton, ginger, and other products, then went to work on indigo.

For years the Low Country people had struggled with this source of blue dye, badly needed by the English woolen industry. While indigo grew well in the West Indies, Carolinians had a difficult problem in handling the leaves so as to preserve their color and bring about a proper fermentation. Eliza Lucas made innumerable tests, asked many questions; and her father sent over an authority to advise her. Watching closely, she concluded that the man was botching the operations for fear that success would provide too strong competition for West Indies indigo. By then Eliza had learned a great deal, and she went ahead on her own.

English merchants received the results enthusiastically, and her neighbors followed her example. They found it possible to dovetail rice and indigo planting,

Other Gateways, Other Entrances to Charleston's Past

using the same workers for both. England paid such a good bounty for the new crop that indigo brought nearly half the return netted by the champion crop of rice.

During the period that she labored over indigo, Eliza married Charles Pinckney, chief justice of the colony. Their sons, Thomas and Charles Cotesworth Pinckney, were to become leading American Revolutionary figures. The widowed Eliza, living to a great age as a grande dame, delighted George Washington when he met her. At her death the first American President asked to be made one of her pallbearers. For even a South Carolina family, this was deemed an honor, and the Pinckneys granted the request.

"The planters are full of money. . . ." When Henry Laurens said this in 1750, Charleston was coming fully into her own as a place without parallel in the South or, for that matter, in the North. She was the South's city-state, dominating her surroundings in wealth, in style, in attitude. What Charleston decreed, others did in the plantations along the Santee River, the Cooper, on the Sea Islands, and elsewhere along the coast. Whatever Charleston thought this season, others thought the next.

For a time no crop in America provided so swift and rich a return as did rice. Since it demanded intensive labor, it gave South Carolina the greatest concentration of slaves in the colonies, and by 1708 the area had as many Negroes as whites. After that every dozen or so years saw the number of whites double, the total of blacks triple. In rural areas slaves were sometimes to outnumber whites 50 to 1, a phenomenal percentage.

Rice called for a series of scattered plantations, and this arrangement meant overseers or managers in each case. Here, as in many other ways, South Carolina reflected the example of the Barbados. The master had less direct contact with his bondsman than he had in other parts of the South, and, as in the Barbados, the massive black population was ruled by harsh slave codes. Movement among the Negroes was rigidly limited, requirements for after-dark passes were strongly enforced. Slave patrols operated to guard against runaways to the Spaniards or to more distant Carolina lands.

The overseer often had considerable leeway; his task was to bring the best possible return from the labor, while raising the fewest problems for the owner. While the Carolina overseers were often kind and fair, at least some showed streaks of hard cruelty, and a number of Carolinians conceded that rice slavery had an unhappy side. The growers knew frequent scares, when word spread of incipient uprisings. Charleston itself had an element of free Negroes, as would other Southern towns as they developed. And here, too, the whites had intermittent alarms.

While the house servants, always closer to the planter or town owner, received special and more kindly treatment, the mass of the low-country blacks remained as a great, submerged element. Largely submerged, too, were the smaller planters in the outlying areas. As in many Latin countries there appeared little in the way of a middle class. Many callers reported that they saw only "opulent and lordly planters, poor and spiritless whites and vile slaves."

In most other places, Americans who could afford a change of scene lived in town or city in the winter and went to the country in the warm months. The Carolina pattern reversed the process. Here the rural areas were moist, malaria-ridden, mosquito-plagued in the summer, while the city had the benefit of breezes from the sea and comparative freedom from hazard. As a result the coming of each summer found the planters going to Charleston to enjoy the light winds in town houses built in a setting of luxury. Then with fall or winter the owners repaired to the Rice Coast, to return at times for the more important social events. As a native put it, this society was constantly on the move.

Clustering about Charleston, Carolina life was urbane, London-oriented, a society of sharp and worldly wit. By contrast the Virginia life was largely rural or English countryside in character, less glittering in tone. The growing Charleston rose like an "American Venice" (many used the phrase), its lines of buildings standing boldly against the water. Because the harbor had shoals, a large area that would otherwise have been devoted to warehouses became the finest of residential places, the Battery of the town, a parade ground, a promenade spot. Charleston as a whole had a half-tropical air with its greenery, its plantings of oleanders, camellias, and gardenias.

In heavy foliage stood the homes of Charleston, their construction an adaptation to scene, climate, and the many origins of the people. Early and late, they had raised first floors to provide greater coolness and to protect against floods. Through the years waters, driven by rain and wind, rose to heights that astounded strangers (and sometimes natives as well). At a fairly early date there arose the famous "single house" that did not face the street but the side garden, presenting, as the saying went, its shoulder to the world. Entry was through a doorway in a small wall, which opened onto the porch. Thus the life of the house remained half-hidden from outside, while the building still offered a pleasant doorway to the stranger.

**Shoulder to the World. The old-time Charleston mansion faced its garden, privacy assured by a unique type of doorway to the gallery.**

A Happy Time Was Had by All. Club life was melodic, or at least energetic, for the Carolinians in Thomas Middleton's lively "Friends and Amateurs of Music."

After the Georgian style took hold in England and America, there appeared adaptations of this "single house"—the narrow end still to the street, the breadth of the residence along the side garden—the whole richer, more elaborate, with handsomely arranged windows and doors. Piazzas or galleries, two or three stories

Above: England Needed Dye Products. She encouraged South Carolinians to use lands for indigo, the shrub with blue-green leaves.

Left: Processing Indigo Was Difficult but Rewarding. Below is basic machine, leading to well providing water, and above, at right, shed for drying. In the machine, water rotted the leaves, which fermented. The juice was beaten with ladles, heated until crystals formed, and the sediment hung in bags to dry.

high, came into vogue, with smaller balconies frequently overhanging the street. In one house might be traced the influence of the Indies; in another there was a hint of southern France. Iron balconies gave a Gallic touch, fine tiles an indication of Dutch taste. And almost all of them tempered the coldness of brick exteriors with stucco coverings in pastel greens, pinks, and blues.

Perhaps more than any other Southern colonial group, the old Carolinians in their town life, away from the plantations, had leisure. The well-to-do Charlestonian acquired fine silver, thick rugs, oil paintings. Sully, Morse, Jarvis . . . as the years passed, a number of leading portrait artists of their day went to South Carolina, while traveling townsfolk sent back likenesses executed by English masters.

The city could claim, in 1733, the first "song recital" ever given in the colonies. About the same period in Charleston horse racing became fashionable, and many began to import blooded horses from England. Gentlemen maintained

Below: Lifeline to the World. As much of Charleston traded with the world, its custom house properly dominated its scene.

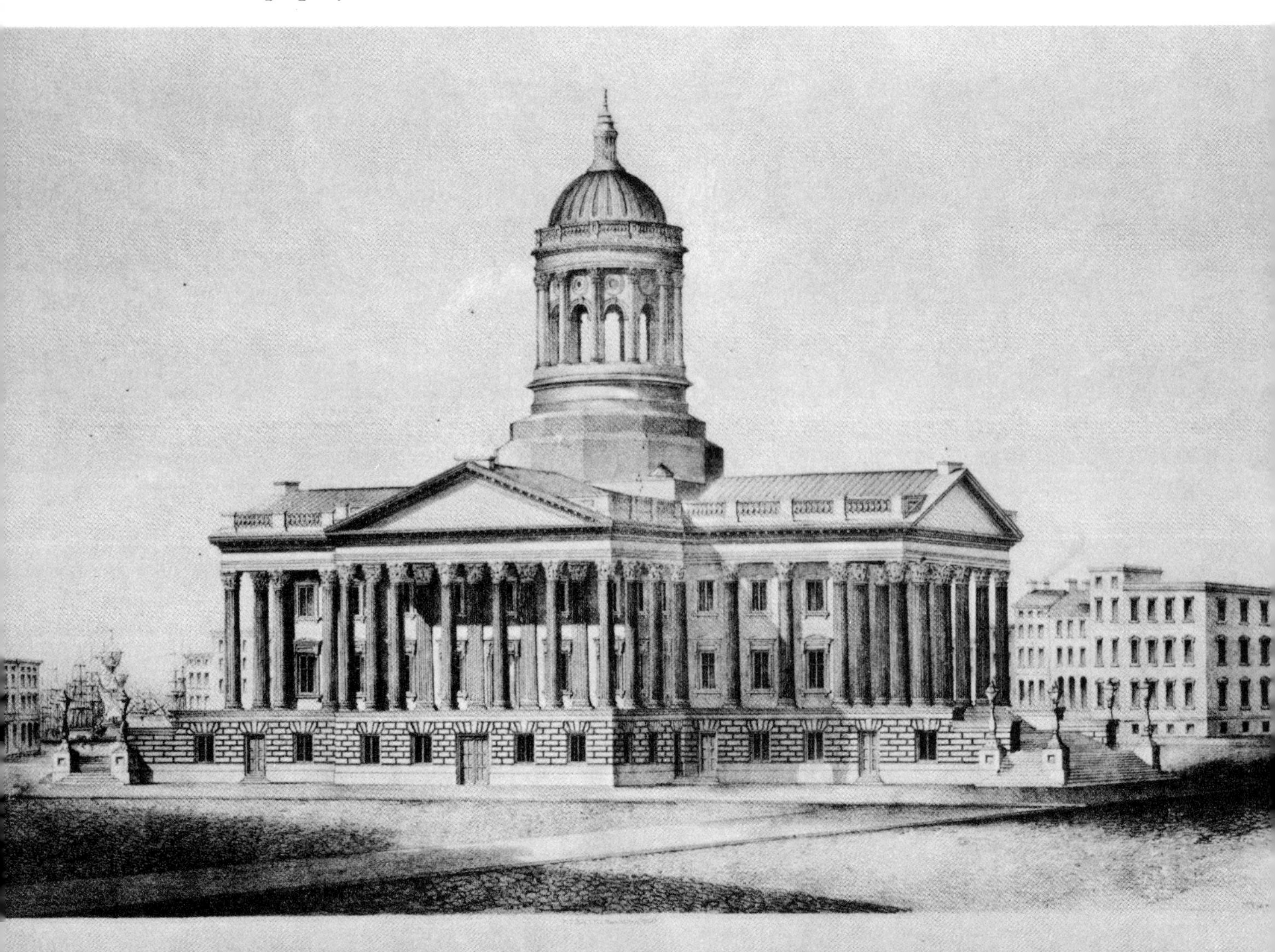

Charleston's "Westminster Abbey." St. Philip's was burned several times, and now dates from 1838.

elaborate stables and formed a pioneer American jockey club. In 1754 a theater company from New York had a successful four-month season, offering Shakespeare, farces and lighter works, although in some other colonies suspicions of the theater's "immorality" prevented such appearances.

Charleston's club life had a particular fervor, many maintained, beyond that of any American community. The city boasted, among others, a Smoking Club, a Laughing Club, Beef-Steak Club, Fort Jolly Volunteers, the St. Andrew's and St. Philip's hunting clubs. Not least was the élite St. Cecilia Society, formed in 1762 and still in existence. The Charlestonians took fencing lessons, heard chamber music, enjoyed cockfights, played cards steadily, and had seemingly endless balls and galas. Assured of a steady cliëntele, dancing teachers flocked there from half a dozen other places.

The Charleston Town Library society was established as early as 1848, and bookstores thrived. Yet education, except for private tutoring, did not progress; the Society for the Propagation of the Gospel maintained a few free schools, but the Carolinians had no college.

Some looked on Charleston as a place halfway on the road to hell. Bishop

In Its High Prime. Charleston's harbor was more crowded than almost any other in the South.

Francis Asbury of the American Methodist Church groaned over it as "the seat of Satan, dissipation and folly." Meanwhile the fashionable milliners prospered, women rode in sweeping laces along the Battery, and their husbands occasionally caroused over their wine. And still, with all their sophistication, the Charlestonians maintained a casual insularity, a happy satisfaction with themselves. Whatever others might do, the native knew that *his* was the right way. A typical townsman paid tribute to the city's two great churches by remarking that he would prefer to be buried in St. Michael's or St. Philip's than to live anywhere else on earth.

A few observers shook their heads over the gaiety. Crèvecœur said: "The climate renders excesses of all kinds very dangerous, particularly those of the table; and yet, insensible or fearless of danger, they live on, and enjoy a short and merry life: the rays of their sun seem to urge them irresistibly to dissipation and pleasure. . . ." Dr. Schoepf put it more emphatically: "The people of Charleston live rapidly, not willingly letting go untasted any of the pleasures of life. Few of them therefore reach a great age." But a Charleston paper made the most telling of comments about certain townsmen:

"Their whole Lives are one continued Race: in which everyone is endeavoring to distance all behind him; and to overtake or pass by, all before him; everyone is flying from his inferiors in Pursuit of his Superiors, who fly before him, with equal Alacrity. Every Tradesman is a Merchant, every Merchant is a Gentleman, and every Gentleman one of the Noblesse." And meanwhile, just above, was the "other Carolina" to the north.

Blackbeard the Terrible. Burning brimstone, and fourteen wives.

For Two Centuries, St. Michael's. Charleston's oldest church dates back to 1752, although plantation churches ("chapels of ease") are twenty-five years older.

The Wealth That Dripped From the Trees

# 7

# HUMILITY, PHILANTHROPY, AND JOIE DE VIVRE

A diverse land, of diverse peoples . . .

ALTHOUGH many have claimed credit, no one can be certain who first remarked that North Carolina, lying between Virginia and South Carolina, was "a valley of humility between twin peaks of conceit." With a smile, North Carolinians have often admitted that they are generally a simpler, more democratic folk than their neighbors.* Few could deny that settlement of the area was long impeded by an accumulation of almost overwhelming problems.

* North Carolinians such as the modern-day editor Jonathan Daniels enjoy stories like the one about the South Carolina grande dame who could never understand the to-do about James McNeill Whistler's portrait of his mother. "After all," the lady observed, "she was just a McNeill from North Carolina."

The coast line was hazardous, obstructed by shifting banks and uncertain shoals, with the riskiest of inlets. Not without reason would a stretch be called "the graveyard of the Atlantic." Through the years men failed to locate a dependable port, and for nearly three-quarters of a century after Walter Raleigh's pioneers disappeared off Roanoke Island, the vicinity remained an expanse of empty sands and silent forests. When people began to arrive again they came, not by sea, but by land, and largely from Virginia.

Several rivers of the Old Dominion led down to Albemarle Sound, and hunters and farmers made little-recorded trips during which they discovered good land, good animal skins, and good trading with the red men. One explorer described cane growing twenty-five feet high and six inches in circumference; the natives had "two crops of Indian corne yeerly, whereas Virginia hath but one." As the years passed, several groups received impressive grants from the king or from Virginia authorities, but the schemes faded, while scattered individuals took whatever stretches of land lay at hand. These included families who found other sections too overcrowded, or who wanted to escape tyrannical governors. At least a few, according to complaints, were runaway indentured servants, seeking a happier life.

Over Albemarle, the "cradle" of what would become North Carolina, several masters hovered. For a time Virginia claimed it; then, when the eight lordly proprietors of Carolina acquired their grant of the 1660's, they took it over. Soon Carolina had two well-separated settlements, as different in nature as any in the New World. The sophisticated Charlestonians and Low Country folk looked askance, when they bothered to look at all, at the isolated locality whose people were small farmers of corn, tobacco, and cattle. The northern Carolinians stared right back.

From Virginia came other signs of disapproval. The high-toned William Byrd, surveying the section near the border, eventually wrote: ". . . 'tis a thorough aversion to labor that makes new people file off to North Carolina, where plenty and a warm sun confirm them in their disposition to laziness. . . . It approaches nearer to the description of Lubberland than any other." Even if this picture were true of one element, the North Carolina that gradually shaped itself had others who worked hard against the odds.

Communication with places outside the immediate area remained difficult. Streams were shallow, and great swamps hindered travel. Not only did the Low Country officials pay scant heed to the distant section, but they neglected to clarify land claims, and the residents of northern Carolina said that rents were rigged against them. Boundary troubles simmered with Virginia, and Virginia tobacco growers frowned on competition from the Carolinians.

Because of harbor difficulties, Carolina settlers sent most of their produce through Virginia, until the Virginians flatly banned such shipments. Here was a harsh setback for a folk poorer than their powerful neighbors, and they deemed it

---

Opposite: His Name, Not His Attitude. Albemarle, "cradle" of North Carolina, honored the Duke of Albemarle. But the doughty North Carolinians wanted nothing to do with him or the other proprietors.

The Animals Were There. Brickell's *The Natural History of North Carolina*, 1737, found many wild creatures to depict, from "buffelo" to "tiger."

nothing less than greediness and oppression. In reply Virginians called the northern Carolinians "theeves," "pyrates," and "rascals."

Through no fault of their own, the northern Carolina settlements continued for years close to the pioneer level, and their people retained frontier characteristics—among them individuality and a certain healthy truculence. To hell with their opponents, all of them! Over and over again the people rose with biting words, and also biting actions, against their rulers. One officer spoke with feeling: "All the Governors that ever lived in this Province lived in fear of the People . . . and Dreaded their Assemblys."

The governors had reason for such dread. They frequently were incompetent or weak or, worse, shabby thieves. The North Carolinians forced one to make a sudden escape; when a successor appeared they replaced him with a man of their own choice. A third individual received a firm order when he showed himself: Get out, and keep out. (He did.) Still another governor was accused of thirteen offenses, including corruption and seizure of estates, assorted properties, and seven pewter dishes. Ordered off, he went. In all, six such officials were run out, amid raging disputes over trade laws, payment of tobacco fees, and related matters.

By 1729 the English crown took over Carolina from the proprietors, and now the northern part became a separate colony. Greater self-government brought quieter days and a growing prosperity. Newcomers settled in tobacco and rice areas along the coast, some with slaves, so that sections acquired the air of the older Virginia. At the same time people of diverse accents and habits arrived. Troubles in northern Scotland between the English and the kilted Highlanders sent thousands of Scotsmen across the ocean, to take homes in the Upper Cape Fear Valley as one of the first and largest such bodies of Scots to move to America. For years they kept the burr in their voices, playing their old-time fiddles in the evening and sending the whine of their bagpipes over the hills.

Bands of Huguenots sought new homes, while Germans of the Palatinate came under the guidance of leaders with land grants. Sturdy Swiss followed, and named New Bern after their medieval city. Other Germans, who had already fixed their identity upon Pennsylvania, rolled on to North Carolina. From Pennsylvania, too, there flowed a wide current of the Scots-Irish, Scotsmen of Northern Ireland, who, to quote the Carolina authority Hugh Lefler, "kept the commandments of God and every other good thing they can get their hands on." And there were Welshmen, Quakers, and others who took up residence in the Piedmont or back country and

The Scots Clustered Here. Fayetteville, along Cape Fear River, became a center of stout Scottish tradition, and the home of a prime Carolina heroine, Flora Macdonald.

eventually spread toward North Carolina's mistily beautiful mountains, so remote that they fostered a distinct, half-hidden existence in distant coves and valleys. In most cases these newcomers were simple farmers who had little in common with earlier Southern growers of tobacco or rice. In religion, they felt no kinship with the Anglicans of the older settlements; they were dissenters, from Methodists to Baptists, from Lutherans to Presbyterians to German Reformed.

A special mark was left by the Moravians, a sect of humble folk who had a part in the beginnings of the Protestant Reformation. Their first leader, John Hus, was burned at the stake. From Bohemia, Poland, and old Moravia, they fled to Germany, later to Pennsylvania and then, in the 1750's, bought a North Carolina interior tract of 100,000 acres. Under harrowing conditions the Moravians made their way from Pennsylvania in Conestoga wagons, fording swollen streams, creaking up and down snow-covered hills.

In their new home the Moravians built settlements with an Old Testament sound—Bethabara, Bethania, Salem. A "plain" folk, they dressed in dark coats without lapels, unadorned hats, and trousers with knee buckles. While many around them clashed with Indians, the Carolina Moravians established continu-

In Many Places, a Rugged South. A farm clung to the mountains, left, along the French Broad in the western section. Right, a settler passed laboriously under "The Lover's Leap."

ously friendly relations. Often neighbors wondered at their customs; usually the hospitable, generous Moravians won them over.

While the community worked hard, music sounded always in the background, and the church was an institution of great choirs and general singing, with trombones, French horns, and other instruments. To greet visitors the Moravians went out with bands and songs of welcome. And in a frontier region the sect constructed compact villages in the German manner. At Salem they erected a group of home and community structures, first of logs, then of stone or handmade brick—probably the South's best examples of Teutonic building style.

In many cases houses were flush with the street, their gardens in the rear. Almost like a scene in Saxony was the panorama of steep roofs with red tiling, "eyebrow" arches over windows, hooded doorways, iron railings before low-ceilinged residences. The church had an onion-shaped dome in the Middle-European manner, and nearby waited the cemetery with flat white gravestones, each the same size and shape because in death, said the Moravians, all men and women are equal. . . . Today at Winston-Salem, two thirds of an original sixty-five buildings remain as evidences of a special Southern past. North Carolina has become the richer for its many elements.

Unlike any other English colony in origin was Georgia, last of the original thirteen. It rose from a hope for a wilderness Utopia, based on man's goodness in isolation from the poisons of civilization, and from a wish to demonstrate that people may be freed from such evils as debt, slavery, and rum. It almost collapsed because the early Georgians did not want any such liberation.

There were other reasons for the colony's creation. England needed a buffer area against the Spanish in Florida. English commercial interests saw Georgia as a source of raw materials, while some had a grand vision of the place as the New World home of the hard-working silkworm. For years England had dreamed of escape from dependence on the worms of other nations; now it would nurture its own in the American South.

First, philanthropy. By the 1730's, Englishmen had become concerned over social conditions at home. Thousands huddled in jails for the crime of debt, and others walked the streets in hollow-cheeked want. Seldom, thought a contemporary, had people of any nation been in so "scandalous nasty" a condition. General James Oglethorpe, member of Parliament, soldier, and man of conscience, succeeded in getting many released from imprisonment. For reasons partly idealistic, partly realistic, Oglethorpe and a group of friends went to the king to seek a charter that would help the oppressed reach an area between the Savannah and Altamaha rivers, extending, like all royal grants of the day, far over to the Pacific. Twenty-one trustees would manage the enterprise for twenty-one years.

Overnight almost all of England demonstrated an interest in Georgia. The government contributed funds. Ministers cried out in praise, gathered money, and encouraged parishioners to give thousands of "elevating books" and other aid. Few colonists underwent such close scrutiny before departure. Going to prisons and elsewhere, a commission sought individuals "of reputable families, and of liberal,

Soldier and Philanthropist. General James Oglethorpe saw Georgia through eyes partly idealistic, partly realistic.

A Quick Bargain. General Oglethorpe worked promptly to establish friendship with the Indians.

The Lord's Prayer in Indian. Tomochichi, chief of the Yamacraws, with his nephew Tooanahowi, was painted in 1734 in London by William Verelst. The chief recited the Lord's Prayer to the Archbishop of Canterbury.

or at least, easy education; some undone by guardians, some by lawsuits, some by accidents of commerce, some by stocks and bubbles. . . ." Ironically, because the sponsors labored so hard to accept only those with a strong possibility of success, only a limited number of debtors were taken.

Knowing little of American climate, some Britons envisioned a New World semitropical paradise. One publication pictured the area as a glorious spot: "Such an air and soil can only be fitly described by a poetical pen, because there is but little danger of exceeding the truth." Fervently it was asserted that an Indian had been found who had passed his three hundredth birthday; his father, still thriving, had reached the age of three hundred and fifty! Even a neighboring South Carolinian, who might have known better, wrote:

> *Then* may the great Reward assign't by *Fate*
> Prove thy own Wish—to see the Work compleat;
> Till *Georgi's* Silks on *Albion's* Beauties shine,
> Or gain new Lustre from the *Royal Line!* . . .
> While the fat Plains with pleasant Olives shine,
> And Zaura's Date improves the barren Pine.
> Fair in the Garden shall the Lemon grow,
> And every Grove *Hesperian* Apples show. . . .

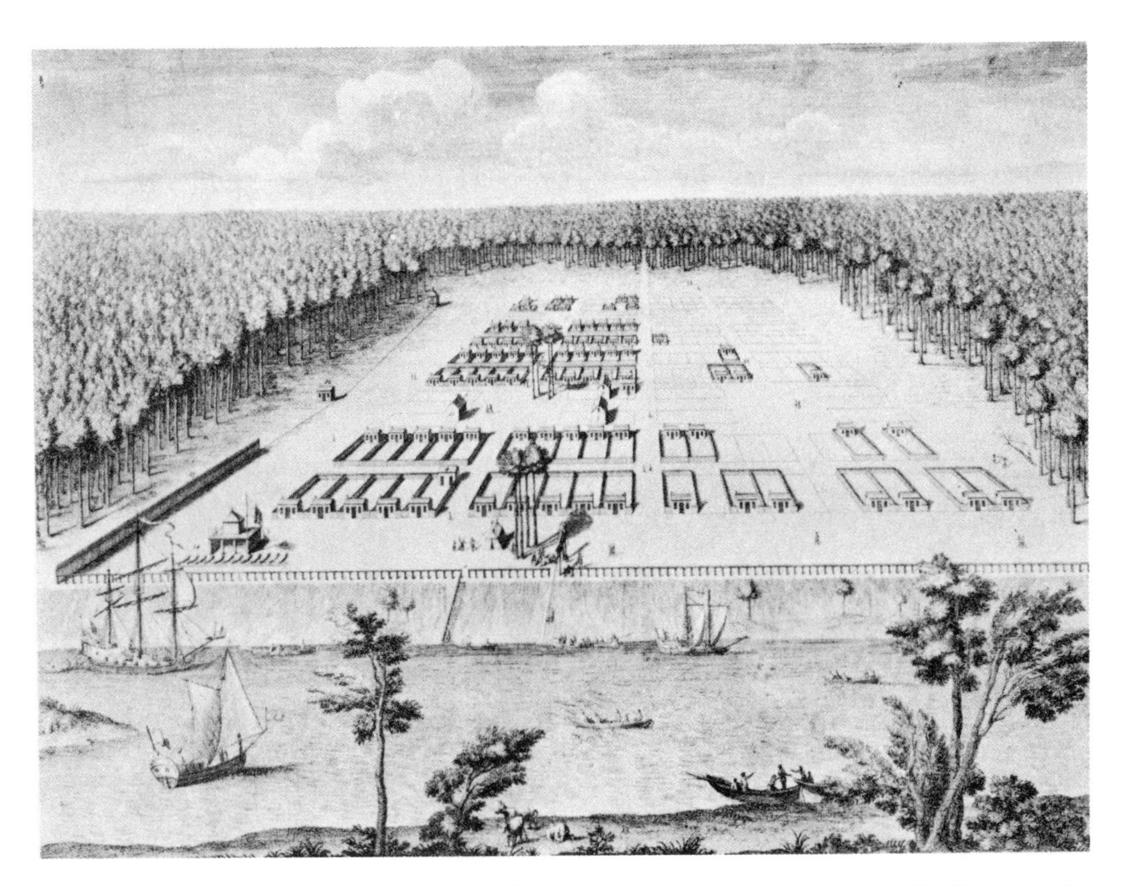

Savannah, Near the Atlantic. Georgia's first settlement was planned on a bluff above the Savannah River. Pines and mossy oaks came close to the edges.

The poet threw in other products: almonds, tea ("China's fragrant Leaf"), limes, pineapple, citron, and similarly glamorous items. . . . With such dazzling prospects before them, a band of 120 rode early in 1733 into a river along the Atlantic coast and stopped at a bluff, the site of Savannah. The town was built from a sketch drawn with sad appropriateness by a debtor who succumbed in an English prison.

To keep holdings small, the deserving settler would get only fifty acres, and these simply for use during his lifetime. To protect poorer colonists from the competition of slavery, bondage was forbidden. People were not to drink (so said the instructions), and all landowners were enjoined to grow mulberry trees to support the silkworms. General Oglethorpe struck a bargain with the Indians, buying land and entering into an alliance with the chieftain Tomochichi. This elderly figure proved a long-time friend of the Georgians. Oglethorpe took him to England, where King George received Tomochichi, as did the Archbishop of Canterbury. The chieftain's nephew sent churchmen into delight as he recited the Lord's Prayer in English and in his own tongue, and Tomochichi became a hero of another kind when, visiting Eton, he called for a holiday for the boys.

Before long the original Georgians were joined by others, many of whom came seeking freedom of worship. They emigrated from Scotland, England, and Germany. The colony acquired an additional mixture with the coming of expert silk makers from Piedmont and unusually large bands of Lutherans from Salzburg. So many of the latter emigrated that at one time Georgia had more German colonists than British. Liberty of faith had been pledged to all except Catholics, and officials were chagrined when Romanists appeared, and Jews as well. Every element was allowed to stay, for Georgia needed every man it could get. Settlement was far more meager than anticipated.

From earliest days trouble with the Spaniards had been anticipated. It

Salem, a Miniature Germany in North Carolina. The Moravians set up a serenely ordered existence. Here is Salem Square as drawn by E. A. Vogler in the early nineteenth century.

"Bathing Rooms . . . next season." North Carolina travel was long, wearing, and expensive, as these documents make clear.

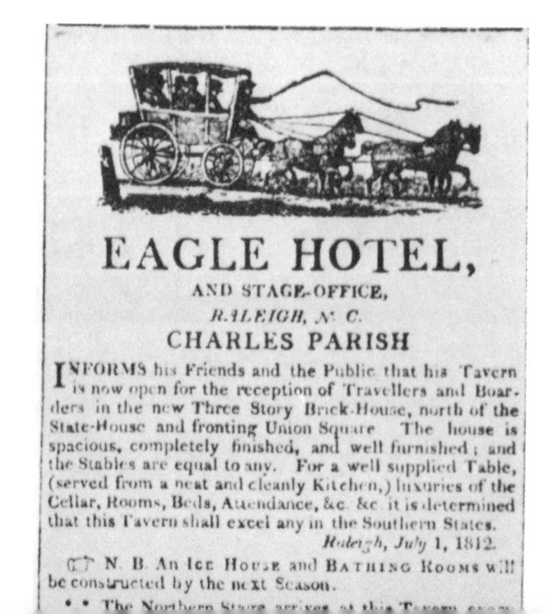

EAGLE HOTEL,

AND STAGE-OFFICE,

*RALEIGH, N. C.*

CHARLES PARISH

INFORMS his Friends and the Public that his Tavern is now open for the reception of Travellers and Boarders in the new Three Story Brick-House, north of the State-House and fronting Union Square. The house is spacious, completely finished, and well furnished; and the Stables are equal to any. For a well supplied Table, (served from a neat and cleanly Kitchen,) luxuries of the Cellar, Rooms, Beds, Attendance, &c. &c. it is determined that this Tavern shall excel any in the Southern States.

*Raleigh, July 1, 1812.*

N. B. An Ice House and Bathing Rooms will be constructed by the next Season.

North Carolina Elegance. The Cape Fear Bank of Wilmington had stairways and balconies with a South European grace.

Left: Stairs at the Riverside. With the passing years Savannah acquired a look of her own.

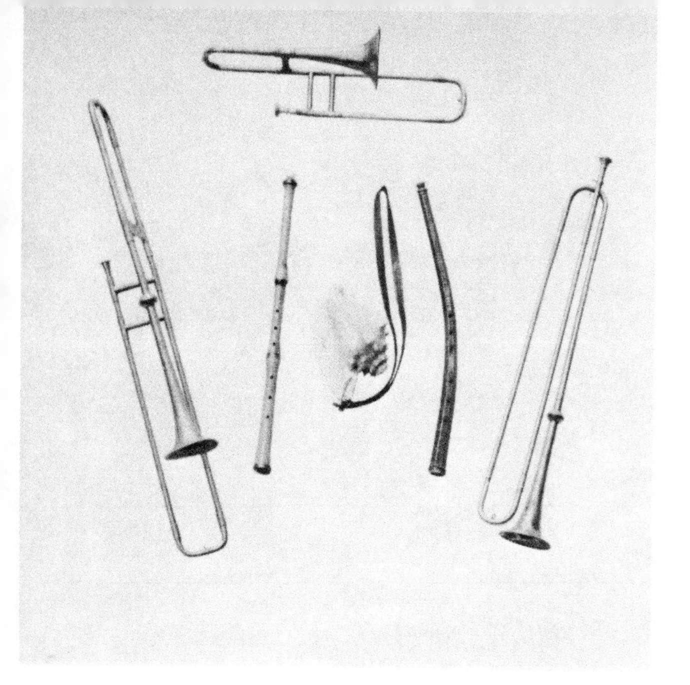

Above: Music Was Ever Present. Ancient Moravian instruments still survive. A chamber-music society, perhaps America's first, was founded at Salem in the 1760's.

Top right: To Protect a People. Fort Dobbs went up in 1755 for Scots-Irish and other settlers against the Cherokee and Catawba Indians, who hunted in the area.

Second from top: Transportation Was Costly.

Third from top: The Indians Pointed the Way. In laying out New Orleans, the French followed an old route of passage used by the red men.

Bottom right: Pine Forests Meant a Living for Thousands. North Carolina's State Seal marks the "naval stores" industry developed by draining the resin from the pines.

Below: North Carolina Pence. Each colony had its own money, as specified by its assembly.

North Carolina No 3629

VIII D. EIGHT PENCE.

Proclamation Money according to Act of Assembly pass'd ye 9th of Ma: 1754

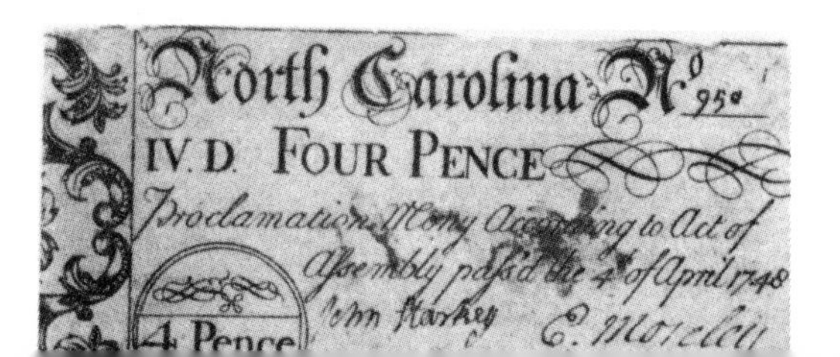

North Carolina No 950

IV D. FOUR PENCE

Proclamation Money According to Act of Assembly pass'd the 4th of April 1748

John Starkey E. Moseley

4 Pence

Printed at the Western Carolinian Office, Salisbury, N. C.

Way-Bill---From Ashville via. Morganton, Statesville, Salisbury, Carthage, to Fayette

| Date. | Passengers' Names. | No. of Seats. | Where From. | Where To. | Fare. $ | Cts. | By Whom Re |
|---|---|---|---|---|---|---|---|
| | Mr Campbell | | Ashville | Fayetteville | | | |

arrived in 1739 with the remarkable War of Jenkins' Ear. An English smuggler, Tom Jenkins, fell afoul of the Spanish along the Florida coast. To show that they were irked, they sliced off his ears and told him to show them to his king. Following the suggestion, Tom went to London, let the government know something of Spain's methods, and the fighting began.

The hostilities had their comic side. At times the warriors could not find their foe; again one opponent stayed inside his fortifications, and the other could not make him come out. Descending upon the well-prepared St. Augustine, General Oglethorpe staged a siege, but the Spaniards outsat him. He left; the Spaniards gathered an impressive army and fleet, and converged on their foes at St. Simons Island. Several clashes and near clashes followed, as each side made magnificent gestures and little else. A man of Massachusetts made the colonists snicker:

From Georgia to Augustine the General goes;
From Augustine to Georgia come our foes;
Hardy from Charleston to St. Simons hies,
Again from thence to Charleston back he flies.
Forth from St. Simons then the Spaniards creep;
"Say Children, Is not this your Play, Bo Peep?"

At one point the Georgians appeared close to annihilation, until the Spaniards committed a gross error in military intelligence. Retreating in the area of Frederica, the Georgians left a detachment hidden in the woods. Seeing nothing, hearing nothing, the Spaniards stopped to eat. At that a Scotsman raised his Highlander cap in signal, and the Georgians swept down, eliminating two hundred enemies at the Battle of Bloody Marsh. When the Spaniards returned to St. Augustine, Oglethorpe's men marched right after them. But the Spaniards would not put their heads out, and the war trailed off. Still, it was more than *opéra bouffe,* for from that time onward, the Spaniards would be a dwindling threat to the English in the South.

These military adventures gave the Georgians a new impulse for independence. Most of them had never been happy as semi-wards of their sponsors, and few of the founders' schemes worked. Several chill blasts ended the fantasies of tropical fruitgrowing. The climate of Georgia was also hostile to the difficult silk culture on which so much hope had been pinned. The worms would not spin as their masters ordered; the best type of mulberry tree could not be, or was not, raised. In any case the New World, where skilled labor had always been costly, could not compete with the Old, where workers were plentiful, low-priced and, most important, long trained in silk production.

The Georgians fretted that they could not have full ownership of land, or access to more than small parcels. Furthermore, they yearned for rum and brandy and slavery. Why should they labor under the sun while the nearby South Carolinians rested on their haunches and made Negroes work for them? Many of the Germans, here as elsewhere in the South, regarded slavery as an evil that injured white and black alike, but they did not prevail.

The population sagged, and more men were leaving Georgia than were coming in. Bit by bit the trustees gave way, permitting liquor distilling and liquor trafficking to spring up, allowing slave traders to smuggle in black bondsmen. The land system was modified, and then, two years before their twenty-one-year charter was to expire, the trustees surrendered the colony to the royal government. As philanthropy went by the board, Georgia took on more of the character of the rest of the South. In a setting of pines and oaks, with neat houses that grew steadily larger and more elaborate, Savannah prospered as a lively port.

Before then a final European power had come to the South—France, Britain's great rival in Europe and Canada. The two nations faced each other ever more directly in a long, relentless duel that extended over thousands of miles in the New World and Old, involving white men and Indians. The French arrived in the South in 1699, later than England itself, but nonetheless took hold of a giant territory covering a third of the present United States from the Alleghenies to the Rockies. The area included the vast spread of the Mississippi and its tributaries, tapping much of the continent's finest soils. If France retained this empire, the English colonials would be completely blocked in any move to push their holdings westward.

As it developed, in population and in philosophy, the South is a different place today because of the pungent, Gallic-Latin subregion that grew up about New Orleans and St. Louis, Natchez and other original French settlements, and because of the hunters, the *coureurs de bois,* traders with the red men, and the priests who trudged the expanses of the valleys. The presence of the French brought generations of conflict but also a new outlook, a *joie de vivre,* a calm acceptance of life, which still survive.

Following Champlain's establishment of Quebec on the high bluffs of that strategic point in Canada, the French waited seventy years before Marquette and his companions set out in 1673 in birchbark canoes for a dangerous trip down the Mississippi. They pressed on until they reached the mouth of the Arkansas. Nearly ten years later La Salle went beyond them in a determined exploration to one of the openings of the Mississippi at its meeting with the Gulf. In this golden-green expanse the French set up a cross and a column claiming all the stream and its tributary areas for their king, and naming it Louisiana.

Finally, in 1699, there appeared the true founders of the Southern colony, Pierre Le Moyne, Sieur d'Iberville, and his brother, Jean Baptiste Le Moyne, Sieur de Bienville, members of a Quebec family recently raised to the petty nobility. Sailing across the sea, the French party negotiated the Gulf to locate the entrance of the Mississippi, staring at the fantastic collections of tree trunks and other

---

Opposite page: She Saved Her Prince. For several years an independent-minded North Carolinian was the Scotswoman Flora Macdonald. When Bonnie Prince Charlie, Stuart pretender to Britain's throne, met defeat, Flora smuggled him to safety. Later she married Alan Macdonald and they moved to America. But, as Loyalists, they lost their properties; Alan was jailed and she escaped to Wilmington, then Scotland, where he finally joined her.

matted debris. After singing a *Te Deum,* the party continued upstream against the powerful current and halted on Shrove Tuesday at a bayou they named Mardi Gras—a meaningful title in a place that was to be celebrated for the Carnival.

For days the newcomers moved along the low banks of the Father of Waters, peering over a semiaquatic land, lush and spring green, with pale birds, alligators, and a strange animal life. After a time they stopped at a slightly higher, still moist plain in a crescent curve of the Mississippi. Even this, many thought, would not support a town, and for nearly a quarter-century the capital remained at different points along the Gulf shore, Old Biloxi and Mobile among them. Only in 1718 did the settlers establish a city in that river bend a hundred miles upstream, christening it La Nouvelle Orléans, setting out symmetrical lines of narrow streets behind a palisade, to form what is now the French Quarter.

The river city received its real impetus from one of the most lurid colonization schemes ever proposed. To the French court earliest Louisiana was a sad and expensive disappointment. After a few years the government farmed it out to a merchant, who soon learned it would not pay. Officials quarreled, made errors in judgment, and few settlers arrived. As a result the government turned to John Law,

The Ursulines Arrive. Though inaccurate in some details, this widely known painting shows the first nuns to settle within the present borders of the United States. They remained through countless disturbances.

a Scottish promoter with gaudy visions of an empire on paper and a Mississippi Bubble that he floated over a bemused nation.

Fecund Louisiana, lustrous estates along the Mississippi . . . in Law's drawings primitive New Orleans became a superb metropolis, center of a glittering empire. "The land is filled with gold, silver, copper and lead mines." Six thousand whites, three thousand blacks were to be brought over. Some people swallowed the tempting bait, but not enough of them. In an effort to make good his pledges, Law's agents scoured towns, urging, then seizing men. "Mississippi bandits" scraped out jails, hospitals, "the kennels and alleys of Paris," while court favorites schemed to send enemies overseas on orders from the king.

When ships sailed to the Gulf, passengers discovered nothing ready for them —only bare sands, steaming in the semitropical sun, and hundreds died of fever in a promised land that turned into a purgatory. Law's Bubble broke, and yet enough men and women survived to give lower Louisiana a start as a settlement. Replicas of Gallic villages rose at far-separated points, with forts and trading posts at Natchez and Baton Rouge and Natchitoches. Teutonic "redemptioners," who agreed to work for stated periods in return for their passage, took small plots of ground to build the sturdy "German coast" of the Mississippi. Now and then the Germans, good agriculturists all, kept New Orleans alive with their produce.

After the court took over Louisiana again, men planted fields in indigo and sugar cane on a minor scale. Although the earth was rich beyond the conception of many Europeans, years had to pass before the colony found its staple crops. Louisiana continued largely a blank expanse. New Orleans, key to many potential treasures, suffered because of over-rigid trade rules, which led merchants to slip in goods from Spanish, English, and West Indian sources. Privateers, smugglers, and outright pirates battened on traffic at which officials winked; the town had a many-hued underside.

The court gave little heed to the troublesome area, and Louisiana existed as a weak, half-forgotten possession. At an early date, however, a high manner of living made its appearance at the tiny, shining court of the Marquis de Vaudreuil, colonial governor. Those of his circle wore powdered wigs, jewels, and rustling satin. With imported wines and rich tapestries and gilded furnishings, they gave balls in candlelighted drawing rooms a few feet from streets ankle-deep in mud in which alligators crawled. An Ursuline nun declared that the ladies, "while ignorant about matters of salvation, are not so about vanity." Women painted "white and red" to hide wrinkles, and added beauty spots for good measure. "In fine, the devil possesses here a great empire. . . ." There was squalor in La Nouvelle Orléans, but also a gaiety which long marked these Frenchmen behind the levee.

But France and England still had momentous issues to settle. For decades the two great nations had carried on their quarrels on varying fronts, in peace and war and semiwar. One fact had a large bearing on the outcome: against an estimated million and a half Englishmen in the American colonies, the French counted only 100,000 or so settlers. A climax came with the Seven Years' War, and sadly the French surrendered Canada, foundation of their New World structure.

To keep the less sturdy Louisiana from dropping into English hands, the

French king in 1762 passed it to his Spanish cousin, in a curious transaction unannounced for several years. When at last the volatile Louisianians learned about it, they cried out in shock and, as their descendants have frequently noted with pride, became the first American colonists to rebel against a master from overseas. When Spain hesitated to take over New Orleans with a strong force, the Louisi-

---

The Burning of Savannah. Despite the fire of 1820, the town survived as a center of graceful dwellings and tall spires. Painting by J. Shaw.

The Look Became Spanish. Old survivor of brick-between-post construction. The Cathedral, founded in 1792. Simple street-corner structure.

anians rose bitterly against the transfer. If France would not have them, they said, they would prefer an independent government of their own. In a memorial they uttered words that Spain later described as the embodiment of "atrocious doctrines": " 'Liberty is the mother of commerce and population. Without liberty, there are but few virtues.' "

Then Spain pounced, executed the ringleaders at New Orleans, and asserted an authoritarian power, in the person of a stout Spanish soldier named Don Alejandro O'Reilly, Irish adventurer in the king's service. Yet the new regime, settling down, proved milder than expected. Officialdom gave way on disputed points and provided a certain efficiency in government. Adjusting to the well-pronounced New Orleans way, it allowed easy smuggling and other violations of regulations from Madrid. As Spaniards married French girls, the result was the Louisiana Creole: dark-eyed and slumbrous, whose women were to excite the admiration of outsiders.

Several disastrous fires swept over New Orleans during the Spanish regime, and when it rebuilt it changed from a town with a French provincial character to one with a predominantly Castilian appearance. Houses of wood and brick stood flush with the *banquette* or sidewalk, and the family life turned toward flagstoned interior courts or *patios.* (New Orleanians used a French word here, a Spanish there, indiscriminately.) The more imposing residences had ironwork gratings and delicate balconies, fanlight windows, murmuring fountains in the courtyards, with lingering traces of France in the Spanish whole. At the high-piled waterfront boatmen and traders caroused and brawled; in their quieter settings the Creoles took their pleasure in a setting as different from North Carolina's as that colony was different from Georgia, or Georgia from Virginia.

Right: He Fathered New Orleans. Jean Baptiste Le Moyne, Sieur de Bienville, explored a moist stretch along the Mississippi, and years later made it Louisiana's capital.

Left: He Floated the Mississippi Bubble. John Law, Scottish speculator, conceived the fantastic scheme that helped populate Louisiana.

Above: Historic Cornerstone. The first French in Louisiana set the base of Fort Maurepas. Right: "Unhappily Assassinated." After tracing the Mississippi to the Gulf Coast, the Sieur de La Salle met death in the new land.

Pelican, Buffalo, Possum. As an early French observer set down the mysteries of Mississippi Valley animal life.

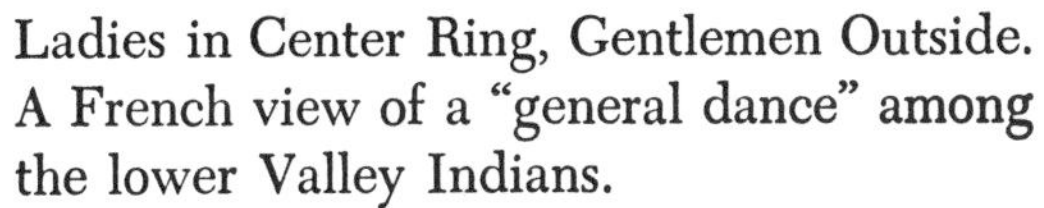
Ladies in Center Ring, Gentlemen Outside. A French view of a "general dance" among the lower Valley Indians.

How To Chase Down a Herd. The French pioneers were fascinated by the technique.

Scalping and Torture. The Natchez Indians, of the region about the fort of that name, were ingenious.

MISSISIPPI OF 'T WYD-BEFAAMDE GOUD-LAND
DOOR DE INBEELDING DER WIND-NEGOTIE

Dit 's 't wond'rc Miſſiſippi Land
Befaamd door zijnen Actie-handel,
't Geen aan den Wind-god is verpand,
En door bedrog en ſnóden wandel
Ontelb're Schatten heeft verkwiſt.
Maar Miſſiſippi, 't is verlóren,
't Is met u achter 't Net geviſt,
Want Schijnſchoon, die u van te vóren
Zoo rijkelijk heeft afgemaald,
Is nu ontmaskeerd, en haar wezen
Word door de Waarheyd overſtraald,
't Geen menig zijn verderf doet vrézen;
Want 't is vergeefs daar Volk geplant
Daar Goud noch Zilver is te hálen;
De hoop die de Acties bragt in ſtand
Ziet zig met ſchande en ſchaà betálen,
En Hennepins verréze Geeſt
Schijnd elk dit opzet af te ráden,
Die niet te ſtout en onbevreeſt,
Het Zijn wil voor den Schijn verſmáden,
Want 's Konings-kiſt ontbloot van Geld,
Waar in de Rotten ſpélemeyen,
Moeſt door deez' Konſtgreep zijn herſteld,
Al zou het de Onderdaan beſchreyen.
(1) Louis leyd naâuw op 't Praal-bed neér,
Wanneer een Schotſſe-wind komt waayen,
En weet zig met een ſchijn van eer
(2) In Orleans zijn raad te drayen;
Hier op word Miſſiſippis naam
Gelijk een Af-god aangebeden
En deez' verdervende Actie-kraam,
Ging boven regt, en deugd, en reden.
(3) Toen klom de grootsheyd, wijl men 't Geld
In Huys brengt op een Kruyers-wagen,
Daar 't op de grond leyd ongeteld,
Als drek, niet waard om naar te vrágen;
Maar ach! die blijdſchap duurt zo kort,
(4) Wijl de Armoede en haar geſpélen
Den Actie-hand'laar overſtort,
En doet hem in haar rampen délen;
Dog wijl de uytvinder van dit kwaad,
Zijn valsheyd door de vlugt laat blijken,
Zoo zal het haat'lijk Actie-zaad
Eerlang ook van de Wéreld wijken,
Want hoe men de Acties ook beziet,
't Is Wind, en Rook, en anders niet.

Bubble Over Central Europe. This broadside about Law's venture, in German, drew men of several nations.

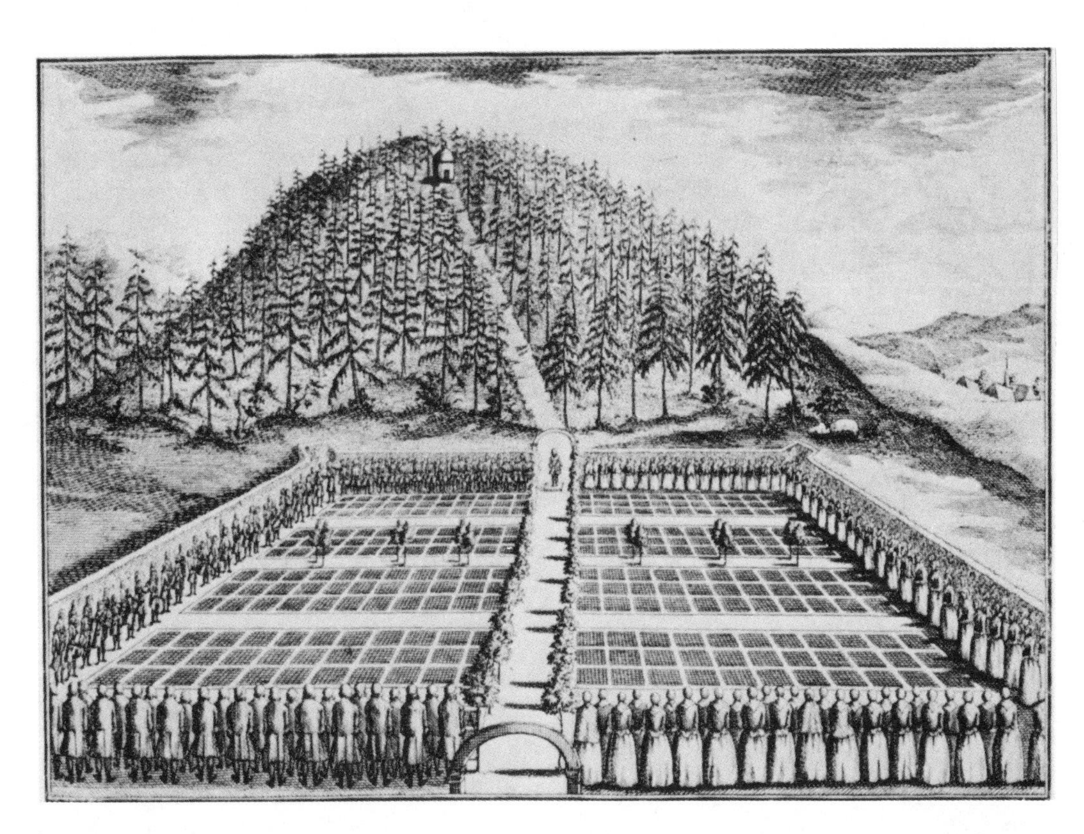

They Were a Peaceful Folk. Top, group marriages among the Moravians, with several couples joining at the same time. Bride and groom might know each other only by sight; partners were "chosen by lot after prayerful consideration of compatible qualities." Below, an Easter liturgy commemorating the deaths of beloved members, at sunrise on Easter Sunday.

For a Time, More Germanic than English. Large bands of Lutherans arrived from Salzburg, and at one point Georgia's population was more Teutonic than British.

The Shakers of Kentucky. In their religious "dance" the sexes remained largely apart.

"Addressing the Almighty with Prayer." Early and late, Negro services reflected those of the whites.

Meetings in the Woods. Again and again thousands thronged to the forest edges to gather about hastily-constructed platforms, in evangelical-style assemblies that might go on for days.

The Baptists Made Converts. Well suited to the philosophy of many Southern individualists were the Baptists. Repeated waves of conversion to Protestantism swept the South.

He Led the First "Awakening." George Whitefield, born in England, stirred tens of thousands of Southerners in the first "Great Awakening" before the mid-1700's, as Methodists, Baptists, Presbyterians spread their denominations over the region.

A Palace Helped Spur a Revolt. The costly palace of Governor Tryon of North Carolina enraged western colonists, in an angry prelude to the Revolution.

# 8
# "THE WORLD TURNED UPSIDE DOWN"

"Could I have foreseen what I have, and am likely to experience, no consideration upon Earth should have induced me to accept this command." —George Washington

It had been long in coming, but some had caught the outline of an American Revolution in premonitory outbreaks and a slowly changing temper among the colonists. A minister of 1759 found the Virginians, for instance, already "haughty and jealous of their liberties, impatient of restraint," so that they could hardly "bear the thought of being controuled by any superior power." Especially in Maryland and parts of North Carolina, other Southerners had grown restive.

Although the revolutionary impulse erupted throughout the colonies, the South had a large role in channeling the increasing discontent, in bringing hostilities to a conclusion and, not the least, in fathering the philosophy of the Revolution, which, more than any other happening in America, changed the world. From beginning to end Massachusetts and Virginia, so far apart in general outlook, gave leadership to a nation in the making.

And in this hour the Old Dominion produced a circle of men whose names would stir later generations to rise for freedom in Western Europe, in the Orient, in Africa: Washington, Jefferson, Madison, Patrick Henry . . . They formed a band such as the South and the country would not know again.

It was a time of many crosscurrents. Over Europe there swept an attitude of enlightenment, a recognition of natural rights among men. Yet England faced unhappy confusion—a Parliament unconcerned about liberty, corruption in high places, a fumbling, pigheaded king, George III.

An important group of Britons felt sympathy with the Americans. Few spoke more vigorously than Edmund Burke, who warned England that it could not "falsify the pedigree" of the English-Americans, "and persuade them that they are not sprung from a nation in whose veins the blood of freedom circulates."

They were becoming a new people, changed by their lands, the tobacco fields of Virginia and the villages of New England, by the trade of Charleston and New York and the rapidly expanding port of Baltimore. But in a way, the new Americans succeeded because they felt profoundly—until the guns roared—that they were still Englishmen like those across the sea, asking only what other Englishmen had fought to obtain. At another time the British genius for adjustment might have settled the quarrels; in the 1770's that opportunity was lost.

Many said that the colonies could never unite. The same English minister who had remarked upon the Virginians' independent manner declared that if the colonials were "left to themselves, there would soon be a civil war from one end of the continent to the other." The people fought incessantly over trade, jockeyed for competitive advantage, and seldom joined those of other colonies even in causes so vital as defense against the Indians. As the mid-1700's went by, harsh colonial conflict developed in North Carolina, Virginia, and elsewhere—not North against South, but East against West, the privileged seaboard against the struggling interior.

Resentment ran highest in North Carolina with the Regulator movement, which some consider an immediate prelude to the Revolution itself. Western Carolinians shook their fists as they protested high taxes, corruption, denial of rights to land, and blamed it all on the more élite eastern elements. In 1768 they formed a mass-scaled organization to "regulate" the colonial government, broke up courts, and in some instances dragged judges about town and burned the homes of officials. Word spread that the Regulators planned to march on the capital at New Bern and set it and the governor's handsome palace afire.

At this point the beleaguered Governor William Tryon called out the militia, largely easterners, and led them against his opponents. Fifteen hundred well-disciplined men met two thousand untrained Regulators in the fierce Battle of Alamance in 1771, and Tryon's followers won. A half-dozen Regulators went to the gallows on charges of treason. More than five thousand accepted clemency, while hundreds of others left for areas to the west, and bitterness rankled.

Before then troubles with England had flared up. On the surface it might have appeared that the Southern colonists had less reason than their cousins in

"If *this* be treason . . ." Patrick Henry's cry before the Virginia assembly stirred the colonists to action.

the North for a break with the old country. New England's manufacturing competed with Britain's, and London had long taken measures to curb it. On the other hand the South's tobacco, rice, and indigo were received warmly by Britain, which also encouraged items such as indigo, tar, and pitch with bounties that made colonials richer. And to help the tobacco trade, the Spanish product was now barred from England.

At the same time, however, people of the South complained that the empire's commercial policies hampered their development, making them pay all-too-high rates by using English vessels instead of continental European ones. Tobacco men raged repeatedly, too, over monumental debts and charges against them that mounted every year on the British merchants' books. "Bloodsuckers," "robbers" were among the words they used. Furthermore, England refused to let coins be exported to any of the colonies, prohibiting the colonies from minting their own, and placed restrictions on the printing of paper money. Colonists had to use substitutes like tobacco certificates and buck skins, from which arose the American slang term "buck." Nevertheless, the historian Clement Eaton concluded, the South could bear the situation until a sudden change occurred, following England's war with France.

The Seven Years' War allowed the colonials, North and South, to learn more about one another. In their battle experience, the colonials acquired a greater mutual respect, and an admiration for men such as George Washington, commander of Virginia's forces. But the very size of England's victory brought the beginning of the end of her empire in America. With the danger of the French removed, the colonials became less dependent on the mother country. After peace came, London decided to remove a basis of future Indian disputes by setting up at least a temporary line; to the east, white men; to the west, the red.

Above: Fair Warning. The Stamp Act gave it birth.

Right: ". . . or give me death!" At St. John's Church, in Richmond, Patrick Henry made his second famous appeal.

From England's viewpoint the proposal made good sense. Yet it collided with the constant colonial pressure to turn Indian forest into settlers' fields. Directly involved were strong Virginia interests, those of planters and investors who had formed land companies to penetrate this region. And soon English officials reached a still more abrasive decision. For years the colonials had lived under varying trade laws, which were enforced sparingly as officials permitted smuggling, charged only token amounts, or took bribes. Now, with peace, the British had large new areas to administer and the cost of the fighting to write off. One source of revenue seemed clear—the colonies that had benefited by the war with France. Thus the government ordered firm enforcement of trade measures, and in 1764 planned its first direct internal tax on America, aimed at licenses, legal papers, and journals: the Stamp Act.

From Virginia came the initial response, in white-hot fury. At the Williamsburg Capitol, a thin, rawboned, redheaded Virginian got up in the House of Burgesses. Patrick Henry was a radical; "son of thunder," some termed him, after hearing his blazing oratory, his short, pounding sentences, with gestures of long hands and elongated fingers. On this day he cried: "Tarquin and Caesar had each his Brutus, Charles the First his Cromwell, and George the Third—" As Patrick Henry paused, the Speaker shouted, "Treason!" and the word echoed from a dozen other lips.

Henry went on: "—may profit by their example. If *this* be treason, make the most of it." (Despite certain questioning of the words quoted in the incident,

An English Satire on the Stamp Act Agitations. Printed in London, 1766.

The Ladies of Edenton. An artist's view of the way Edenton, North Carolina, acted in the matter of non-drinking of English tea.

The War Came Steadily Closer.

Henry's best biographer accepts it.) The orator had introduced seven vigorous "resolves," declaring colonists entitled to all the liberties of Britons, insisting that Virginians alone could tax Virginians. Only five passed, and by narrow margins, but the acts and Patrick Henry's words, "in a strain never before heard in the Royal Capitol," struck fire. "An alarum bell to the disaffected," said the Governor of Massachusetts, and the bell rang loudly and clearly. As one colonial assembly after another took similar action, the "ball of Revolution" rolled. . . . No one was more affected than a student of law, standing in the doorway, who wrote later that to him Henry "spoke as Homer wrote." He was Thomas Jefferson, and he never forgot the episode.

Soon "Sons of Liberty" were forming, to erect "Liberty Poles," hold torchlight marches, break windows, punch heads, and threaten tar-and-featherings. Again and again the colonials forced Stamp Act officials to escape or make public resignation of their assignments. Wilmington and Brunswick, North Carolina, witnessed massive demonstrations that alarmed conservatives. In 1765 nine colonies sent representatives to a Stamp Act Congress in New York, which asserted loyalty to the king—yet demanded that colonials receive all rights due to Englishmen. The ball of Revolution still rolled, but slowly. The Americans boycotted British goods, and thousands of workmen lost jobs.

After long argument Parliament repealed the obnoxious Stamp Act, and at Williamsburg, Charleston, and other Southern centers crowds shot fireworks and heard joyful speeches. For a time, however, the colonials did not know that just as Parliament gave way in the matter of stamps, it passed another measure reaffirming its right to tax the colonies. Ten years followed, during which new disputes crackled, quieted, broke again. The mother country took steps to require colonials to quarter troops; it adopted levies on imports, including tea, and ordered revenue violators taken overseas for trial.

Each step stirred Southern resentment. For a time Virginia acted hesitantly, but in the Old Dominion liberal western elements gained strength over the calmer Tidewater. Discontent grew until 1769, when on learning that Boston rioters were to be tried in London, the Virginia burgesses struck out so sharply that the disturbed royal governor dissolved their assembly. Thereupon members went over to the Raleigh Tavern and signed an agreement to reject British goods—and slaves. The motion was presented by a farmer-member who had recently resigned from the Virginia military, George Washington of Mount Vernon.

When that dispute calmed, Virginia legislators of 1773—among them Thomas Jefferson, Patrick Henry, and George Mason—formed a committee to keep in touch with other colonial representatives. Co-operation was coming closer. That same year the Bostonians staged their Tea Party, dumping the cargoes into the harbor. In retaliation the English shut down the port, and a new apprehension ran through the South. Might not Charleston suffer the same way, or Baltimore or Savannah?

---

Opposite page: A Man Six Feet Two Inches. George Washington of Mount Vernon, Virginia, became commander in chief of the American forces.

Simple Home, High Tradition. At Bridges' Creek, Westmoreland County, Washington was born in this plain house, which had four rooms on the ground floor, several in the attic, heavy chimneys at each end.

Charleston and the other ports forwarded food and general help to the Bostonians, and at Williamsburg, Virginians took steps that brought the break with England still nearer. They asked a "Day of Fasting, Humiliation, and Prayer" and implored "Divine Interposition, for averting the heavy Calamity which threatens Destruction to our civil Rights, and the Evils of civil war." As before, the governor dissolved the Assembly, and members again repaired to the Raleigh Tavern. With Jefferson taking a leading role, the burgesses asked for a colonial congress to develop a uniform plan for the preservation of rights. That act did much to bring the First Continental Congress, called by Massachusetts.

At the Congress, Peyton Randolph of Virginia presided over a long debate regarding method of representation. Patrick Henry helped settle the issue when he called out: "The distinctions between Virginians, Pennsylvanians, New Yorkers, New Englanders are no more. I am not a Virginian, but an American!" Six months later, at St. John's Church in Richmond, Henry made his famous demand for arming of the militia. "Is life so dear or peace so sweet as to be purchased at the price of chains and slavery? Forbid it, Almighty God. I know not what course others may take, but, as for me, give me liberty or give me death!"

Events moved rapidly. In North Carolina, fifty-five women took a much-talked-about step. "We the Ladys of Edenton do hereby solemnly engage not to conform to that pernicious practice of drinking tea, or . . . [using] ye wear of any manufacture from England." Burning their supplies of English tea, they sipped a beverage made from dried raspberry leaves, at this Edenton Tea Party. At Annapolis townsmen burned a tea ship in their harbor.

Then, in April of 1775, British soldiers fired on colonials at Lexington and Concord, Massachusetts, with "the shot heard round the world," and the fighting was on. At the Second Continental Congress, George Washington, an imposing man of six feet two inches, in the red and blue uniform of a Virginia militia colonel, solemnly received the title of commander in chief of the American forces.

During the following June of 1776, Thomas Jefferson labored for several days of a stifling summer, putting down sentences, pausing, trying others as he composed the Declaration of Independence. (His own state had already galvanized most of the South by declaring her separation from England.) Not happily the young Virginian saw the delegates remove his strong castigation of England for fastening a system of human slavery on the colonies. It was taken out,

Congress Voting Independence, July, 1776. Painting by Robert Edge Pine, 1788; completed by Edward Savage.

A Declaration by the Representatives of the UNITED STATES OF AMERICA, in General Congress assembled.

When in the course of human events it becomes necessary for one people to dissolve the political bands which have connected them with another, and to assume among the powers of the earth the separate and equal station to which the laws of nature & of nature's god entitle them, a decent respect to the opinions of mankind requires that they should declare the causes which impel them to the separation.

We hold these truths to be self-evident; that all men are created equal; that they are endowed by their creator with certain inherent & inalienable rights; that among these are life, liberty, & the pursuit of happiness; that to secure these rights, governments are instituted among men, deriving their just powers from the consent of the governed; that whenever any form of government becomes destructive of these ends, it is the right of the people to alter or to abolish it, & to institute new government, laying it's foundation on such principles & organising it's powers in such form, as to them shall seem most likely to effect their safety & happiness. prudence indeed will dictate that governments long established should not be changed for light & transient causes: and accordingly all experience hath shewn that

Facsimile of the original draft by Jefferson of the Declaration of Independence

Above: The Declaration of Independence. Its sentences were to ring down the centuries, around the world.

Right: Jefferson Was the Author. Franklin Adams, Livingston, and Sherman assisted, but Thomas Jefferson did the great work on the Declaration of Independence.

said Jefferson, "in complaisance to South Carolina and Georgia, who had never attempted to restrain the importation of slaves, and who, on the contrary, still wished to continue it." He added: "Our Northern brethren also, I believe, felt a little tender under those censures; for tho' their people had very few slaves themselves, yet they had been pretty considerable carriers of them to others."

Nevertheless the Virginian had achieved a statement of principles that would live on as one of history's great documents. "We hold these truths to be self-evident: that all men are created equal, that they are endowed by their creator with certain unalienable rights: that among these are life, liberty, and the pursuit of happiness . . ." Here was a brave time, a shining hour.

It was to be, to a marked degree, a civil war, with neighbor often raising gun or ax against neighbor, with families bleakly watching members align themselves on both sides of the quarrels. Certain strong Southern elements favored the king, among them conservative Anglican churchmen, various merchants who hoped that their trade would continue, and a section of large planters and their attorney-connections, who saw a general threat in the too democratic talk around them. Here and there, small planters of the back country refused to join the Revolution, mainly because Eastern growers favored it. A number of important figures shifted as events progressed; one would be repelled by British military acts, another horrified by the fury of the rebels. At the beginning Georgians held apart from the Revolution; comparatively new, the colony had close ties to England. Ever-conservative South Carolinians would frown on the fighters against the king, yet one of their privileged element, Christopher Gadsden, formed a "Liberty Tree" movement that drew thousands of artisans and workingmen of Charleston.

Left: He Provoked Virginia's First Resistance. Lord Dunmore, the governor, ordered gunpowder moved from Williamsburg's public magazine to a warship. To hamper the rebels, he also declared all slaves freed. Then he bombarded Norfolk from his ships.

Right: Norfolk Aflame

During the long years of the war many of the revolutionists cursed the fates as they saw their cause all but given up. Often it appeared that only a handful of foolish men had faith in their purposes. The colonists squabbled; the Congress intrigued, failed to provide men or materials, undercut officers in the field. Soon after taking command, George Washington wrote of his difficulties: "Such a dearth of public spirit, and want of virtue, and stock-jobbing, a fertility in all the low arts to obtain advantages . . . I never saw before and pray God I may never be witness to again. . . ." For Washington it was only the beginning of a long-drawn-out ordeal.

Over the war towers the figure of this Virginian. Without Washington, his patience, his unvarying determination, the struggle might have ended at any of a dozen points. Many underestimated him, wondering at the choice of a commander. He was stolid, never a highly communicative man. He lacked wit, brightness of mind and spirit. He had a reserve that repelled some of his well-wishers, and those around him frequently surpassed him in intelligence and the ability to articulate. And at times it was easy for his early contemporaries to consider Washington as little more than a shrewd and ambitious man, who had missed few opportunities to advance his interests. (Ultimately he owned sixty thousand or more acres.)

Yet the master of Mount Vernon had a fundamental character, an integrity that would serve well his fellow Southerners and fellow Americans. His courage

**Left: Virginian of 1776**

**Above: General Nathanael Green. Next to Washington, perhaps the best revolutionary soldier in the South.**

was rare, his capacity to stand up under disappointment and setback little less than phenomenal, and he possessed in great measure the old-fashioned quality of personal honor, bringing into public affairs "the severe standards of private morals."

Nevertheless Washington was also, despite the storybook portraits, a quite human being. For years he cherished a silent love for a woman who was already married. He could go four nights in a row to the Williamsburg theater to gaze dreamily on the beauty of a popular actress, and he admittedly liked "pretty little frisks." He loved to dance, and sometimes did so for hours; again, in high humor among friends, he could tell his quota of earthy stories. And, although he was eventually to speak out against war, he once said: "I heard the bullets whistle, and believe me, there is something charming in the sound."

He was a methodical man, who planned everything and acted with caution. At the moment of decision, however, Washington could strike with startling speed. As the war advanced he gained the confidence of officers and men in remarkable demonstrations of military daring. He grew in stature as the struggle wore on, as he fought against lack of supplies, lack of financial support, lack of men. Several times he had to agree with his subordinates that everything seemed lost; and yet he held on, doggedly, unsparing of himself.

Early in the war a British fleet moved on Charleston and Wilmington, its officers hoping to crystallize Tory sentiment there. The venture failed. Fighting in

The Swamp Fox and His Potatoes. The traditional painting showed how Francis Marion offered his customary meal to the Englishman.

these first years centered largely in the North, in Massachusetts, New York, New Jersey, Pennsylvania, and also Canada. Despite successes, the invading forces could not win vital points, and late in 1778 the British advanced southward. Savannah, then Charleston, fell, and both states were heavily scourged.

From the backlands of Virginia, the Carolinas, and Georgia emerged huntsmen with an uncanny skill, marksmen who picked off enemies like forest animals. They formed a nondescript crew, their "uniforms" whatever hunting dress they could find: greasy trousers, ripped coats, buckskin and fur caps. South Carolina saw the services of formidable bands of partisans in guerrilla operations. Francis Marion, the "Swamp Fox"; Thomas Sumter, the "Gamecock"; and Andrew Pickens each had his role, but it was Marion who captured the imagination of the region.

Francis Marion was a bold fighter, whose deeds, retold many times, border on folklore. In civilian life his manner had been quiet, hardly prepossessing. Small, slim, dark-complexioned, with sharp chin and sharper nose, Marion was an unimportant Carolina planter who, early in the war, had become an officer in the Second South Carolina Regiment. When that army surrendered, the area lay silent for a time. Then the raiders crept about to cut British communications, seize supplies, and crush isolated units.

Francis Marion's bases were remote recesses of the Low Country, a place of wet, shadowed cypress lands. Roads skirted the section; to an outsider it ap-

Left: Washington's Camp Chest

Right: Their Own Money. The colonials had their own treasuries and their own bills.

A Western Virginia Heroine. This romantic episode occurred near Wheeling. Elizabeth Zane defied Indian fire to bring powder to beleaguered colonists.

The Indians Grew Restless. In 1777 Indians from western Virginia struck at settlers. Along Wheeling Creek Major Samuel McColloch found himself trapped, and saved his life by leaping over a precipice. But five years later other Indians ambushed him and, according to legend, each member of the band ate a piece of his heart, to "give bravery."

peared impenetrable, and even a native might be lost there. The locale was made for the Swamp Fox, a retreat from which he and his men could materialize in a moment, strike a hard blow, and vanish in the echoing waste. The raiders slept under trees, around fires, and Marion shared the hardships of his mixed crew. They attacked at night, at bright noon; sometimes they broke up temporarily, to gather again at another point.

For thousands Marion was a Robin Hood, celebrated for his red jacket and blue breeches, the plume of his black-visored helmet lifting and falling as he swept across the land. That romantic headgear had a crescent of silver with the engraved words "Liberty or Death." And Marion figured in a favorite story of the British officer who went to his camp under a flag of truce. Invited to dinner, the Englishman discovered only a handful of baked potatoes on the table. The stranger asked if this were the regular fare. No, Marion assured him; since they had a guest, it was rather more than usual!

Marion's opponent was Colonel Banastre Tarleton, "Bloody Tarleton" who, said the rebels, had slaughtered men after they surrendered. "Remember Tarleton. No quarter!" they cried. In those days the fighting in the South became more and more of an outright civil war, patriots slashing at Tories in a murderous conflict. Local officials seized Tory property, hanged some, sent others into bitter exile. Loyalists who survived frequently joined the British armies and showed no more mercy than the rebels, burning, killing, and mutilating their opponents. And hundreds in the patriot ranks, hungry and despairing, deserted to the enemy.

Yet repeatedly the revolutionists of the South stood the test without flinching. They were, militarily speaking, often a rabble with guns. They fought in casual fashion, on impulse, and thousands had an unfortunate habit of slipping off home when the fancy struck. "The weather's just got too cold." Or: "The old 'oman says the kids need me to home. I'll be back." Often they did return.

Late in the war, Congress dispatched General Horatio Gates to South Carolina, where his patriot followers at Camden suffered a resounding defeat, losing two-thirds of their forces. By contrast, at Kings Mountain Southern frontiersmen turned the tables and sent the trained English and Hessian soldiers, together with Tory allies, into headlong retreat. General Nathanael Greene, who took the place of the unlucky patriot Gates, employed his limited band of fighters with skill and resource, withdrawing whenever he had to, keeping men and spirit intact. At Cowpens there occurred an important battle that proved that a small band of militia, handled with care, could smash a superior force of expert soldiers. The revolutionists set a trap, and in less than an hour an imposing British army was slashed to a fraction of its size. Similar demonstrations of backwoods tactics would crop up in later conflicts in the South.

England's old opponent, France, intervened on the revolutionary side, to tip the scales with her fleet and other aid. With French help the conflict came to a climax when action turned to the vicinity of Williamsburg in Virginia. In the peninsula of Yorktown, an old tobacco port, England's Lord Cornwallis set up his forces. From the New York area Washington hastened south. With Lafayette near him, a French army and a French fleet of twenty-eight ships, Washington prepared for a joint attack on Cornwallis. Here, military authorities agree, Washington showed superlative generalship, perhaps the greatest of his life. In an inferno of smoke and bullets the English put down their arms, and their mournful musicians played the meaningful notes of "The World Turned Upside Down."

George Washington returned to his beloved Mount Vernon on the Potomac, only to leave it as the country's first President. After a second term the Virginian went back gratefully to his acres, to give his final years to the congenial but difficult task of managing his large estate. "How much more delightful to an undebauched mind," he once declared, "is the task of making improvements on the earth than all the vain glories which can be acquired by ravaging it."

As much as did any Southerner of his day, Washington became an experimental grower. Turning from the old one-crop tobacco economy, he tried a range of many crops on his five separate farms, tested new types of cultivation, new breeds of animals. In an effort to arrest the ruin of overused soil, from which all of Virginia now suffered, he labored to fertilize his land in a way that few of his neighbors attempted. Among other honors he received a premium from an agricultural society for "raising the largest jackass."

Through the years Washington had changed a small, plain residence into a graceful mansion, a place which, in his own lifetime, Americans of South and North considered a shrine, almost a public establishment. Ruefully he once noted that Mount Vernon seemed to be like a "well-frequented tavern." The house, crowning a rise along the Potomac, is a superior example of Georgian Colonial with its delicate cupola, curving arcades, and a series of balanced outer structures, and remains a monument to the calm, slow-thinking man of principle who did more than any other to keep his country alive in the agony of its birth. For many years its central hall has held a significant object, a symbol of liberty for the nations. It is the key to the Bastille, taken when the French people broke into that stronghold of oppression. Lafayette presented it to him.

Beginning of the End. The surrender of General Burgoyne on October 16, 1777. Painted by Trumbull.

Washington's, and the Colonists', Friend. The gallant Marquis de Lafayette won revolutionists' hearts by support of their cause.

"The World Turned Upside Down." The music had a sad note as the British surrendered their standards at Yorktown.

Left: The Climax Approached. Charles, Lord Cornwallis, opposed Washington as the dénouement came near at Yorktown in Virginia.

The Closing Phase: Martha and George Washington

But Then, and for Generations Afterward, the World Visited. George Washington called it a "well-frequented tavern."

The Last Days Were Largely Serene. In his "little village" that was Mount Vernon, George Washington spent his final years as a farmer.

Greatest Voice of the South. Though high-born, Thomas Jefferson nevertheless believed in a natural aristocracy of "virtue and talents," and he became America's first spokesman for democracy.

# 9
# THE MAN OF MONTICELLO

"The Creator has made the earth for the living, not the dead."
—Thomas Jefferson

America was free, but would she continue free, or even continue as a country? With the confusion of the decade after the Revolution the new government came close to foundering. In the salvaging of the United States and the shaping of the nation that emerged, two Southerners had determining roles—George Washington and Thomas Jefferson. It was the latter who established a "Virginia Dynasty" that governed America for twenty-four unbroken years.

In the early postwar days many expected the country—the original thirteen colonies and the new settlements extending irregularly southward and westward toward French Louisiana—to collapse like a jerry-built structure. Under the old

Alexander Hamilton, the Pessimist View. Jefferson's astute opponent devoted himself sincerely to the cause of "the rich and well-born."

Confederation the government proved a weak "league of states," with little authority, without an executive, without power to stop brawlings over trade and customs and a dozen other matters. As Washington put it, "There are combustibles in every State which a spark might set fire to."

After many complaints and demands, with Virginia taking a leading part, a Philadelphia convention of 1787 went to work on a Constitution. Day after day competing interests, rival beliefs clashed. The world had known town-size free governments, but could one operate successfully over so many miles and so varying a scene, from New England dock to Carolina plantation to frontier hut?

The Constitution that emerged provided for a stronger national organization with a responsible President and a rough balance between executive, judicial, and legislative branches. In certain areas the Constitution was silent, and controversy would recur for generations, South and North, over its interpretation. Some elements were appalled; it made the President a king, the government a bloated monster, they said. Others contended that it gave too much to the propertied, too little to the plain people.

The issue of slavery threw an uneasy shadow over the proceedings. For the apportioning of representatives in Congress, the South demanded that its bondsmen be counted as "persons." But, various Northerners retorted, didn't the South claim its Negroes were simply property? Delegates reached a compromise, with a slave classed as three-fifths of a person. While many insisted that the arrangement gave the South far too large a power in government, the ratio carried.

Throughout the country men felt at least twinges of conscience about the existence of slavery in a government dedicated to equality among men. Nervously the Constitution passed over mention of the word, referring only to "service" or "labor." Powerful forces both North and South demanded an end to the bloody, barbarous slave trade. Again, an adjustment; the slave traffic would be halted in twenty years.

George Washington after his election as the first President said he left Mount Vernon with the emotions of a culprit headed for execution. During the eight years that followed, Washington served the nation well by setting up workable

As an Enemy Saw Jefferson. A caricaturist summed up all his conservative enemies' hostility to the man's policies.

For Years, a Muddy Southern Village. Generations of callers found Washington City ugly and uncomfortable. But then it acquired a quality of its own.

Gradually, a Beauty. In time the capital took on a beauty of wide avenues and many buildings.

machinery, bringing men together in unity and good will. He established procedures and precedents in situations left uncertain by the Constitution; he created a national credit, assisted commerce by sea. In spite of strong protests, he made use of presidential authority to curb an uprising in a state, when western Pennsylvanians staged their "Whisky Rebellion" against a new tax.

The two outstanding men in Washington's Cabinet were respectively a New Yorker and a Virginian, who represented philosophies which have struggled ever since, in one form or another, to control the American experiment. The former was Alexander Hamilton, his Secretary of the Treasury, a small and handsome man, briskly efficient. Hamilton, though the natural son of a West Indian merchant, was an aristocrat by temperament, and labored hard for his adopted class.

Hamilton's conservatism was grounded in a pessimistic view of humanity. The great error was to "suppose mankind more honest than they are. Our prevailing passions are ambition and interest." He saw two elements, "the rich and well born" against "the mass . . . turbulent and changing," and he set out to give the first group "a distinct, permanent share in the Government." Regarding him, Woodrow Wilson was to comment: "a great man, but not a great American."

The opposite view was held by Jefferson, Washington's Secretary of State. Lean, tall, and gangling, carelessly garbed at times, his talk could be unemphatic in style, though studded with fact and reasoned observation. Born to a privileged place in the Virginia Piedmont, Jefferson spent much of his life in an aristocratic group, and yet he struggled through the years in behalf of democratic principles. He favored a "natural aristocracy," based on "virtue and talents" rather than "wealth and birth." He also said: "I hold it, that a little rebellion, now and then, is a good thing, and as necessary in the political world as storms in the physical." And again: "The tree of liberty must be refreshed from time to time, with the blood of patriots and tyrants. It is its natural manure."

This man of earnest study and conviction had a fundamental faith in his fellow beings. To Jefferson the human mind was "perfectible to a degree of which we cannot as yet form any conception." He had "no fear but that the result of our experiment will be, that men may be trusted to govern themselves without a master." He was to become America's first great spokesman for democracy, and to make himself perhaps the greatest of Southerners. He failed in details; at many points the times were to be against him, and still he would stand forth as the nation's finest advocate of the democratic movement.

Although at home in Tidewater drawing rooms, Jefferson had the frontier in his soul. His father, a successful land surveyor, married a young woman of ranking family; in his boyhood Thomas watched many a backwoodsman and neighbor in hunting garb and coonskin cap. After early training the youth went to William and Mary College at Williamsburg where, under able teachers, his intellect broadened. Originally Jefferson was shy, ill at ease with crowds. Appraising his gaunt cheeks, big hands and feet, freckled skin and light eyes, some considered him the ugliest man on the campus. Yet even such observers liked him; throughout his life Tom Jefferson made and kept an amazing variety of friends.

The young Jefferson studied as long as fifteen hours a day. At the same time he profited from the high-spirited life of Williamsburg, the ballrooms and taverns; he had a good hand with a fiddle, if an occasionally awkward one with a number of young women, including the "fair Belinda" with whom he danced. He married a well-to-do widow of the Tidewater area, went to Albemarle as a lawyer, but before long developed a distaste for the profession. Early and late Jefferson preferred to think of himself as a farmer, and his heart remained with his plantings. Democratic government, he felt, could "endure only so long as the great majority of the people were farmers."

Here was a complex individual, a many-faceted one, yet also a man of simple common sense, and as the years passed his appeal to Americans grew in a surprising way. For he was no orator at all; he had nothing of the military record with which many Southerners, and also Northerners, frequently unqualified, have leaped to public office. At first politics repelled Jefferson, until he became a quiet master of the art, a deft hand at adjusting differences. Through the prerevolutionary days his voice was heard more and more often in vital deliberations. Then, as Virginia's governor during the war, Jefferson worked hard and effectively to implement his views.

In a sustained fight he ended the system by which great estates were held intact after a man's death and passed to an eldest son; other Southern states followed Virginia's lead. Here, as in many struggles, he tried to loosen the "hand of the dead." "Can one generation bind another, and all others, in succession forever? I think not," he declared. He labored for religious freedom, attacking Virginia laws which made the Church of England a tax-supported institution, although other denominations now had larger memberships. He tempered inhuman laws, ending capital punishment for lesser offenses. He strove to bring public schools to all districts of Virginia, with three years of fundamental instruction, followed by several more years in a higher school and a university at the top. From each school only the qualified would advance, with the government assuming costs for those unable to pay. (He included even girls.) While Virginia did not adopt the plan, his efforts eventually had some effect.

Above all, Jefferson worked against slavery. Under his regime Virginia did more than any Southern state to encourage emancipation, and led the region in action to abolish the African slave traffic. As a result of Jefferson's efforts a law permitted masters to liberate Negroes by "will or deed." (Until then this had been legally difficult.) He urged a graduated emancipation; he asked that any slave brought into Virginia be free after twelve months. Although some of his proposals were rejected, he could still write: "Nothing is more certainly written in the book of fate than that these people will be free." Once more: "I tremble for my country when I reflect that God is just; that his justice cannot sleep forever."

To the Confederation's Congress in 1784, Jefferson proposed that slavery be ended within sixteen years in the wide Federal territory extending to the Mississippi. (States had not yet been formed there.) He lost—by a single vote, and Jefferson spoke in sorrow: "Thus we see the fate of millions unborn hanging on the tongue of one man, and Heaven was silent in that awful moment!" Had his plan carried, a slow process of freedom might have spread over all of America.

Jefferson Was Its First Tenant. In the "President's House" Thomas Jefferson created a certain dismay by ignoring protocol, but he also made it a place for the meeting of great minds.

A Capitol To Match an Enlarging Nation. After vicissitudes, the structure became an impressive mass.

With such programs Jefferson inevitably made enemies among the more powerful elements of the society in which he moved. Now and then he tempered his efforts, only to resume in another way at another time. Often he hesitated; always he was ready to take a short step back in order to make a long one forward. Through it all his concern was man, his mind, his spirit, his opportunity for self-realization. The Virginian's curiosity was remarkable, the range of his interests phenomenal. He played the violin; he studied ancient Anglo-Saxon languages; he pored over models of steam engines, assembled facts about American Indian civilizations, taught himself Spanish on a nineteen-day ocean voyage to Europe and, while minister to France, made a full investigation of French and German vineyards for the guidance of Americans. He invented a swivel chair and a "polygraph" to make copies of his letters and devised a unique range of household gadgets to make his life simpler. Jefferson was America's closest approach to the Renaissance man. Still, he pointed out, "I am not fond of reading what is merely abstract." To a high degree Jefferson had the American bent toward the useful and the practical.

Such was the Virginian who served for a time in Washington's Cabinet, not altogether happily. Although a moderate, Washington largely supported the views of the firm conservative and nationalist, Alexander Hamilton. By contrast Jefferson favored a simple government, rural in background. The Hamiltonians looked

But Some Disapproved. Robert Cruikshank's aquatint was entitled "President's Levee, or all creation going to the White House."

"A Glimpse of Kentucky." Men entered it by the well-patronized Cumberland Gap.

to a broad construction of the Constitution, permitting the government various powers, while the Jeffersonians advocated a more narrow interpretation. Yet Jefferson, ever a flexible man, was to change his attitude in specific cases.

He was Vice President under Washington's successor, Adams, when the Federalists wrote into law their harsh Alien and Sedition acts, which permitted imprisonment of anyone publishing "false, scandalous and malicious writing" against the government. Twenty-four editors whose papers had opposed the administration were arrested, and Jefferson and his allies saw a clear violation of the constitutional protection of free speech and press. Jefferson promoted the famous Kentucky and Virginia Resolutions which called the two acts void and asked other states to join against them. No other states did so, several insisting that the Supreme Court was the only agency to declare laws contrary to the Constitution. (Only some years later did the Court assume that authority.) This explosive issue helped Jefferson and his Republican party, an organization of small farmers and townsmen who opposed the conservative elements. And yet, as some have forgotten, Jefferson retained a strong belief in a national union, and worked hard against later threats of secession by other sections.

In 1801 Jefferson won the Presidency by a two-vote electoral majority over the enigmatic Aaron Burr. Hamilton, Jefferson's great rival, used his strength to break a tie. While he considered Jefferson a man of "bad principles," Hamilton said, Burr was one of "no principles at all."

Many predicted wild days for the Republic under the "dangerous" Jefferson. The president of Yale fulminated that the Virginian's radical program would bring "legal prostitution" for the daughters of good Americans. Others foresaw, at the least, financial ruin and civic chaos. Nothing of the sort happened, of course, and Jefferson gave the country a quiet administration in which he made few domestic changes while he coped with endless problems in turbulent foreign relations.

To the White House of Jefferson's regime came guests of varied backgrounds and interests. Skillfully he drew them out, tossing in provocative questions, watching reactions. He never strove for status as others might have done, but insisted on a new simplicity in official life. To the horror of ambassadors and American dowagers, he abandoned protocol as the first President to be inaugurated in the newly laid-out capital on the Potomac, named for George Washington. For years the District of Columbia would seem a horror to those who had to be there, a muddy, barren waste with only an occasional finished building. With the village of Georgetown adjoining it, Washington would ultimately become one of the handsomest of world capitals. For the time being, residents of the uncomfortable Southern village could only dream of the day when it would change to something else, in the words of the poet Tom Moore:

> Though nought but woods and Jefferson they see,
> Where streets should run and sages ought to be.

In this setting Jefferson reached one of his most important decisions as President, one that altered the shape and future of his South and of the United States. As an old saying went, If hell were out West, Americans would jump over heaven to get to it. For years the Southerners had been pushing steadily beyond their old

---

The Tread of Pioneers. In his famous, romanticized painting of Daniel Boone leading his party, George Caleb Bingham epitomized an era.

bounds. In colonial days innumerable parties had crossed the Appalachians and followed river or mountain gaps to the rich hunting grounds of what were to be Kentucky and Tennessee. Wanderers, traders, and speculators went alone or with pioneer families from Virginia, North Carolina, Maryland, and other colonies.

Richard Henderson, "Nolichucky Jack" Sevier, James Harrod, Jacob Brown . . . these were only a few of a variegated band. Indians sometimes destroyed their settlements, or disapproving officials quarreled over their right to the land. Along the Ohio, in Tennessee, and the bluegrass section of central Kentucky men had to be sturdy, and also sturdy-willed, or die overnight. In the "dark and bloody ground," as the red men named Kentucky, new arrivals fought animals, Indians, disease, and the elements. And one report declared that of 255 men who in 1780 organized an early government of Tennessee, there were ten years later not quite a dozen survivors, and only one of the original band died of natural causes.

For those who survived in Kentucky, it frequently appeared to be a beckoning paradise of virgin forest and flashing waters. Often quoted is the remark of a local preacher. Heaven, he assured his listeners in terms of utmost praise, was a "perfect Kentucky of a place"! In 1792 Kentucky became a state, and four years later Tennessee followed. For years afterward, Americans were stirred by stories of the colorful Kentucky frontiersman Daniel Boone. Trapper, trader, and possessor of a restless pair of legs, Daniel moved from North Carolina to Florida and many another area before he returned to the bluegrass state to blaze a trail through the Cumberland, a trail which would be known as the Wilderness Road.

Daniel had become a master of the woods, an adept student of its secrets. Captured once by Indians, he was adopted as a chief's son, a role he greatly enjoyed, and as he often said, he learned to "think like a red man." In later years

Left: Protecting His Family. In an idealized scene, admired in another day, Daniel Boone saved his wife and child from a tomahawk.

Right: Daniel's Tree, Near Jonesboro, North Carolina

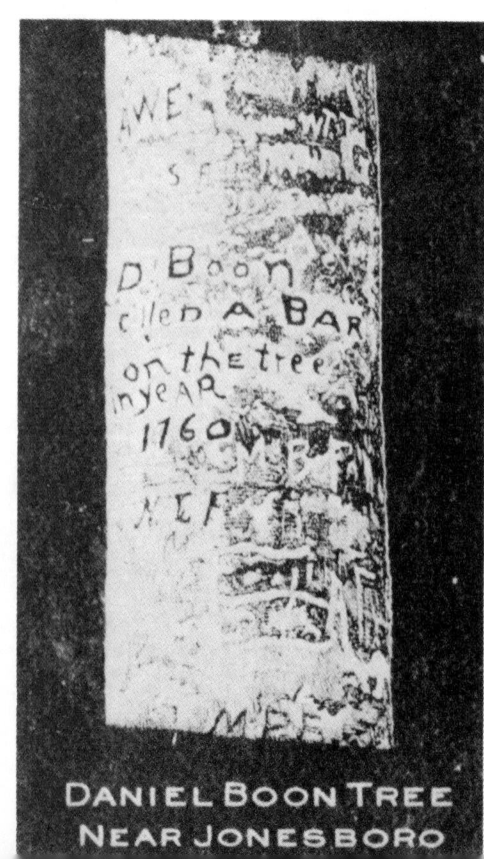

Daniel was asked if he had ever been lost. He couldn't say he'd been *that,* but admitted he had once been "bewildered for three days."

Settlers who followed Boone, taking acres pointed out to them by land speculators, found a demand for their produce—flour, corn, bacon—if they could get it to a market. Their natural passageway lay down the Mississippi and its tributaries to the Gulf. The frontier people had to reach New Orleans or die of economic strangulation. Through the 1700's and early 1800's lines of keelboats, flatboats, and other craft came down the river to the Crescent City, where the frontiersmen disposed of their goods and started the long trip home on foot or by horse.

But Louisiana, originally French, was now in Spanish hands, and Spain looked suspiciously on the forthright rivermen. Then the Spaniards began to clamp down, selectively. Some Americans could use the port, while others could not. It was a game of carrot-and-stick, its purpose evident: to persuade the practical-minded frontiersmen to break away from the United States. At first rivermen shouted defiance and talked of organizing flatboat-loads of settlers to sail down and seize the place. Others hesitated, and a surprising number of Westerners seemed to see merit in the Spanish cause. Some took bribes to work secretly for Spain.

Perhaps, they argued, their interests did lie with any nation that held this vital entryway to the continent. Besides, what did the Eastern states care about *them,* except to sell them out whenever they could? As a matter of fact, many influential Easterners tended to regard the American users of the Mississippi as rambunctious troublemakers. Such people made up almost another nation, with far different interests, far different purposes. Let them go!

For years the issue hung in uncertain balance. Washington once declared that the Westerners stood "as it were on a pivot," and "the touch of a feather would turn them any way." By 1793 the West boiled with a new excitement. The Revolution had broken over France, sending to the United States a special envoy, Citizen Genêt, who came to promote, among other things, a fantastic scheme. The French, now hostile to their former Spanish friends, had a plan: assemble the rivermen and lead them against New Orleans, to take it and nearby Florida for France! The revolutionary government was even prepared to order vessels to assist in this exotic enterprise.

These were remarkable times indeed. The effervescent Genêt gave the frontiersmen military commissions in an *Armée du Mississippi* and an *Armée du Floride,* and the excited Westerners put up new Liberty Poles and started to call one another "Citizen McIntire," "Citizen Johnson," and the like. Clearly Genêt's operations would tend to disrupt the young Republic. The American government protested firmly to France, and *l'affaire Genêt* collapsed. (The unconventional envoy, unwilling to go back to the spreading revolutionary terror across the sea, decided to stay, and eventually married a rich American.)

Then, in mid-1801, the sorely pressed President Jefferson came into a piece of amazing intelligence. In a secret treaty France had persuaded Spain, now under Napoleon's tight control, to cede all of Louisiana back to her, the original owner. The Corsican envisioned a new Gallic empire, a glorious realm including North America and, as an added bauble, the island of Santo Domingo. Already

The Older Daniel. The woodsman was ready for whatever the later years would bring him.

"Kentucky's First Fort." Boone erected it in 1775 at Boonesborough.

an overpowering expeditionary force was moving toward the island, to crush an inconvenient Negro uprising there. Let that minor disturbance be quieted, and the fleet would sail on to New Orleans.

With that information Jefferson had to choose between consistency and his country's interest. A strong, aggressive French neighbor would be a very different one from tired Spain. Jefferson had always been a friend of France, but now he made a historic decision. "The day that France takes possession of New Orleans . . . we must marry ourselves to the British fleet and nation." Overnight the Spanish intendant, still in charge at the Creole city, shut the port tightly to Americans. With this black development the Westerners burst into fury: Take the damned city; march down, ride down the river and show the world!

At any moment war might break, but Jefferson practiced his usual calm and also a shrewd diplomacy. Persuading Congress to vote a then-heavy appropriation of two million dollars for international dealings (details kept extremely vague), he dispatched James Monroe to Paris. The United States was ready to give up to 50,000,000 francs for New Orleans and Florida. If that proposal failed, Monroe would suggest three-quarters of the amount for "the island of New Orleans," or perhaps only a portion of land there to receive American goods for transshipment to the world. If *that* did not work, Monroe should seek a French guarantee that the American people could have permanent use of the river and port facilities at its mouth. Finally, if none of these dealings succeeded, the American agent must get in touch with the British—to negotiate a strong alliance against France.

As Jefferson waited, world changes were in the making. French armies in Santo Domingo melted away; disease as well as the Negroes, who fought bravely for their land, had won, and one of the bastions of Napoleon's proposed empire had vanished. War was about to begin once more in Europe, and Napoleon needed funds. Now, too, he would have to contend with England's powerful fleet, and could anything keep it from taking New Orleans out of his hands? If the United States were in possession of this large tract in the heart of the continent, he would at least be helping to create a great future force against the nation he hated. And so, to the astonishment of the American minister, Talleyrand of France quietly asked: What would the United States give for the whole of Louisiana?

Such a possibility had never been considered. Louisiana of that day was a 900,000 square-mile empire, as large or larger than the states themselves. How could they absorb this fantastic spread of territory? More than that, were the American representatives authorized to bid for it? Monroe and his colleague weighed the odds, then grasped at the chance. They entered into negotiation and agreed to a price of $15,000,000, or four cents an acre. At home President Jefferson debated with himself, but only briefly, since the ever-uncertain Napoleon might change his mind.

Was such a purchase permissible within the Constitution? Many Jeffersonians, advocates of a narrow interpretation, would say it was not, and the President himself had strong misgivings. But, as he had said, "The Creator has made the earth for the living, not the dead." He accepted and pressed the matter through Congress. Opponents taunted him with this reversal, and some men of the upper Atlantic, of New England in particular, attacked the proposal heatedly. It would lessen the influence of the East, give the West and South more power than ever. New Englanders, complaining that the basis of the Union had been broken, threatened secession.

Still others balked at the thought of the peculiar Louisianians: "A hotchpotch, a mixed race of Anglo-Hispano-Gallo-Americans who bask on the sands of the mouth of the Mississippi." As for the Louisianians themselves, many of the élite Creoles groaned at the prospect of union with Americans. A connection with loud-mouthed barbarians from Virginia and Georgia and Boston and those other crazy places . . . *Mon Dieu,* what would happen to them and their civilization? But firmly, determinedly, Jefferson carried out the program that would rank among his greatest monuments.

Among Jefferson's many interests, architecture ranked high. He rejected the popular Georgian style, and turned instead to the classic. He studied Greek and Roman structures in Europe, and returned to design some of the best of the Old South's historic buildings. Near Charlottesville, Jefferson built his Monticello, a majestic house with a Doric portico and white-domed upper section. Seeing it, the Marquis de Chastellux termed him "the first American who has consulted the fine arts to know how he should shelter himself from the weather." A place that grew with the owner's changing ideas, Monticello had disappearing beds, hidden staircases, a remarkable clock operated by weights and pulleys—and an ingenious

Plain Tennessee-Kentucky Mountaineers. As others saw them.

A More Opulent Era. The icehouse at Henry Clay's Ashland estate demonstrated the statelier aspect as Kentucky grew settled.

dumbwaiter by which meals could be served, without distraction, from pantries below.

Jefferson also planned Richmond's noble state Capitol, probably the finest public structure in the Old Dominion, an adaptation of the Maison Carrée, the Roman Temple at Nîmes. It influenced many others, and Thomas Jefferson is considered one of the fathers of the stately classic style that came to characterize, beyond any other, the South of the 1800's. In Virginia, in the District of Columbia, wherever he went, he proselytized for it; enthusiastically he brought it to attention of plantation men, town people, riverbank residents, urging them to produce their own versions and adaptations.

In his later years Jefferson saw Virginia accept a project close to his heart and to his mind, a project that combined his concern for architecture and his passion for learning—his beloved University of Virginia. He drew the designs for one of the great structural groups still intact in the South and in America. At Charlottesville he envisioned a collection of "academic villages," with teachers and students sharing a life of study. The dominant building was the Rotunda, suggested by the Pantheon of Rome. Along a terraced central lawn stood five large pavilions in the shape of temples, with long rows of structures behind colonnades. Against the rolling Albemarle area, the warm red bricks and white columns have gained in mellow beauty with the years.

It was America's first university without narrow denominational basis, one dedicated to "the illimitable freedom of the human mind. For here," said Jefferson, "we are not afraid to follow the truth wherever it may lead, nor to tolerate any error, so long as reason is left free to combat it."

This follower of the truth, wherever it led, lived to be eighty-three, and his final years were shadowed. Through all his days he had been prodigal of his heart and his means, and he had drained himself of funds. Nevertheless, as in the case of George Washington, the world called; sometimes there were as many as thirty uninvited guests for dinner, many for a weekend or a week—whole families in a body. He received them all.

At the edge of bankruptcy, Jefferson hoped for assistance from the people of Virginia to whom he had given so much. They provided help, but not enough to remove his concern about his heavy debts. Yet, despite hours of despondency, his eternal optimism returned. Barely able to walk, he still managed to ride his horse, inspecting his handsome acres at Monticello. Three weeks before the end he bought a book; he had never lost his zest for learning, for new information. He died on the Fourth of July, 1826, the day to whose meaning his life had contributed very much. He was invited to join a Washington celebration of this fiftieth anniversary of American independence, but the old man declined with his characteristic simple eloquence:

> All eyes are opened, or opening, to the rights of man. The general spread of the light of science has already laid open to every view the palpable truth, that the mass of mankind has not been born with saddles on their backs, nor a favored few booted and spurred, ready to ride them legitimately, by the grace of God. These are grounds of hope for others. . . .

Jefferson's Masterwork. Few achievements meant so much to Jefferson as his "academic village," the University of Virginia, combining his interest in classic building and in education.

But Many New Orleanians Cried. The French flag lowered, the American rose at Place d'Armes.

He Negotiated for an Empire. Jefferson's emissary James Monroe acquired a fantastic addition to the new country, the Lousiana Purchase.

Night March. Latin in origin, New Orleans in embellishment, Carnival approached a high point in the years just before the war with the North. An impressed Englishman drew this version of the 1858 procession.

A Touch of France, a Touch of Spain. A postwar Carnival ball with grotesque heads and garb.

Parade Coming! Nurses, praline sellers, matrons, babies, all appeared on the streets and balconies of the French Quarter.

Left: To See and To Be Seen. The grand tier of the New Orleans Opera House during a Carnival ball.

Below: Only Henry Clay Seemed Unmoved. Mardi Gras around Clay's statue on Canal Street in New Orleans.

The Gin Also Meant More Houses in the Deep South. They were wide-galleried, high-ceilinged, often had basements with flood protection, and occupied semitropical settings.

# 10

# ENTER COTTON, AND THE SLUMBROUS DEEP SOUTH

"A cotton crop . . . became a golden fleece."—ULRICH B. PHILLIPS

A NORTHERNER of Northerners, journeying to Georgia on a quiet teacher's errand, set in motion a series of events that brought on an economic revolution in the South, a revolution that was to alter, in one way or another, the lives of practically every man and woman in the region.

During later years, certain Southerners would swear consistently at "the Yankees." Logically they might have directed their wrath at the well-meaning Northern schoolteacher Eli Whitney. For his cotton gin gave the South a wealth such as it had never before known, but in time brought it close to destruction. The device that the young man from Massachusetts created set the region apart from the rest of the nation and, in the opinion of many, made inevitable the war that broke out in 1861.

Fields whitening steadily in a fervent sunlight, heavily pressed bales piled at the river landings, unprecedented holdings that materialized in a single season, with new slaves multiplying in the tens of thousands . . . all of this appeared swiftly after Mr. Whitney made his contribution. And just as swiftly there arrived a roaring land boom, speculation on a scale such as the country had never seen before.

The cotton gin came into being at a decisive hour in the 1790's. In one place after another slavery had begun to sicken, dwindling in Virginia and Maryland, proving an economic burden in other Southern areas. Tobacco prices were dropping badly. In colonial days England had supported South Carolina indigo by a subsidy; with that gone the crop died away, and now rice growing suffered from certain basic difficulties. George Washington, along with many others, tried to develop a balanced farming program, but slavery did best with staple plantings, under a day-in, day-out routine.

In the older South a general decline was in progress as the soil became ever more depleted. In a number of coastal colonies, population diminished by 50 per cent in only fifteen years, when estates were broken up and big houses left in neglect. After some years even Jefferson's superb Monticello was to go for less than four thousand dollars. Before 1795 bondsmen were in oversupply, and a typi-

From New England, a Southern Revolution. Eli Whitney gave the South the fateful invention that set the base of its great prosperity.

cal grower regretted that practically every year he had to sell a few to get food for the rest. Thus "they eat each other up."

George Washington advised a correspondent to give up slaves for other property. "Were it not that I am principled against selling negroes, as you would cattle in a market, I would not in twelve months hence be possessed of a single one as a slave." Another Virginian, the sardonic John Randolph of Roanoke, declared that if conditions continued to deteriorate, "the slave shall not elope from his master, but his master will run away from him," and the Negro would "advertise for the return of his owner." After a stay in Virginia the Marquis de Chastellux observed that the growers were "constantly talking of abolishing slavery and of contriving some other means of cultivating their estates." Many expressed the belief that the system would wither away as it proved unprofitable.

Would the result have been a spread of general farming such as obtained in other areas, and a gradual increase of industry, trade, and commerce? Many Southerners welcomed the thought. Developments abroad and in the New World were to dictate another answer. In England inventors had perfected engines that could spin and weave with amazing rapidity. Cloth could be produced far more cheaply than ever before, and a great new market for cotton goods had opened. English woolens, long supreme, soon had to give way to cotton. Woolen interests fought fiercely against the trend, even implying that the delicate cotton was immoral and un-English because it promoted "erotic" feelings in chaste women who wore it! Yet the momentum of cotton in the economy could not be stopped; suddenly the mills needed much more cotton and still more.

Hour of Harvest. Eventually, in the warm sun, came the long process of picking the fleecy product.

Left: Cotton Fields of Fervent Growth: Mississippi, Alabama, Tennessee, Louisiana, Georgia

Below: Pressing Cotton for Bales. The lint went into a press for baling. Cotton bagging covered each bale, with metal ties for security. Eventually bales weighed up to five hundred pounds each.

Cotton had been a very minor Southern crop from the first years at Jamestown. A special type, the long staple, thrived on the limited area of the Georgia Sea Islands; the short staple could be grown with ease over a wide range of soils. The short variety, however, had a serious drawback. To remove the seeds took far too much effort, far too many hours, far too much labor. Americans had contented themselves with tiny patches, while a few even bought small amounts of cotton from overseas.

By the 1790's a vast new market awaited the Southern growers if they could only evolve a machine to take out the seeds. At this point Eli Whitney, a recent graduate of Yale, accepted an offer of a position as tutor for a family in South Carolina, near the Georgia line. Embarking on a coastal schooner, he met the lively, handsome young widow of General Nathanael Greene. There had been a misunderstanding about the amount the teacher would receive, and, uncertain what to do, Whitney accepted an invitation to visit the widow's Mulberry Grove estate near Savannah, a property given to the Greenes by the grateful state.

There the New Englander heard considerable talk about the cotton "situation." Before long the hostess noted that young Whitney could "do anything with a machine." As he wrote to his father: "There were a number of very respectable gentlemen at Mrs. Greene's, who all agreed that if a machine could be invented . . . it would be a great thing both to the country and to the inventor. In about ten days I made a little model. . . ." As a matter of fact, Whitney devoted five or six months to careful testing, and evolved a device that greatly interested Phineas Miller, another Northerner, who had become Mrs. Greene's plantation manager and who would later be her husband. Miller provided the necessary financial backing, and he and Whitney agreed to split profits.

In time the two surveyed a machine that would "make the labor fifty times less." The gin ("engine" in shortened Southern style) was a wooden cylinder with spikes like porcupine quills; as the cotton rolled by, the seeds fell out. Hurriedly Whitney went to the East for one of the new Federal patents, and within a year he and Miller had gins in manufacture. Demand was phenomenal. "The people of the country are running mad for them," Miller wrote to his associate. The cotton poured out of the fields to the machines, and cultivation raced through Georgia and the two Carolinas, spreading to counties that had never tried cotton, then jumping to adjoining states.

Unsympathetic witnesses called it "the cotton mania," but the mania paid. Some thought the crop the closest thing to the Southern gold for which the Spaniards had hunted. Before Whitney's invention the nation (mainly the South) exported less than 140,000 pounds of cotton; two years later the figure reached 1,600,000. On all sides, alas, others copied the simple machine, and the monopoly that Whitney and Miller tried to enforce meant little. The two men realized only a modest return on their labors, and spent years in hopeless lawsuits.

By then cotton was transforming the South, its economy, and its thinking. Cotton became the great crop of the region, far more important than tobacco or rice. With every decade production practically doubled. At the beginning of the 1800's, some 100,000 bales were produced; by 1860 the figure had gone above

Cotton, Cotton Everywhere. The Charleston docks shipped it out to the world.

Ready for the World. Guilmartin & Company of Savannah did a thriving business, as shown in this photograph, taken about 1860.

4,500,000. The South sent out an ever-larger proportion of the world's cotton, and eventually accounted for two-thirds of the world's total production. Cotton took on a soaring importance as the nation's main export, with more than half the value of all the others combined. And, significantly, three-quarters of the nation's slaves were to work in fields devoted to the crop.

The cotton rush was on, a cotton kingdom in the making, from the edges of the upper South down across part of the future Texas and up to Arkansas and Missouri. At many points in the early South men substituted cotton for tobacco, transforming their economy. But it was in the newer South that cotton achieved its greatest revolution.

The swiftly expanding crop intensified pressures on growers, big and little, to find fresh lands to the south and west, toward the Gulf, toward the Mississippi and beyond. Vast areas of the Louisiana Purchase beckoned, and into the future Alabama, Mississippi, and the lower Louisiana territory went landseekers by boat or wagon packed with household and planting supplies, their farm animals with them and also their slaves. Western Tennessee, in the vicinity of Memphis, was a favored spot, as was the rest of the land bordering the lower Mississippi.

Everybody wanted to get there first, take the untouched soil, and turn it into white fields. The pattern was clear: Locate land near a river, set the black workers, or your own family, to their tasks, and watch yourself get rich. The newcomers were of every stripe: old Virginia planters or new Georgia ones on the economic make; men who sold large possessions in the Atlantic coastal areas to invest everything in Louisiana; others who had saved for years to buy three or four slaves and move southwestward.

Especially privileged individuals would send an overseer and a band of slaves ahead of him and his family to clear the land, put up a house, and make the way easier. Others, however, rode broken animals, changed to rafts, and trusted to God that they would somehow reach fine land, to turn it into their own. And here and there throughout the states of the Deep South rose the sprawling properties of absentee landowners, who stayed in Virginia or the Carolinas and reaped their rewards at a distance.

Steadily the center of cotton production shifted to the newer South. By 1830 more was being grown in areas near the Gulf than along the Atlantic. Power follows riches; while the Old Dominion clung to its old ways and habits, the lower South and Southwest came to the front rank, and with them they brought new attitudes, new ways of doing things. This land was different from the Atlantic coastal areas—loamy river valleys and lowlands stretching from horizon to horizon; giant forests ending suddenly in acres pale with the cotton bolls. The Deep South had a somber, prodigal beauty that could be violent: dim swamps, silent as if asleep, but teeming with a half-malevolent life; plains bright with a half-tropical spring beauty.

It was a lush land and a cruel one, in which man could live off a heavy bounty of nature, or suffer destruction in a day from disease, fever, pestilence. For miles the stranger met little delicate gradation of light—a shadowed wood, and then a dazzling patch of sunshine on stream and open field. And everything grew furiously in an endless cycle of procreation, birth, decay, death, and new birth. Often the heavy heat caused the inhabitants to seem indolent. But if that was so, the climate also bred strong emotions, bitter opinions, insistently held, and furies that could sweep down like a Gulf storm. Decidedly this new South was a more excitable, more impulsive place than the earlier one.

Slaves were, of course, in steadily increasing demand, and their prices would rise until they reached what many thought fantastic levels. It just wasn't fair, mister, to have to pay so much. . . . Most of the Southern states, like the Northern ones, had outlawed the grim overseas slave trade, and in 1808 Congress ended it on a national basis. Nevertheless the cotton South demanded bondsmen and bondswomen, and until the war men continued to smuggle in loads of slaves for high fees.

Simultaneously a vigorous and profitable traffic in Negroes went on among the states. From the older places streams of black people were taken to the new land, chained in small groups or loud clanking parties on journeys that lasted for hundreds of miles. No matter what some of the Virginians and Marylanders thought, such older states became slavebreeders for the newer ones. Only the sale of Negroes, year after year, kept many old-time plantations from bankruptcy. Under these conditions the earlier movements to free the bondsmen underwent a slow decline. The new leaders of the Deep South had little of Jefferson's or Washington's concern over slavery and its evils.

It would be hard to find a "typical" planter of so far-flung a country, among men who were openhanded and tightfisted, naïve and cunning, hard and gentle. The plantation of Burleigh in Hinds County, Mississippi, was probably a pleasanter one than many others, and Susan Dabney Smedes wrote an unusually detailed memoir to show what its life was like. In 1835, at thirty-eight, Thomas S. Dabney left a good-sized Chesapeake property to buy a group of farms in the lower South. Recently remarried to a girl of sixteen, Thomas was to have a second family of sixteen children. In an area that was part hilly, part lowland, he eventually owned four thousand acres, and in an exceptionally good year he reaped a heavy return.

Their house at the beginning leaked terribly, and Thomas Dabney often had to sit up in bed, holding an umbrella over his wife and baby. The crop had to be hauled in wagons for forty miles, and the master accompanied each vehicle to safeguard it from accident. During such trips he slept under the wagon. But soon conditions improved for Dabney, and he resumed a life much like the one he had known in Virginia. Eventually he had under his charge the destinies of five hundred slaves, including those of his family connections.

Neighbors considered Burleigh a "model" plantation, Dabney's daughter tells us, and other growers asked his rules. He worked his slaves five days and a half rather than six, and Dabney said he got more out of them this way. Every week during a four- or five-month cotton-picking season he gave prizes for best performances—a dollar for first place, a Mexican coin of 87½ cents for second, and so on. "The master gave money to all who worked well for the prizes, whether they won them or not. When one person picked six hundred pounds in a day, a five-dollar gold piece was the reward." On most plantations 350 pounds was a good day's work, but at Burleigh many handled 500.

Thomas Dabney was a proud man, and liked to dress in broadcloth with plated buttons. He rose late, insisting that "it did not so much matter when a man got up as to what he did after he was up." Burleigh plantation had a certain punctilio.

Cotton Wagon Train

For dinner, "Everybody was expected to be ready, and sitting with the family in the hall or drawing room or dining room not less than five minutes before the last bell rang." Nevertheless Tom Dabney made an effort to accept some of the rules of his simpler neighbors. Invited to help in a house raising, he arrived with a gang of his blacks and ordered them about as he sat on his horse. The plain folk let the planter know that they were not impressed.

The cook at Burleigh had always a scullion or two to help her, besides a man to cut her wood and put it on the huge andirons. The scullions brought the water and prepared the vegetables, and made themselves generally useful. The vegetables were gathered and brought from the garden by the gardener, or by one of the half-dozen women whom he frequently had to help him. A second cook made the deserts, sweetmeats, etc. As children, we thought that the main business of the head cook was to scold the scullion and ourselves. . . . Four women and a boy

Classic Homes Grew Larger. Ever wider porches, ever more elaborate capitals and spreading lawns . . .

were in charge of the dairy. . . . Two of the women milked; the third held the semi-sinecure office, taking charge of the milk; and the fourth churned.

During the spring and summer, lambs were butchered twice a week, or oftener if required. The hides from the beeves almost supplied the plantation with shoes. Two of the negro men were tanners and shoemakers. A Southern plantation, well managed, had nearly everything necessary to life done within its bounds. At Burleigh there were two carpenters in the carpenter-shop; two blacksmiths in the blacksmith-shop; two millers in the mill, and usually five seamstresses in the house. In the laundry, there were two of the strongest . . . women on the plantation. Boys were kept about, ready to ride for the mail or to take notes around the neighborhood. There were twenty-seven servants in the service of the house.

By coincidence a last great staple crop reached the Deep South at almost the same moment as cotton. The scene was the environs of New Orleans, the plant sugar cane, and it transformed the lower Mississippi. For generations the French and Spaniards of Louisiana had sought a dependable major crop. Cotton did not do well in the moist land so close to the marsh and Gulf. Indigo served for a time, but by the early 1790's a plague of caterpillars almost wrecked that source of income, and ruin confronted the planters.

Louisiana's earliest settlers had speculated about the area's fitness for sugar cane, the "thick grass" that thrived in the warm islands of the Caribbean. From Santo Domingo, Jesuits brought the makings of a crop and slaves to cultivate it. The cane juice, however, did not crystallize well; it was little more than a brownish marmalade that leaked out of the barrels on ocean trips. Doubt was often expressed that Louisiana was close enough to the tropics to support a successful sugar culture. After 1790 the slave rebellion in Santo Domingo sent large groups

Left: Stealing Cotton by the Handful

Right: It Granulated. Etienne de Boré, once a king's *mousquetaire* in France, first proved that sugar could be produced commercially in the South, giving Louisiana its special crop.

of refugees to Louisiana. They gave New Orleans a new sophistication, a new taste for music and theater—and, not least, contributed a real skill in sugar making.

One or two of the newcomers tried their hands at various experiments. Then Etienne de Boré, a well-to-do Louisianian, staked everything on an expensive trial. Constructing a sugar house, "drying room" and other structures, he would find out if the product could be made on any sizable scale. The future of much of Louisiana hung on a tense moment as a crowd gathered silently around a large, steaming vat. A hand dipped a container into the thick mixture; it rose, and a cry burst over the green delta: "It granulates!"

That first year De Boré became Louisiana's hero and a man wealthier by $12,000. From New Orleans a sugar fever spread along the river and adjoining areas. Other sugar houses were hastily erected at the edge of the Mississippi and on waterways with names like Bayous Terre aux Boeufs, Teche, Boeuf, Lafourche. Near the swamps and the prairies that lay in the direction of Texas, small growers built more limited plants, mainly for syrup, but for the most part the sugar industry had no place for small operations. A new arrival needed heavy capital for plant and equipment, land and slaves. A current saying held that a man "has to be a rich cotton planter before he can start as a poor sugar planter."

Above all, the cane planter required a sizable labor force to work doggedly

"Cut the stalk at its peak . . ."

with the weather—and also against it. In the West Indies the absence of frosts allowed stalks to mature easily. Near the Gulf of Mexico the grower had to keep his eye both on the calendar and on the thermometer. At some point before the cane fully matured the order would have to be given: Start out with the cutting knives; signal for the machinery to begin! From then on, it was a race with frost and wind, and at times planters lost much or all of a crop, and the sick stench of soured cane spread over the lowlands. And while cane roots gave new crops for twelve years in the Indies, in Louisiana replantings had to be made after two or three seasons, all of which added still more to the planter's fixed costs.

Nevertheless, in less than a decade more than eighty sugar plantations had sprouted. When the United States acquired Louisiana in 1803, the sugar experienced a new upsurge, as more growers flocked to the new territory, with large amounts of capital at their command. The wealthy Wade Hampton of South Carolina heralded a new movement in 1811 by going to Bayou Lafourche to the west of New Orleans, and an unimpressed French observer remarked that the Americans "flock over all of Louisiana just as the holy tribes once poured over the land of Canaan."

Creoles, descendants of early French and Spanish, filled some stretches of the waterways, while Anglo-Saxons established beachheads on others. The two elements looked askance at each other, though gradually they began to merge. The first Creole girls who married "Américains" caused eyebrows to be raised. But slowly the enterprising newcomers—planters, merchants, land speculators, officials—dominated the region. In New Orleans a "French downtown" area continued intact for generations, while an "American uptown" operated as almost a separate city. Stuccoed Creole houses with ironwork balconies symbolized one influence, Greek Revival the other.

Through the years cane growers improved their crop. Sugar mills became more elaborate; planters produced varieties more resistant to cold, and learned better ways to cope with the climate. They operated in a special subregion, much of it blanketed with a shimmering summer heat and blessed with a winter climate sufficiently bland to attract winter vacationers to the Gulf coast in increasing numbers.

Above all, this was an area of the Mississippi, created by the river, nourished by it. Most of the section had been built over the centuries by the down-thrusting current, with the highest land left by seasonal deposits at the river and bayou edges, sloping toward the tattered shores or the empty marsh and swamp. As the years passed, sugar planters built artificial mounds or levees on top of the natural ones. In earlier days, breaking through from time to time, the river had often lost part of its momentum as it rushed southward. Now, unfortunately, the stronger the levees, the worse the effect if one gave way along a settled stretch. When the mounds heightened, the current between them pushed more and more powerfully against the barriers, trying to force its way out.

In springtime, with high water, gasping white men and Negroes would work feverishly, putting emergency topping along the banks, fighting the threat of seepage at this point or that. Nevertheless a whole section might suddenly collapse. A thumping sound, a shout of "*Crevasse!*" and a roaring sheet of water would pour through, to spread for many miles, leaving houses standing forlornly in inundated fields, mills isolated above the ruined cane.

True, each break left a thick new covering of earth, the cream of America's soil, dropped by the river. If a planter could hold title to his establishment he might have a better plantation than before. But a single crevasse could destroy him financially. And through the early decades of the 1800's, as the Mississippi's level rose each spring, men with guns patrolled the river edge to prevent others from saving their own lands by breaching the levee at a downstream point.

For years other hazards persisted. The dripping warmth of the lower Mississippi encouraged epidemics and infestations that gave the area the reputation of a pesthouse. New arrivals, their systems unadjusted, died by the thousands. Worst

In Full Blast. Sugar was an agricultural-industrial enterprise, as it made, and cost, fortunes.

of the plagues was yellow fever, which sent countless residents fleeing a city or town. Men and women dropped in the streets and bodies rotted in homes while officials fired cannons, set bonfires, and tried other measures in an effort to "clear the atmosphere" of "miasma" and "effluvia."

Annually a large part of the population left New Orleans, Baton Rouge, Donaldsonville, and Plaquemine, to remain away until the first frost, the traditional signal that the hazard had ended. As they departed they often slapped angrily at mosquitoes, recalling the words of an early missionary: "This little insect has caused more swearing . . . than had previously taken place in all the rest of the South." Not until much later did Southerners realize the connection between the bothersome creatures and the death that came to them on the warm breezes.

Sugar cane spread to parts of Georgia, along the Altamaha and Satilla rivers and the Sea Islands; to South Carolina and to Tampa and northern coastal areas of Florida, and ultimately to Texas, about the Brazos and San Bernard rivers. Yet predominantly, Southern cane meant Louisiana, the Sugar Bowl where more than 90 per cent of the crop was to be grown. By 1827 about 300 plantations had 21,000 slaves; by 1850 there were 1,500 estates, 100,000 slaves. In that peak year Louisiana produced nearly a fourth of the world's exportable sugar. If cotton were king, Louisianians could regard sugar as his crown prince.

Sugar and cotton seesawed for rule in the state. The central and northern parts, with the loamy alluvial earth along the Mississippi, Red, Tensas, and Ouachita rivers, proved ideal for cotton, and thousands raised it in the hills. In areas where both cotton and sugar could grow, a bad cotton year would send men hastening to convert to cane. Then, when sugar suffered, scores transferred to cotton—and perhaps returned to sugar a few years later. For those who managed to cling to it, the life had opulence. John Burnside, of Houmas House along the Mississippi, was reputed to be the wealthiest man in the South, holding 7,500 or more improved acres and 22,500 acres of all kinds, and nearly 1,000 slaves with a value of a half-million dollars. Burnside's land itself was appraised at a million and a half, an enormous fortune for the day. Burnside was a great host, and coped with the climate by encouraging guests to immerse in portable bathtubs filled with chilled water and hunks of ice. A short way off, French-American trappers and fishermen lived in flimsy cabins at the swamp edge, and pieced out a marginal existence by fishing and by trapping alligators.

In the words of a memoirist: "More land and more niggers, more niggers and more land, was the ruling passion of the cotton and sugar planters." And it was in this lower Mississippi delta, about the châteaux of the sugar growers, that America's second great war reached its high point.

Watermelons on the James. The *Pocahontas* was a famous James River steamboat, carrying a cargo everyone valued.

Many Were Nicked. Southerners suffered like others under Jefferson's Embargo Act, which sought to avert war by keeping vessels from leaving American ports. "Ograbme" was "embargo" spelled backward.

# 11

# "OLD HICKORY" —FROM NEW ORLEANS TO THE WHITE HOUSE

"The Union must be preserved, without blood if this be possible,
but it must be preserved at all hazards and at any price."
—Andrew Jackson in the South Carolina nullification crisis

The War of 1812 was a strange conflict, one that most Americans and most Britons did not seem to want. Neither side won, and the United States gained none of the ends for which it entered into the war; yet, in the end, it can be said to have benefited the country and the South in a way that few would have predicted. And it introduced a new era in American history, one dominated by a Southerner who added a new flavor, highly peppered, to American democracy.

Formal conflict with France or England might have occurred at almost any moment after the Union was established. With each nation the United States had fuming disputes over maritime matters. In the early 1800's the arrogant Napoleon laid particularly violent hands on American shipping. The English seized American vessels too, but, as James Madison commented, the French took even more of them.

According to the usage of the times, British naval officers took Englishmen from American vessels, but all too often the men happened to be American rather than British. Yet New England, the seafaring section that presumably suffered most from this practice, wanted no war and struggled bitterly against it. The clash might still have been averted had it not been for an active, ambitious element of the new South and West, clamoring for a fight. It had a strong interest in land: the large British holdings in Canada and stretches in the Louisiana Purchase area, protected for the Indians by the treaty ending the Revolution.

To Congress came a band of expansionists, or "War Hawks," including two young Southerners—Henry Clay of Kentucky, the ever-engaging "Harry of the West," and John C. Calhoun of South Carolina, an intent, poker-stiff man whom some would later call the savior of the South, while others thought him a zealot who impelled the South relentlessly toward destruction.

The War Hawks shouted for freedom of the seas and also for Canada, which, according to their boast, the United States could swallow in a few weeks. The

War Hawks of the South. John Calhoun, "Cast-Iron Man" of South Carolina, left, and Henry Clay of Kentucky, worked steadily, skillfully to bring on a conflict that many did not want.

sharp-tongued John Randolph of Virgina protested: "Agrarian cupidity, not maritime right, urges the war." And still the Hawks had their way. Only two days after the United States' declaration of hostilities, England suspended the trade measures that had occasioned much of the resentment. But by then it was too late.

The young America was almost totally unprepared. When Congress authorized the President to call for 50,000 volunteers, 10,000 assembled. The original American strategy proved extremely bad. "On to Canada!" went the cry. Though they launched an invasion, the United States armies achieved, in the main, only failure or stalemate. On the water the American Navy scored several brilliant successes in which Baltimore frigates demonstrated true seamanship—a good augury for the future. Yet these victories did not change the war's course, and thus far England, absorbed in her bloody duel with Napoleon, had given little close attention to events in the New World.

By 1814, however, the Corsican had been eliminated, and the English could mount several strong offensives. In August of 1814 a British force of 4,000 men

The Taking of Washington City. Contemporary engraving of 1814 was a panorama of action on sea and land.

reached Chesapeake Bay, and 7,000 Americans took a stand at Bladensburg, a few miles from the District of Columbia. President Madison and friends rode out, confidently anticipating a diverting game of watching-the-enemy-run. The two forces made contact; about sixty-five Americans fell, and the others left the field, officers thoughtfully showing their men the way home. This fiasco has been dubbed since then "The Bladensburg Races." Yet a small naval squadron held bravely until defeated. . . . At the White House, supper had been kept warm for James and Dolly Madison, but they had to decamp on short notice, snatching up as many national relics as they could carry, and a number of the English officers ate the meal in their place.

The British, in brief control of Washington, ordered the firing of public buildings in retaliation for recent burnings of Canadian towns, including Toronto, capital of Upper Canada. Smoke-blackened shells were all that remained of the White House and Capitol, and the priceless library of Thomas Jefferson was destroyed, a library that included thousands of books on America that could never be reassembled. (Jefferson's collection had been purchased for the new Library of Congress, over the protests of ignorant opponents who thought the volumes "immoral," too "literary" and, worst of all, occasionally written in "foreign languages"!) Interestingly, English officers protected Washington's Mount Vernon from destruction by their soldiers.

The invaders withdrew from Washington and continued on to Baltimore, where the militia behaved more bravely than did the capital's defenders. For long

Well-Smoked Shells. The Capitol and President's House were burned in retaliation for American firings in Canada.

hours the enemy vainly bombarded Fort McHenry, and as Francis Scott Key was rowed ashore on September 14, 1814, he wrote the words of his—and soon the nation's—"Star-Spangled Banner."

The United States was nevertheless in a sad plight, its government in wretched confusion, its finances almost wrecked. As had happened before and was to happen again, a strong threat of secession arose, this time from New England. The people of Massachusetts and their neighbors, resenting the war, charged that the Union was rigged against them and that their interests were being flaunted. At a Hartford convention they demanded guarantees that their rights would be protected; otherwise they would form their own government. To this the editor of the influential Richmond *Enquirer* answered: "No man, no association of men, no state or set of states has the right to withdraw itself from this Union." A majority of states would have to consent to secession, he said, and until then any such act was treason. Fifty years later Virginia and New England were, in effect, to reverse positions.

Negotiations to end the sorry fighting had begun in England when, late in 1814, a massive British force rolled toward New Orleans for a co-ordinated amphibious operation. If the English took this entryway to the nation, they might tear away the new South and West. And many Americans distrusted the recently annexed Franco-Spanish element at the river city. Suppose the odd folk, who read

They Left a Warm Supper. President James Madison and his lively Dolly abandoned their meal to British officers.

French newspapers and still talked that language, turned against the United States, or simply would not fight?

Similarly the Creoles of Louisiana had scant faith in the Americans. That faith shrank further at their first sight of the man who would command them, the awkward, leather-faced frontiersman Andrew Jackson, not quite recovered from a Nashville street fight involving Thomas Benton. The Southwesterners called the doughty, violent-tempered Indian fighter "Old Hickory," but the Creoles exchanged worried glances. *Ma foi,* was this a general?

When a minor English force went to Pensacola in Florida, to receive a welcome from the "neutral" Spaniards there, the forthright Jackson acted without authority, pounced on the town, and subdued it. Although Easterners cried outrage at this action against a third country, Jackson did not let the protests bother him. (In such cases, he seldom did.) Riding back to New Orleans, he gathered his forces, the Creoles and the Southwesterners whom he had brought with him. He managed to arrive a short time before the English, but then permitted them to surprise him.

The result was one of the incredible battles of modern times. Slipping through the inlets and bayous below the Creole town, the English, eight thousand strong, advanced over marshy ground toward the Chalmette and Villeré sugar estates, a point hardly seven miles from New Orleans. They had expected help from a

The Bombardment of Fort McHenry. Near Baltimore the English fired steadily in an effort to take the American fortification.

Left: He Wrote at Fever Heat. Francis Scott Key.

Right: "The Flag Was Still There." The new anthem's first publication. The tempo was "con spirito."

First, Movement Against Spanish Pensacola. Although Congressmen shouted protest, Jackson ignored international law and quieted a threat.

band of smugglers and pirates of Barataria along the Gulf. "Hellish banditti," Jackson once termed the Lafitte brothers, Jean and Pierre. Under the new (and fairly unpopular) American government of Louisiana, the crew of corsairs had suffered a growing interference, and they had several good reasons for accepting a British offer of cash and protection.

But, surprisingly, the pirates sided with the Americans, and so did the Creoles. They took part in a series of preliminary clashes involving land, lake, and river-edge fighting, and then came the main Battle of New Orleans. On January 8, 1815, with Sir Edward Pakenham in charge of a superbly trained body of troops, the English moved steadily, relentlessly, toward fresh earthworks where waited the piebald American forces: fringe-shirted Southwesterners, Frenchmen, Spaniards, Indians, "free men of color," grimy sailors, representatives of seven or eight nations.

Then a miracle in the delta. From their positions behind ramparts constructed of mud with a few cotton bales here and there, the Western marksmen and Louisiana hunters picked off their foes with rifle fire and blasted them with cannon. Courageously the British marched on, doomed and now aware of it. Long lines fell, reformed, fell again, reformed, were butchered. Finally the battle ended. In half an hour some two thousand Englishmen died, and only a single general officer lived. The United States lost thirteen men, with about sixty injured.

It was America's great victory of the war, and the nation wept in joy. The battle had taken place after the signing of the peace treaty at Ghent, and it did not affect that settlement. What might have happened had the British taken New Orleans? No one would know, and yet the episode, it seemed, had saved the Union, giving Americans a pride in their country they had not known before. The American experiment had a new life.

The end of the war brought rapid expansion to the South and Southwest, with new settlers, new produce moving down the river. Veterans of the fighting stayed along the Mississippi or returned with their families. As national pride grew, internal improvements, financed by the Federal government, gained fuller acceptance. More and more influential were the views of a Virginian named John Marshall who became Chief Justice of the Supreme Court just before Jefferson assumed the Presidency.

In earlier years the court had little importance. Justice Marshall, a Federalist with a firm belief in strong central government, gave the court a new rank. Could that body declare unconstitutional an act passed by Congress? On this as on other matters, the basic law did not speak. During Jefferson's Presidency a minor case arose, and in a carefully worded ruling John Marshall asserted the authority of the Court. No overt clashes between Jefferson and Marshall ensued, although Jefferson complained then and many times later of Marshall's ruling, but to no avail. The direction of future decisions was set.

John Marshall served as Chief Justice for thirty-four years under five administrations. A conservative, he favored property over other rights; he also worked to develop the concept of the United States as a unified government rather than a confederation of states. And the Presidency was soon to go to a man who, though

Left: His Destiny Approached at New Orleans. Before the battle Andrew Jackson's fight seemed almost hopeless. Above: A Harassed Governor. William Claiborne, Louisiana's first American governor, felt peril on all sides.

he differed with Marshall on many points, labored to strengthen this view.

The nation's center of gravity was extending southward and westward as it experienced a rapid explosion of growth. Between 1790 and 1820 the number of Americans doubled to 9,500,000, and after that almost doubled with every twenty years. More and more people were gaining the ballot; the old Virginia Dynasty, which meant rule by a comparative aristocracy, though often an enlightened one, neared its conclusion. Between 1828 and 1900, eleven of the eighteen Presidents were to come from states within the borders of the Louisiana Purchase.

Resolutely Andrew Jackson, far different in background and temperament from any previous President, moved toward the White House. Once he wrote: "Do you think I am such a damned fool as to consider myself fit for the Presidency?"

But few in his position persist in such views. The Hero of New Orleans grew more convinced of his own capabilities, as support for him mushroomed in every direction. In 1824 he received more ballots than his opponents, yet lost in the Electoral College. Four years later, after a campaign violent even by the standards of the increasingly free-and-dirty American politics of the day, he won by a landslide.

This man who represented the new democracy lacked both formal education and a closely defined philosophy of government. The son of Irish immigrant parents, the lank, freckled Jackson had lived through a hard childhood, moved to Tennessee as a young lawyer, become a public prosecutor, speculated in lands, sold slaves, and run a small store. He planted and raised cotton, prospered, and built for himself a large white-pillared house, the Hermitage. Jackson possessed courage, a vast drive and a vaster understanding of people, their good points and their meaner ones. While the more refined sniffed at his frequent truculence, his back-country bluntness, and some regarded him as "little advanced in civilization over the Indians with whom he made war," he could charm a dowager with his courteous and considerate ways. And he struck the simpler, plainer Southwesterners as their man, who, like them, despised banks, monopolies, and silk-shirted Eastern privilege.

In certain respects Jackson was like Jefferson; both believed in an agrarian society, in the will of the majority. Still the Tennesseean lacked Jefferson's breadth of conviction, his wide-ranging intellect, his comprehension of underlying social and political forces in American life; and Jackson's violent feelings let him be taken in by others. His regime was far from tranquil.

Thousands of old-time Southerners flinched on reading of the near free-for-all on Jackson's inauguration day. A horde of supporters pressed into the White House, stood on brocaded chairs, jostled and elbowed until the new President had to get himself out by a window. To the disapproving it recalled the French Revolution; but it was only the new Southern and Western democracy, there to hail its champion. And in many ways "Old Hickory," like Jefferson, proved far from the radical his enemies predicted. He dismissed fewer job-holders than expected and made fewer general changes, although he collided spectacularly with banking interests and then, no less spectacularly, with the redoubtable John Calhoun.

The South has produced few more provocative characters than the paradoxical Calhoun, who made South Carolina his personal property. "The cast-iron man, who looks as if he had never been born and never could be extinguished," the Englishwoman Harriet Martineau described him. No section has had a representative of more penetrating logic, and few men have pursued their aims with a greater sense of complete rightness. A rigid Calvinist, he had deep-set eyes that burned with his zeal; tall, stoop-shouldered, he drove himself harshly, making himself almost an automaton. If Jackson was, as his critics said, "simply all action," Calhoun was "all theory."

The philosopher-politician rose from simple Scots stock of the Carolina back country. As a boy he worked hard on a farm. After study at Yale, Calhoun practiced law and took an interest in public affairs. He married a cousin, Floride Bonneau, a Huguenot with high Charleston connections. Although a number of the rice aristocrats looked down on Calhoun as a rustic, they accepted him. Now he had his own Negroes, went to Congress and, as we have seen, became one of the "War Hawks" who urged the break with England.

When those hostilities ended, Calhoun, Clay, and their adherents promoted the cause of a unified government. Following in Alexander Hamilton's steps, they asked for a manufacturers' tariff, a protected market for farmers, and Federal public works in the form of a "national road." In the South Carolinian's words, the country was increasing "greatly and rapidly–I was about to say fearfully," and he proposed roads and canals as a "most powerful cement" to hold the parts to-

Jackson's Creole Headquarters. The Tennessean occupied Macarté plantation near the scene of the conflict.

Mud Ramparts and Bravery on Both Sides. The Americans watched warily, and the English marched steadfastly to annihilation.

gether. To that end he made a statement which, coming from him, would later have a strange sound: "I speak not for South Carolina but the nation."

Now, however, the issue of slavery broke in a way that threatened to tear the country apart; reverberations would be many in the South. Since early days North and South (non-slave and slave areas) had been more or less equal in population and number of states. With the end of the War of 1812, men hastened to Missouri and especially to St. Louis, a former French trading post. They included slave-owners in large numbers, and Missouri took on a more Southern aspect. But when a measure arrived to make Missouri a state, Southerners were jolted by an amendment halting further admission of slaves.

Sullen debate changed to raging controversy, and in his retirement the aging Jefferson wrote: "This momentous question, like a fire bell in the night, awakened and filled me with terror." After long argument Congress adopted the Missouri Compromise of 1820. Maine had asked admission as a separate state, and it would come in as a free one. Missouri was to enter as a slave state but, by agreement, no additional states recognizing slavery would be admitted in the Louisiana Purchase area beyond Missouri.

Calhoun came in as Jackson's Vice President, and it was generally understood that the South Carolinian would succeed "Old Hickory" four years later. As much as any American, the "cast-iron man" was bitten by the presidential bug. Matters, alas, were not to be so simple. Soon Calhoun began to hear unhappy voices at

"In Mud Up to My Ears." In this sharp contemporary cartoon John Bull lamented his condition, between a Kentucky rifleman and a Louisiana Creole.

home. The tariff, which he had thought would bring mills to the South, had done nothing of the sort, and poorer days had fallen on his state. After years of heavy use, the soil gave diminishing returns. The tariff had increased, and Carolinians protested that it, as well as Mr. Calhoun's Federal works, were taking money from the South for the benefit of the North.

As his constituents held furious meetings, Calhoun had to change his stand—and, more than that, try to alter the government's policies. Without using his name, he sent to his state legislature an *Exposition and Protest* which began a new Southern era. As New England had done, unsuccessfully, South Carolina took a stand against an American majority, asserting a view of state rights that went beyond anything previously proposed.

Chief Justice Marshall considered the United States a national government

Death of a Commander. British General Pakenham died with his officers under the aim of the motley American army.

with broad powers. Calhoun, on his side, argued that a state continued fully sovereign with the right to decide whenever a Federal law violated the Constitution. It could then refuse to obey, and nullify the measure. Years earlier the Virginia and Kentucky "resolves" had maintained that joint state action might negate an act of Congress. But South Carolina proposed that a single state could declare a law unconstitutional. Former President Madison spoke coldly, calling this a "preposterous and anarchical pretension" for which there was no "shadow of countenance in the Constitution."

The question hung ominously over the country. How would President Jackson, himself a Southerner, act? On Jefferson's birthday celebration of 1830, Jackson faced Calhoun, and the clouds lowered. With every eye in the room on him, Jackson faced Calhoun and lifted his glass: "Our Federal Union—it must be pre-

Cotton Bales Were Used Defensively. Jackson directed backwoodsmen, militia, Indians, free men of color. But the bales were few and not of great help.

served!" Calhoun got up, hand trembling, face white. "The Union—next to our liberty, the most dear!" When the gathering dissolved, the issue had been drawn.

More titillating personal differences contributed to a break between the two men. Washington society simmered over Peggy Eaton, the bright-eyed daughter of a former boardinghouse keeper, a girl whose behavior had been informal, to say the least, before she married her close friend, Jackson's War Secretary. The other Cabinet wives fumed, and none more so than the aristocratic Carolinian who was Calhoun's wife; the ladies coldly ignored the glamorous Peggy. At the same time Calhoun's enemies brought to Jackson an earlier incident in which the other man had worked against him, and the President turned his back forever on the spokesman of nullification.

The storm fell. When a new tariff went into effect, Calhoun and his state struck at the Federal government. In 1832 a Carolina convention declared the tariff unconstitutional; the state would pay no heed to it. The Carolinians ordered an army raised. Let the government try to enforce its law!

Andrew Jackson, furious, declared that any state's claim to nullify a law of the country was "incompatible with the existence of the Union." How, he asked, could a state stay in the Union and follow only the measures it liked? Then, he added: ". . . if this thing goes on, our country will be like a bag of meal with both ends open. Pick it up and it will run out." Furthermore, the President swore that he would "hang every leader" of these "infatuated people," and asked Congress for authority to use the Army and Navy to collect the disputed revenues.

Jackson's act brought support from many men in many areas, while South Carolina found no other Southern state to follow her course. "Old Hickory" also said, however, that he thought the recent tariff too high, and a bill was sent to Congress to reduce it. Under these conditions both sides gave way to a degree. On the same day Andrew Jackson signed two measures—one to permit military action against South Carolina, the other to cut the tariff. In South Carolina a convention repealed nullification, then performed a last act of theoretical defiance by declaring the Federal military measure "null and void"!

Some expressed the view that the South Carolinians had shown how a state could use threats to get almost anything it wished. Still, Jackson had saved the Union, beaten back the claim of nullification. The matter of minority against majority would lie dormant, but it would rise again in another, different, and more sinister fashion. But before that happened, the South was to enjoy a flowering like a burst of bloom in a hothouse.

A New Authority, Another Direction. The Virginian, John Marshall, gave the Supreme Court a fresh importance and changed the country's course.

"Our Federal Union . . ." Jackson's answer to Calhoun was inscribed on the base of his equestrian statue before the White House.

Wearied but Still Determined. After many hard years President Andrew Jackson directed a sturdy fight against John Calhoun and South Carolina.

In Jackson's Path. Directly or indirectly, the Indian hater Jackson contributed to the steady repression of Southern Indian tribes, sometimes with great injustices. Thousands were removed from Georgia when he permitted that state to nullify a Supreme Court decision. But for years the Florida Seminoles resisted determinedly. Picture shows destruction of Indian Key Village in August, 1840.

At First, Canals Along the Rivers. Southern interests launched ventures, sometimes unsuccessful, for canals such as this one along the James River.

Right: They Conquered the Swampland.

Below: Horse Power, Sail Power. Early "railroads" were largely rails and engineless cars.

The South Had the Country's First Locomotive Built for Actual Service. "The Best Friend" was constructed in New York for the South Carolina Railroad, and arrived by ship. After experimental runs, here is the first excursion on January 15 of 1831.

They Had Music, Too. The second American locomotive built for service was the "West Point," also constructed for the Charleston Railroad, making its first excursion on March 5, 1831.

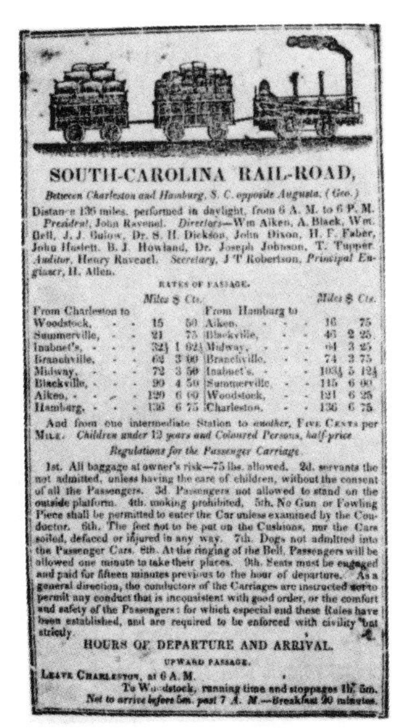

SOUTH-CAROLINA RAIL-ROAD,

*Between Charleston and Hamburg, S. C. opposite Augusta. (Geo.)*

Distance 136 miles, performed in daylight, from 6 A. M. to 6 P. M. *President*, John Ravenel. *Directors*—Wm Aiken, A. Black, Wm. Bell, J. J. Gulow, Dr. S. H. Dickson, John Dixon, H. F. Faber, John Haslett, B. J. Howland, Dr. Joseph Johnson, T. Tupper. *Auditor*, Henry Raveael. *Secretary*, J T Robertson, *Principal Engineer*, H. Allen.

RATES OF PASSAGE.

| From Charleston to | Miles | $ Cts. | From Hamburg to | Miles | $ Cts. |
|---|---|---|---|---|---|
| Woodstock, | 15 | 50 | Aiken, | 16 | 75 |
| Summerville, | 21 | 75 | Blackville, | 46 | 2 25 |
| Inabnet's, | 32½ | 1 62½ | Midway, | 64 | 3 25 |
| Branchville, | 62 | 3 00 | Branchville, | 74 | 3 75 |
| Midway, | 72 | 3 50 | Inabnet's, | 103½ | 5 12½ |
| Blackville, | 90 | 4 50 | Summerville, | 115 | 6 00 |
| Aiken, | 120 | 6 00 | Woodstock, | 121 | 6 25 |
| Hamburg, | 136 | 6 75 | Charleston, | 136 | 6 75 |

And from one intermediate Station to another, FIVE CENTS per MILE. *Children under 12 years and Coloured Persons, half-price*

*Regulations for the Passenger Carriage.*

1st. All baggage at owner's risk—75 lbs. allowed. 2d. servants the not admitted, unless having the care of children, without the consent of all the Passengers. 3d. Passengers not allowed to stand on the outside platform. 4th. smoking prohibited. 5th. No Gun or Fowling Piece shall be permitted to enter the Car unless examined by the Conductor. 6th. The feet not to be put on the Cushions, nor the Cars soiled, defaced or injured in any way. 7th. Dogs not admitted into the Passenger Cars. 8th. At the ringing of the Bell, Passengers will be allowed one minute to take their places. 9th. Seats must be engaged and paid for fifteen minutes previous to the hour of departure. As a general direction, the conductors of the Carriages are instructed not to permit any conduct that is inconsistent with good order, or the comfort and safety of the Passengers: for which especial end these Rules have been established, and are required to be enforced with civility but strictly.

HOURS OF DEPARTURE AND ARRIVAL.

UPWARD PASSAGE.

LEAVE CHARLESTON, at 6 A. M.

To Woodstock, running time and stoppages 1h. 5m.
*Not to arrive before 5m. past 7 A. M.—Breakfast 20 minutes.*

Left: Early Schedule Making. Right: Facilities Improved in Many Places. Scene on a Baltimore & Ohio coach in 1861.

Above, and below left: The Horses Still Pulled. Baltimore & Ohio passenger car about 1830, and a New Orleans one of a later date.

Below, right: They Burrowed Into Mountains.

Left: North Carolina Pioneer. The Raleigh & Gaston Company obtained a charter in 1835 in a race with rivals. Eventually the state had to help finish both lines.

Right: Coffee and Fried Chicken. No diners had yet been installed on the Chesapeake & Ohio.

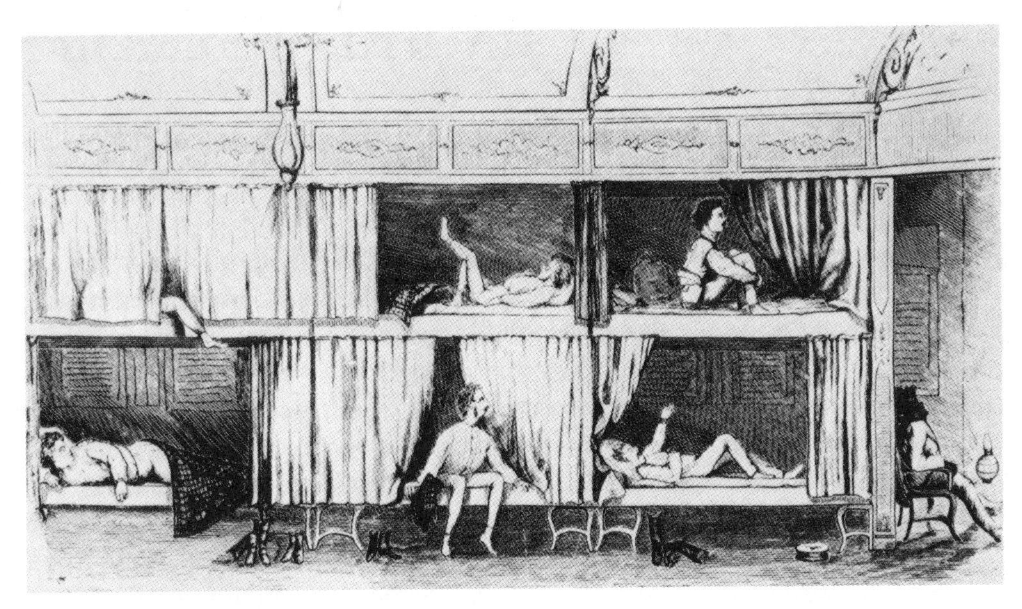

A Sleeping Car of the 1850's

Above: Rafts, Keelboats, and Flatboats. They arrived early on the Mississippi, and swept on through the years.

Left: Fur Traders Floating Southward. George Caleb Bingham portrayed them for a future America.

# 12

# "BRIDES OF BABYLON" ON THE MISSISSIPPI

"Steamboats are built of wood, tin, shingles, canvas and twine, and look like the Bride of Babylon." —CLYDE FITCH

SOME have called those thirty years before 1860 the golden days of the Deep South, and to Southerners they must have seemed that. Many were aware of the increasing tensions and discontents, but for most of the people of the lower South and the Mississippi Valley it was an era of steadily expanding good times. The endlessly flowing master river and the liquid tentacles of its tributaries became pathways of opportunity, of higher and higher hope, as the heart of the continent opened to new settlement. New Orleans, Baton Rouge, Natchez, Memphis, St. Louis at the upper end of the region—each was the center of a teeming new life and a growing prosperity. And there was the world of the rivers and the riverboats, part elegant, part hard and crude, that had no counterpart in America.

For a century or more a thriving traffic had rolled down the Mississippi in primitive keelboats and flatboats. The former, narrow and long, slid more or less steadily downstream; on the return, if crews did not go north on foot or by horse, they might laboriously work their way by poling along the edges. The flatboats, bigger, more ungainly, had the appearance of boxes on rafts, which is more or less what they were. A hairy, rambunctious band, the rivermen yawned, scratched themselves, fought and defied anybody who crossed their path.

These were the prototypes of the "half-horse, half-alligator" element who, like the legendary Mike Fink, claimed they could "out-run, out-jump, out-shoot, out-brag, out-drink an' out-fight, rough-an'tumble, no holts barred, any man on both sides of the river from Pittsburgh to New Orleans an' back ag'in to St. Louiee." They had little respect for rank, and the story is told of the time a keelboat captain carried the Duc d'Orléans, later Louis Philippe of France, and his two brothers, on the way to New Orleans. When the vessel stranded, the captain yelled: "You kings down there! Show yourselves and do a man's work, and help us three-spots pull off this bar." The kings got to work.

In the Creole city the boatmen tied a whisky bottle on a pole to tell the world they were ready to sell their grain, hides, and pork. Then, with their pockets filled, they would start the wearing trip back home. It was a treacherous stream, with "boils" that whirled men to death, hidden sandbars that brought prompt destruction, and floating trees that could rip out a boat's bottom. It was estimated at one time that a third of the men who made these trips disappeared en route. "Last seen on the Mississippi," "never heard from below Memphis . . ." The river had hazards other than those of nature, for gangs of pirates clustered along the stream to overpower them or lure them ashore with false appeals or promises. Along the Mississippi life was risky and also cheap.

Nevertheless the traffic flourished. From 1805 to 1823, more than twelve thousand flatboats, exclusive of other types of vessels, arrived in New Orleans. Few dreamed of the revolution on the water that was in the making. Since the late 1700's Americans had tried to apply steam to ships. No single individual can be said to have "invented" the first vessel; rather it evolved from a series of largely unsuccessful tests by James Rumsey of Kentucky, John Fitch of Connecticut, and others. By 1811 Robert Fulton evolved his version, and Nicholas Roosevelt, associated with him, made a memorable pioneer trip. Hundreds watched in wonder (or derision) as Roosevelt's *New Orleans*, deep-hulled, with a low-pressure engine, started down the Ohio from Pittsburgh. How could a thing like that—a "floating sawmill," in the words of one man—hold its own against the vast Mississippi?

At river towns, along the route, entire populations ran out to behold the sight. Several times disaster brushed the *New Orleans*. As the passengers held their breaths the vessel plunged into the falls of the Ohio, shivered, headed under the water, righted itself, and rode on. When it neared New Madrid the worst earthquake in American history split the ground apart, sucked islands to the bottom of the river, opened hideous fissures in the banks. A number of people believed the steam contraption was somehow responsible, and Indians sent war canoes against it.

There were other lively events: the *New Orleans* caught fire, and Mrs. Roose-

The People Packed It. The *Belvidere* was the precursor of many more elaborate steamboats.

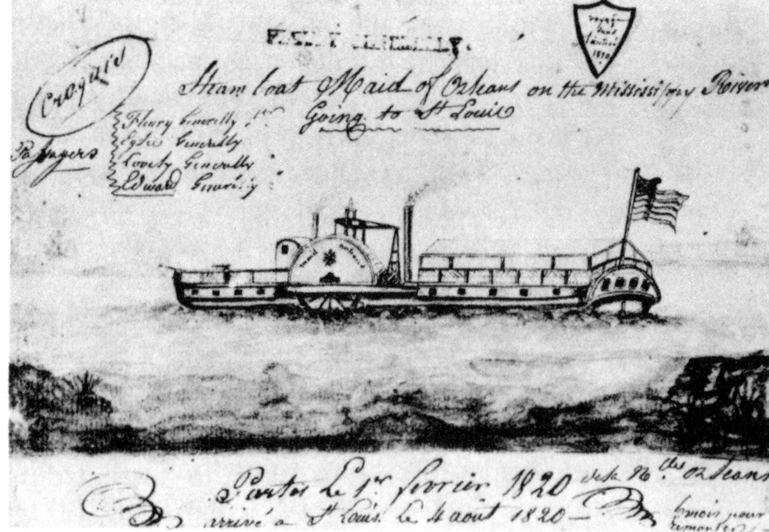


*Maid of Orleans.* Early paddle wheeler, with French comment on her trip of 1820.

velt took time out at Louisville to have a baby. Then, on a January day of 1812, New Orleans wildly celebrated the craft's safe arrival, and Nicholas Roosevelt took the natives on short upriver trips to prove his steam vessel could perform against the currents. Other steamboats made short runs along the lower stretches until 1816, when Henry Shreve came along with a quite new design.

Shreve took his ideas from the flatboats. To navigate so dangerous a stream, with its hidden sandbars and obstructions, he needed every inch of clearance, and he designed a vessel with the shallowest draft possible. He lifted the machinery to the main deck, installed high-pressure engines, and added an upper deck for extra space. Someone said it looked like "a floating wedding cake," and the description was not inappropriate.

For these "Western waters," the Mississippi and tributaries, the steamboat seemed almost to have been invented. An editor told the world: "The puny rivers of the East are only as creeks, or convenient waters on which experiments may be made to our advantage." Here was an empire awaiting the development that only steamboats could bring it. To the heart of America, said James Madison, the Mississippi was "everything . . . the Hudson, the Delaware, the Potomac, and all the navigable rivers of the Atlantic States formed into one stream." In 1820 some sixty steamboats moved up the river and connecting waterways; by 1840 the number reached four hundred, and by 1860 a thousand or more.

Travel, commerce, communication—all were revolutionized, as an army of men, women, and children ambled or hurried aboard the steamboats in greater and greater numbers. New Orleans to Vicksburg, Port Gibson to Memphis to St. Louis . . . steamboat life had a swift, zestful tempo. Past the decks swept a panorama of the South: towns at the muddy river edges, cities on occasional breeze-swept heights; bobbing shanties, houseboats, flatboats, isolated huts perched on a shelf of land at the riverside.

For thousands the steamboat was a floating hotel such as they had never seen before, a place of flashing display and promenade. It was a world between paddle-wheels: reigning planters, cigar-smoking lords of the realm; small growers with limited produce, half-timorous, half-defensive as they looked from side to side; broad-skirted, narrow-bonneted girls with their aunts, grandmothers, and Negro maids trailing them, on their annual trip for the social season at the St. Louis or St. Charles hotels in New Orleans or with friends in Natchez; Pennsylvanians or New Jersey people enjoying (or perhaps not quite enjoying) their first appraisal of a florid existence; long-faced, unshaven men who lolled about the lower deck, riding at the cheapest rate—perhaps only eight dollars downriver, five dollars up-river to Pittsburgh; ladies of the evening and the inevitable neatly attired gentlemen who turned out to be experts in fleecing the unwary.

There were also rich Europeans making a grand tour of America, and less well-to-do visitors going as immigrants to Missouri or Arkansas; singers like Jenny Lind, evangelists with a holy fervor in their eyes, land speculators, the simple-minded, the rascally. Everything was fair cargo. On one trip a circus owner took

The Flatboats Filled Their New Orleans Landing. People said a man could walk a full mile from deck to deck.

aboard his cages of lions and a bear, and no one thought that unusual. The mate yelled at the Negro roustabouts who carried cargo on and off; planters exchanged toasts in brandy and bourbon; tall-hatted men boasted, told stories of record crops, groaned over the market's vagaries and schemes to reduce acreages, chewed and spat everlastingly about them—a habit that observers thought all too prevalent in the South.

Steamboat days had an excitement: coquetry on the upper deck, runaway marriages, domestic dramas, the "insult" of one colonel by another, a low-voiced challenge to a duel. For this time of surging wealth and soaring tempers brought the code duello to a prevalence never previously witnessed in America, with river towns keeping score of the week's clashes, and New Orleans leading America in a fantastic recourse to formal games of murder. At one spot, "Under the Oaks," a single day sometimes saw as many as ten encounters. Jean de Buys dueled with a man and wounded him, not fatally; quarreled later, dueled again, again without death for either, and had a third encounter, still without fatalities.

Others were more homicidal. Alcée La Branche, speaker of the Louisiana House, dueled with an editor, a Mr. Heuston, because the latter had taunted him for never having fought a duel. They met along Gentilly Road outside New Orleans, and exchanged three fires without incident except for a bad scalp wound for Editor Heuston. Most of the two hundred spectators (a good duel merited a lively audience) called for a stop to the thing. Bleeding heavily, Heuston still insisted that it go on, and received a bullet through the lungs. For an hour he gasped in agony, pleading to a friend to shoot him through the head. . . . Many protested the grim encounter, but the next day's dawn witnessed still another grim and futile duel.

Now and then steamboat life brought death of another kind. A youth who had lost the family holdings in a card game would go to the end of the deck and send a bullet into his head. But most of the professional gamblers found it easier, and safer and more profitable, to relieve a man of five hundred or a thousand dollars at a time. George Devol, one-time greatest gambler of the river, told of a career built upon a long train of such medium-sized bilkings.

Signs on the steamboats read: "Gentlemen who play cards for money, play at their own risk." Such warnings stopped no one, especially the plausible men who worked with "cappers," equally bland-looking confederates who carried on elaborate performances during which one, then another lost as they baited the suckers on. By arrangement with the bartender, decks of cards were marked in advance; a "new" deck would be called for, to allay suspicion. But sometimes the sharpers would be found out, and consultation with the captain followed. The vessel would be halted during the night, and the rascals would be landed on shore or a sandbar. They might be lucky if they missed a volley of bullets from the deck. In such cases the prudent gambler automatically jumped into the water for safety until the steamboat had chugged away.

A more innocent kind of game also fascinated onlookers. In one case a pair of passengers reportedly played without interruption for two days and ran up a bar bill of $600. (That included free drinks for the audience.) And another man, who had no taste for such unrelaxed pleasures, was said to have stayed at the bar for three days, imbibing periodically as he clung to the rail.

With the years steamboats became richer, gaudier, until, as one man said, they resembled "brides of Babylon" on the Mississippi. Charles Dickens observed that steamboats were "foreign to all ideas we are accustomed to entertain of boats. . . . Except that they are in the water, and display a couple of paddle boxes, they might be intended, for anything that appears to the contrary, to perform some unknown service, high and dry, upon a mountain top." Nevertheless steamboats could be considered efficient, with some reservations, as we shall see. And operations gradually improved.

Until about 1840 the riverboats would almost never leave on time. A prospective passenger might race to a landing, jump out of his carriage and receive assurance: "Yes, sir, goin' in a few minutes." With that he could wait eight hours or twelve, a day or three days. When the captain had all the freight he thought it likely he would get, and a maximum of passengers, he would depart, and only then. But with the years service improved, quickened, and the steamboats generally took to leaving on schedule.

Every 5:00 P.M. in New Orleans saw lines of packets preparing to head, one by one, into the river.

Stepping aboard, passengers divided into two classes: main deck and upper level. The first remained among the machinery, merchandise, flotsam and jetsam, anything that was pushed aboard, and made way for it. The second ascended

Left: Innovator in Steam. Robert Fulton's pioneering *New Orleans* touched disaster many times on its downward journey.

Right: Low Water in the Mississippi. Such drawings as this by F. F. Palmer show the romantic view of life along the river.

Cotton Bales and Jigging Time. They went together, according to this popular view.

Steamboats and a Pillared House. The owner's sugar plantation is in the background.

the ornate branching stairway to the upper deck and private rooms that lined the sides, with their small outer walk and usually, at the end, a kind of Southern porch in which they could "catch a breeze." The pioneer Henry Shreve supposedly named rooms for the individual states, hence the term "stateroom." When Texas entered the Union as the biggest of all, the final deck above, or the hurricane deck, became the texas. Here, in semilordly isolation, lived the officers.

Above everything else, literally and otherwise, stood the pilot in the pilothouse. As the saying went, his post gave him the right to be arrogant to anybody on earth. Master of the fate of all on board, the pilot scanned the river, made decisions, snapped orders to the engineer and his helpers in their blazing quarters below. While the vessel moved, no one could countermand him.

Ruler of another kind, a compound of benevolence and the imperial manner, was the captain, a figure who strode his world like God's overseer on the river. The universe beamed upon the captain and listened deferentially—all of it except, of course, certain prized customers among the river gentry, who did their heavy shipping every season and bowed before no one on land or on the Mississippi. Curious as it sounds today, many vessels would halt at nearly any point to drop off freight or pick it up, take on goods and passengers. Someone, usually the slave of one who lived nearby, would stand for hours, then signal with cloths or burning brands. Captains performed shopping services for the wives of planters, and delivered purchases to the shore, from a new gown prepared by a Royal Street shop in New Orleans to a set of chairs made to order in Memphis. Good will counted.

Each vessel had its own trade-mark, a gleaming insignia. While the steamboat carried no figurehead, an enormous paddlebox might be ornamented by a painting of a mountaintop or a castle; the pilothouse frequently displayed one. But the most popular spot was the space between the soaring chimneys, and here a ship would have a golden crescent, a silver star, a replica of a tall hat or a resplendent cotton bale.

The steamboats' titles and feats were legendary—the *J. M. White,* the *Natchez,* the *Belle Creole;* when an old, celebrated one disappeared, its successor inherited the name. The bigger vessels became showplaces, with rival interests using greater and greater luxuries of food and service to draw passengers. On the upper deck an orchestra, advertised up and down the river, would play at the end of the long, gleaming tunnel of a main cabin filled with greenery, oil paintings, and statuary. Lines of chandeliers were reflected from mirrors and ornamented spittoons, and the scene repeated itself many times in mirrors that stretched into the distance.

One packet boat had a cabin 270 feet long, 28 feet wide, and its floor carpet had been woven to size in Belgium. One of the *Natchez* boats cost $200,000, and the carpets alone cost more than $4,500. Mulatto maids attended the lady passengers while slick-haired bartenders, "right from New Orleans," concocted mixed drinks from gin fizzes to mint juleps to tropical punches. A number of steamboats had barbershops and also bridal suites with pink and blue wall decorations of Venus and Cupid. One counted 28 honeymoon chambers.

"Wooding Up" Along the Way. The floating palaces were always hungry for fuel.

Far left: "Woodchoppers Along the River." A grimmer picture of a cramped, malarial existence among those who served the steamboats.

Left: Scenes and Faces on the Steamboats

For honors in cuisine, captains competed like hotel managers, offering towering constructions of jellied meat, platters of game, ragouts, fricassees, gumboes, thick soups and thin soups, hams and chickens, desserts creamed, desserts enriched with spices and nuts. With good reason, guidebooks warned travelers of the perils of overeating. Many, not accustomed to such fare, especially the heavily sauced Creole dishes, suffered accordingly, but nevertheless did not fail to return for the next meal. Who in his right mind would pass up such celestial, and also free, food? Steamboats carried live chickens, live farm animals, to be killed, then quickly served. And as soon as Negroes cleared tables and chairs from the main cabin, the steward's helpers piled broken meats, game and fish in one enormous metal container, the sweets in another, took them to the main deck, yelled "Grub stock" and left it all for the lesser folk below.

These main-deck passengers had a special service to fulfill; they must help "wood up" along the river. Engines were hungry for fuel, and usually twice every twenty-four hours the vessel stopped at a point at which woodchoppers had large stores ready. Men jumped out, worked swiftly by early morning light or in the glare of bonfires, while the captain fretted over the minutes lost. The second the last piece had been dragged on, or before that, the vessel rolled away.

Steamboat life was not all glamorous. Eliza Ripley has told of a childhood ride, about 1840, on the *Gray Eagle*. She occupied an upper berth, which was "so narrow that in attempting to turn over I fell out and landed in the wash basin, on the opposite side of the room! My sister had to sit on the lower berth to braid my pigtails, then sent me forth so she could have room to braid her own."

By this time the vessels were growing ever more ornate, ever more tinsel-gaudy. Gingerbread fretwork appeared everywhere, with colored glass at the windows, and in time the style spread to land. Here was a taste far removed from the simplicity of Thomas Jefferson's Greek and Roman temples, but much of the later Southern life had the rococo touch. Classic columns became taller, wider, with Corinthian capitals and florid ornamentation.

Behind their elaborate façades steamboats were far from durable. According to estimates, the average vessel lasted only four or five years, but profits came so high that owners accepted their temporary losses. Start work next week on a new one, and bigger than the old. . . . While captains spent money for lavish exteriors, they skimped elsewhere. Inferior and untested engines were the rule; little heed

Down the Chute. To speed cotton to the steamboat, some sections built facilities of this sort.

was paid to the engine-room personnel. A barrel of whisky was always standard equipment in the lower rooms. It "encouraged" the men, and also a general carelessness. Steamboats ran aground, or were caught by hidden snags; they took fire, they exploded. Those who rode the river could see the shore lined with an irregular file of wrecks, the corpses of packets that had met disaster.

The South shuddered at stories of hideous death as men and women were thrown toward the sky or forced to jump from blazing decks. The river itself remained a perilous place of passage. Although the Federal government spent large sums to remove navigational hazards, the Mississippi continued to change its shape, building islands, losing a stretch of land at one bank, building another opposite it. Mark Twain claimed that by his time, all thirteen hundred miles of La Salle's original stream had become land, as the river shifted to left or right. And the pilot had to study water surfaces, judge the speed of currents, changes in sandbars—and even alterations in landmarks like big trees and clumps of bushes. A difference of a foot in the water level, or an inch, might mean death. One ship was wrecked because, it was claimed, its pilot used to listen for the bark of a feisty dog at a certain point. A dark evening, the usual bark . . . But the dog had been unchained, and moved to another spot!

An equal hazard arose from actual navigation: slackness and the wish to save time, flaunting of the most elementary of precautions so that boilers were overheated and sudden blasts ripped through flimsy woodwork. . . . Nevertheless the steamboat that reached the landing first took the business, and a captain survived by the reputation he built and maintained for quick delivery.

Steamboat speeds increased by spurts. In 1817 the New Orleans-Louisville run took 25 days and two hours; by 1828 the time dropped to 18 days and 10 hours; by 1834, 8 days and 4 hours, and by 1858, 4 days, 9½ hours. Races occurred at a moment's challenge or by careful prearrangement. The psychology was irresistible; delicate-souled women who had previously quivered at the suggestion of a race found themselves clinging to the rails and crying encouragement. In some cases vessels were stripped, furniture removed, spoiled meat and tallow tossed in the boilers to raise the pressure. To reduce all possible weight, one captain said he got a new haircut! Engineers tied down safety valves, tried assorted tricks, while those aboard one vessel shouted taunts at the other.

Some sources claim that more than 4,000 persons were killed or injured in river accidents between 1810 and 1850. One out of eight vessels was destroyed between 1831 and 1833 because of human error. Dozens of volumes provide catalogues of horror on the Mississippi. A few examples:

In April of 1832 the *Brandywine* roared along near Memphis in a race with the *Hudson.* Sparks set fire to crates on the deck; the woodwork flamed, and a blaze darted through the ship as if through straw. The pilot steered for the bank but never reached it, because the *Brandywine* was caught on a bar. Half-crazed, panicky passengers and crew members piled into a yawl, which overturned, and the boat itself burned to little more than a crisp. The death toll was more than a hundred.

In the early hours of May 9, 1837, the *Ben Sherrod* trailed the *Prairie* in a race near Fort Adams. A flash of sparks, and in a moment the *Ben Sherrod* was aflame. Again the pilot headed for land, but the tiller ropes were gone and she went out of control. Boilers burst and then gunpowder exploded in the hold, breaking the boat to pieces. Officers of the rival *Prairie,* seeing the fire, declined to turn back but "made a report" at Natchez. Another vessel, the *Alton,* rode up and plowed through the survivors, drowning many as they clung to bits of wood. Toll, over two hundred.

At times the less fortunate did not die. When the *Princess* exploded in 1859 victims were brought to shore near Baton Rouge, hideously burned and scalded. So terrible was their plight that sheets were thrown hastily on the ground, flour was poured on them, and men, women, and children were rolled in the white coating. And the worst of all river explosions occurred in 1865 when the *Sultana* burst apart outside Memphis. Nearly 1,550 were lost within sight of land—more than died on the *Titanic.*

All the newer South benefited by this procession of the steamboats, but New Orleans gained the most. For several generations the Creole city served as the glittering capital of the Southern empire, queen of cotton and sugar and river trade with the world. Years earlier, Jefferson had predicted: "The position of New Orleans certainly destines it to be the greatest city the world has ever known." By 1840 the town in the crescent bend of the Mississippi had become the fourth largest in the United States.

For a decade or so before midcentury, New Orleans sent out more goods than New York; 50 per cent of the nation's exports passed through it. It was at this period that the tonnage on the Mississippi and its tributaries exceeded that of the whole British merchant marine. With each decade after 1820 the value of goods that rolled down to New Orleans doubled itself. And, though some might not talk quite so proudly of another aspect of the city's pre-eminence, it was the great American slave center, the biggest slave market in the world.

The actor Tyrone Power in 1834 found three miles of the New Orleans levee "bordered by tiers of merchant shipping from every portion of the trading world, and close against it, those of the greatest tonnage, having once chosen a berth, may load or unload without shifting a line; a facility derived from nature that no other port in the world can rival." Power was overwhelmed by the range of storehouses, cotton presses and shops, "numberless steamboats of all sizes," fleets of "rude rafts and arks constructed by the dwellers on the hundred waters of the far West."

Hour after hour laborers, sailors, bargemen, and draymen "cheer and order and swear in every language in use amongst this mixed population." The visitor, pushing his way "amongst tens of thousands of bales of cotton that actually cover the Levee for miles," saw wealth "on all hands accumulating with a rapidity almost partaking of the marvelous." Another observer termed the New Orleans waterfront the "master street" of the universe, and still another said, simply, "This is one of the most wonderful places in the world."

How could she fail to outstrip all other American cities, with the vast produce of the West pouring down, trade going back up the Mississippi at the same time, and the wide plantation region of the lower South to feed it? In the early 1820's, Eastern merchants were expressing this fear in mournful words. Through the years until 1860 the value of mercantile operations increased steadily, so that the place appeared about to burst its seams.

And yet . . . Flushed as it seemed, New Orleans had grown less healthy economically, along with other Southern centers and supporting rural regions. The trend of American economic development was away from the river capital and from the South as a whole. By 1825 the Erie Canal connected New York with the Great Lakes, and a swift new waterway lay open to the upper Mississippi River and

Like a Front Porch on the River. The upper deck of a steamboat resembled a Southern plantation gallery.

the West. Little understood by many in the South, this was one of the most drastic changes in the pattern of American progress. Only fifteen years later more grain shipments went by that Northern route than through New Orleans. Before the canal was dug, Western goods made up nearly 60 per cent of the city's trade; by 1860 the figure had fallen to less than 25 per cent. And other canals were dug, to feed the process of diversion from the South. America was growing prodigiously—in another direction.

True, New Orleans received a larger total of goods from the upper valley than it ever had. Yet to maintain its place in an expanding nation, it should have received far more. Just as important, or more so, was the fact that the railroads had arrived, and the North and East soon had more of them than the South, joining more towns, larger towns. Baltimore, Charleston, and other Southern centers were pioneer rail centers, but the Northern cities outdistanced them, at first gradually, then not so gradually. And the rail lines moved from East to West rather than North to South; the old pattern of river traffic was being broken. New York advanced steadily to rank as the largest city of the country, and the major point of entry to the West and to the nation as a whole.

Most New Orleanians, however, still showed little alarm. Around them Cotton extended his realm, expanded his importance: more planters, large and small; more slaves, more gray bales. New Orleans and the South as a whole concentrated their energies, their interests, banked their future on the staple. Let other sections go as they wished; cotton was New Orleans' destiny, King Cotton its monarch, and the South's as well. And the South soon received its last great addition of people and cotton fields, from the lands to the west of the Creole city.

Scenes and Faces on the Steamboats

Lower Deck and Engines. The less-privileged passengers lounged, talked, waited, while the engine attendants worked at the furnaces.

"The Arkansaw Traveler." A visitor to a remote rural area far from the more cosmopolitan river.

A Steampipe Burst. In a moment the *Western World* was in flames.

Left: Race on the River! The classic of classics was between the *Natchez* and the *Robert E. Lee.*

Right: A Losing Battle. In spite of every effort, the Louisiana levee was soon to collapse.

Left: Great Fire at St. Louis. On May 17, 1849, the waterfront suffered a major disaster.

Right: Show Time on the Mississippi. The "Floating Palaces" brought drama and excitement to the river.

Steamboat Disasters Immortalized. Thousands sighed as they sang it at the piano.

Left: The Steamboat Went Nearly Everywhere. Alligator shooting from the decks.
Right: A Watery Back-Country Mailbox

Left: Levee Giving Way! With the spring-swollen river held within embankments, the steamboat rode high above the surrounding land.

Right: Miles of Ground Swallowed by the River. For the people of the Mississippi banks, it meant terror and tragedy.

"A Friendly Game of Poker." Excitement, rivers, and chance-taking went together.

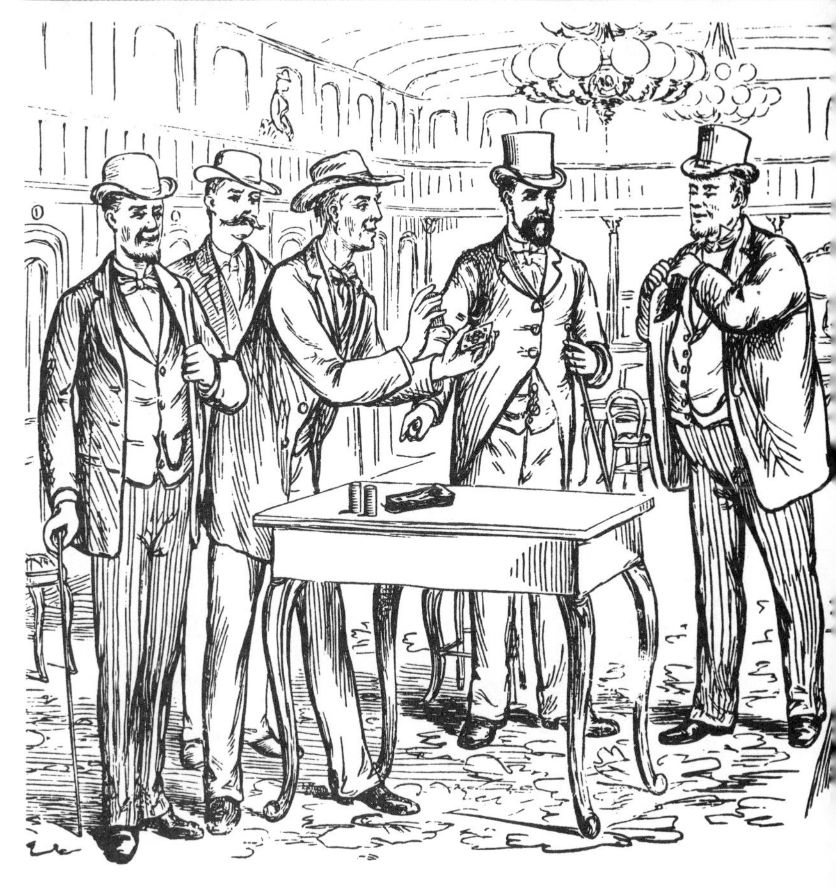

Top: "Nothing Like It!" A style very much *sui generis* was that of the steamboat interior, exemplified here by the *Grand Republic.*

Bottom: Sharper's Paradise. Many a fool, and many a more or less wise man as well, was parted from his money.

Left: Fur Trade to Cotton Market. St. Louis, center of an old-time French traffic in pelts, became a humming river capital.

Right: The French Missouri Manner. The Chouteau Mansion.

Left: It Was Not Quite Elite. At this "Natchez Ballroom" the ladies smoked as they danced with the boys, in an on-the-scene, contemporary sketch.

Right: Vicksburg. A town that would play a major role in the war that was coming.

"Red Stick" of Louisiana. Baton Rouge, eventually capital of the state, had its sugar country, a Walter Scott castle—and politics. England owned it for a time as part of "West Florida," and Spain took it during the American Revolution. East Florida, after being shuttled from Spain to England and back to Spain, was sold to the United States.

Great Interior Cotton Market. Memphis drew the Lower Mississippi cotton from many miles in the surrounding area.

Natchez Came Into Its Own. Elegant manner on the high bluff, and raw fun at Natchez Under the Hill.

Queen of the River. New Orleans would be the world's greatest city, Jefferson predicted.

The Rivers Could Be Graveyards, Too.

Left: Travelers' Peril. Highwaymen and murderers waited at the forest edges, and many a man was never heard of again.

Right: Near the Meeting of the Mississippi and the Gulf. The pilots' settlement in a world of grass and many waters.

The Dividing Line. To one side of Canal Street lay the downtown French New Orleans, to the other the uptown American section.

Notorious Natchez Trace. For more than a century men used this Southern-Western roadway to the Mississippi, its soil worn deeply by travelers' wheels and horses' hoofs.

"Breathing Spot" of the Creole Town. The Cathedral, Cabildo, and Presbytère faced the Place d'Armes in the center, with the long Pontalba Buildings to each side. In time it became Jackson Square.

Cities of the Dead. In low-lying New Orleans, burial had to be aboveground.

View in Rear
of
St Louis Cathedral

Vignettes. New Orleans had the air of a European town, French and Spanish, with a suggestion of the West Indian.

Dueling Capital of America. "Games of murder" took place generally on the outskirts of New Orleans.

Creole City Cockpit. Popular in many Southern places, the "sport" reached a peak here.

A Wilder, More Raffish Side. The baiting of a bull and a bear at New Orleans.

Cool to Enigmatic, Coy to Haughty. They were beauties of the Old Dominion, which gave them high rank in any Southern belledom. Usually they married well.

Left: Fashion, Flirtation, and Health, Too. To the White Sulphur Springs of Montgomery County went the elegant, the would-be-elegant, and those so secure that they need not bother how they looked.

Right: Fauquier White Sulphur Had Eclat. Six hundred guests at one time, two big hotels, ninety double cabins, and a ballroom for everybody.

"Permanent" Bath-Keeper at Berkeley Springs. John Davis, eighty, spent forty years on the job. He left the spot once in his life, when drafted briefly into the 1812 militia.

Fashions at the Hot Springs

Greatest Sight of All. The Natural Bridge of Rockbridge County was considered the finest of Virginia's natural attractions.

Big Spring Cavern. A spot for pleasant sightseeing, socializing, and the like.

Tapestry Room, Weyer's Cave, for the Still More Adventuresome. Ladies (chaperoned) accompanied gentlemen to the caves.

"Delightful, Isn't It?" Getting healthier might involve a grimace and a special effort.

For the More Adventuresome. Falling Springs, Bath County, drew those who liked novelty.

Romantic Interlude, Then Failure. About 1718 a French military colony, Champ d'Aisle, began in Texas. It did not last long in the raw wilderness.

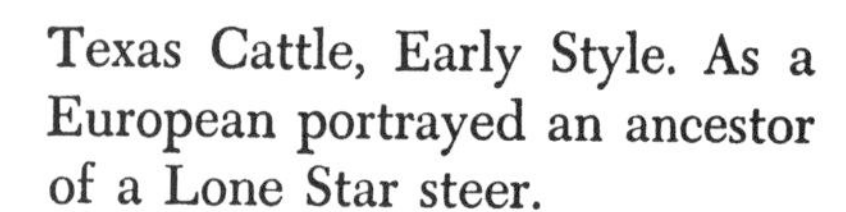

Texas Cattle, Early Style. As a European portrayed an ancestor of a Lone Star steer.

# 13

# G. T. T. MEANT "GONE TO TEXAS"

"Volunteers from the United States . . . Come with a good rifle, and come soon. . . . Liberty or death!" —SAM HOUSTON

FOR YEARS Southerners had been turning speculative eyes toward the expanses of Mexico, its Gulf sands and its rolling plains, extending from the Louisiana border. Men spoke grandly of "manifest destiny," the inevitable drive of Anglo-Saxon Americans toward the Far West. Uneasily the weakening Spanish rulers attempted to halt individuals or small bands who crept across the line, forcing out some of the land-hungry intruders, shooting others.

But the *Yanquis* could not be stopped; soon after the Louisiana Purchase a

New Orleans man commented that people from the United States were "spreading out like oil upon a cloth." Then in 1821 Mexico fought her way to freedom from the Spanish overlords, and a year later, after some hesitation, the new nation admitted the first of some carefully screened colonists to the Brazos River with the pioneer Stephen Austin as *empresario*, or manager.

Mexico tried to impose regulations that would prevent the general area—later known as Texas—from becoming a paradise for gringos. Settlers were to embrace Catholicism and live under Mexican laws like any other residents. Newcomers from over the border nodded, made promises, and carried on as they always had, putting up replicas of the places they had left. From Louisiana, Tennessee, Alabama, Kentucky, Mississippi they rode alone or in small bands to build settlements with a generally Southern look.

"G.T.T.," "Gone to Texas," read the signs they left behind. One element consisted of men who yearned simply for fresh acres, who were propelled by the same motives that had possessed their ancestors. Another was an unsettled group, restless and anxious to escape sterner obligations like sheriffs' summonses. In the beginning Texas presented a raw, primitive aspect, as a place of crude discomfort and frequent brawls. It was true, as one early housekeeper said, that "Texas is a heaven for men and dogs, but hell for women and oxen."

Many families brought slaves, to set up cotton farms in the fertile valleys of

Left: On the Way to Texas. In the early 1800's Joshua Shaw captured the details, outlook of travelers to the West.

Right: Plain-Style Ferry, Comal River. Texas was "heaven for men and dogs . . . hell for women and oxen."

eastern Texas, and the Southern air grew more pronounced. Within fifteen years an estimated twenty-five thousand had established themselves, with their several thousand bondsmen. Such areas, long empty under Spain, began to benefit, but the Latins and the *Yanquis* had marked differences in outlook, in basic beliefs, and trouble crackled.

The newcomers fumed over Mexican delays and red tape in government; Mexican officials resented the protests and demands for greater rights, and adopted stricter laws to hamper or halt immigration from the United States, and to stop, or try to stop, the trade between Texas and lands to the east. The last thing Mexico wanted was a healthy commerce between its territory and the United States.

Nevertheless a great element among the Anglo-Saxons on Mexican soil became ever more confirmed Southerners—with a difference. If only because of their isolation in a "foreign" locale, the Texans showed an independence beyond that of most of their fellow frontiersmen, a lusty, go-to-hell attitude toward anyone who stood in their way. And Texas pride mushroomed. A United States official who visited there about 1830 proclaimed the place a "most delightful champaign

Left: He Fathered Anglo-Saxon Texas. Stephen Austin became *empresario* of a band of pioneers along the Brazos, tolerated by Spanish elements.

Right: Spain's Stamp Was Clear. For generations the military plaza at San Antonio had an unmistakable air of Spain.

*Declaration of the independence of Texas.*

The Louisiana Herald, contains a copy of a declaration, issued on the 23d of June, by the supreme council of the republic of Texas. The following extracts contain all that would be interesting to the American reader.

The citizens of Texas would have proved themselves unworthy of the age in which they live—unworthy of their ancestry—of the kindred republics of the American continent—could they have hesitated in this emergency, what course to pursue. Spurning the fetters of colonial vassalage, disdaining to submit to the most atrocious despotism that ever disgraced the annals of Europe—they have resolved, under the blessing of God, to be FREE. By this magnanimous resolution, to the maintainance of which their lives and fortunes are pledged, they secure to themselves an elective and representative government, equal laws and the faithful administration of justice, the rights of conscience and religious liberty, the freedom of the press, the advantages of liberal education, and unrestricted commercial intercourse with all the world.

"Animated by a just confidence in the goodness of their cause, and stimulated by the high object to be obtained by the contest, they have prepared themselves unshrinkingly to meet, and firmly to sustain, any conflict in which this declaration may involve them.

"Done at Nacogdoches this twenty-third day of June, in the year of our Lord 1819.

JAMES LONG,
*President of the Supreme Council.*

BIS'TE TARIN, sec'ty.

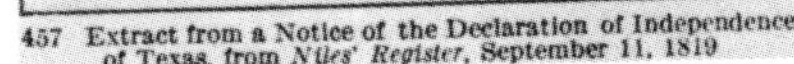

457 Extract from a Notice of the Declaration of Independence of Texas, from *Niles' Register*, September 11, 1819

Left: "Most Atrocious Despotism." This early declaration of Texas independence proved abortive.

Right: Baroque in Texas. Not quite like anything else in the South were the Churrigueresque stone carvings at the Mission San José of San Antonio.

[meaning champagne] country." The new Texan went further, calling it, with single-minded vigor: "Finest land in the New World, or the Old, either."

Fine land or not, the Mexicans wanted no slavery there or elsewhere, and ordered the system abolished. Settlers insisted that they had a right to keep their Negroes, and although they obtained concessions on the issue, new sources of friction mounted. Then in 1832 the Mexican Santa Anna launched a revolution against the government, and he pledged the *Yanquis* a more generous regime. Once in office, however, *El Presidente* proved a devious dictator, and the Texans lifted their banners in the rebellion of 1836.

"Liberty and Texas!" The Anglo-Saxons shouted it as they gathered in their log cabins, in adobe huts, at the crossroads. They oiled their hunting guns, sharpened butcher knives and any other weapons they could find. In the words of one of the volunteers: He could not be sure of the precise role the majority expected to take toward Mexico. Some favored full independence, others wanted rights promised previously by Santa Anna, and some were "for anything, just so it was a row."

In the United States the public watched events with interest. At New Orleans, Memphis, Louisville, and other Southern points men were quick to offer their services. "Volunteers from the United States . . . Come with a good rifle, and come soon. . . . Down with the usurper!" Late arrivals received a meaningful promise —"liberal bounties of land."

"Remember the Alamo!" When the Mexicans stormed it, the Texans fought on to the last man and to future fame.

Spain Plus the New World. They combined in the plaza and church of El Paso.

There ensued two bloody actions that galvanized the Texans and their sympathizers. At the old Alamo Mission in San Antonio, 188 men stood together under Colonel William B. Travis, originally of South Carolina. As Santa Anna came steadily closer with more than 6,000 fighters, the little group had the opportunity to escape or surrender, but it chose to remain, in a stirring saga of determination and courage.

Among the Alamo band were Jim Bowie, a vigorous borderland character who struck out often in deadly accuracy with the knife that bore his name, and the redoubtable Davy Crockett of Tennessee, a rip-roaring, near-legendary figure. With rare bravery the men of the Alamo fought from building to building, room to room, bayonet to bowie knife. Jim Bowie, sick at the time, died in his bed, still fighting. Before the last Texan sank in hand-to-hand combat, 1,500 enemies lay dead or injured.

About two weeks later, at Goliad, there was another grim slaughter. . . . J. W. Fannin, a former Georgian, had been organizing forces along the Trinity, when, heavily outnumbered, he and his men gave up. On orders of President Santa Anna, about 325 were taken out, shot to death, their bodies burned. From then on the Texans used "Remember the Alamo!" as their rallying cry. Others shouted a variation: "Remember Goliad!"

Soon afterward the United States stirred to news of the activities of Sam Houston. The burly Sam was an individual who, once seen, would never be confused with anyone else. He had a natural flamboyance of dress and manner. As a youth he had lived among the Cherokees. A protégé of Andrew Jackson, Houston became Tennessee's governor at thirty-four, only to quit after a domestic tragedy. For a time he had gone back to the Indians, who called him "The Raven" and also "Big Drunk." Now he found himself in Texas, on his way to rank as a hero.

Leading an outnumbered band near the Gulf, Houston retreated for many days. Then, discovering his chance, he swept down to astonishing victory in the Battle of San Jacinto. As Santa Anna dozed through the siesta hour, Houston waved his hat in signal, and his men crashed through the grasses that hid them. Within twenty minutes of their roaring assault, the Mexican Army ran off in disorder, leaving Santa Anna himself a prisoner.

Texas became an independent republic, to continue so for ten years. Most Texans wanted to join the United States, but entry was delayed for reasons political, tactical, and ideological. Advocates of "manifest destiny," to say nothing of most Southerners, wished Texas in the Union. The empire of empty land, the South reasoned, would be a dazzling acquisition, which could eventually be

Left: Early Capitol of Texas at Houston

Right: He Fought and He Flirted. The brave, burly Sam Houston struggled ably against Mexico, then "flirted" deftly for Texas with Britain and the United States.

Southerners and Americans Did Not Forget. Ruins of the Alamo, honored for more than a century.

Davy the Ripsnorter. Davy Crockett, frontiersman-philosopher-humorist, delighted Congress. Now he headed for Texas.

broken into four or five slave states. By the same token New Englanders opposed the step, and their advocates called proposals to acquire Texas a "slaveholders' conspiracy." The South heatedly denied the charge.

In Texas the wily Sam Houston flirted purposefully with England, which had sizable investments in the area, and dropped hints that Texas might align itself with Britain. Then, to the discomfort of some Southerners, elements hostile to slavery were beginning to show themselves in Texas. In time there would be twenty thousand Germans, a hard-working element that wanted nothing to do with bondage. And to complicate matters, Mexico made clear that annexation of Texas would bring war with the United States.

At this point John Calhoun, South Carolina's logician-philosopher and unsuccessful nullificationist, came back to the national scene. The "Cast-Iron Man" had quit Jackson's Democrats to join the highly conservative Whigs, but only temporarily. The play of politics served Calhoun again when the President, the Virginian John Tyler, named him to the strategic post of Secretary of State. Here he labored hard, but far from well, to get Texas admitted to the Union.

A treaty of 1844, ushering Texas in, approached a Senate vote. In his zeal Calhoun performed one of the most foolish acts of his career. As Secretary of State he declared in a letter that Texas *must* enter as a slave state because if it were a free one, it would invite runaways from the South. The fat was in the fire. As a contemporary declared, Calhoun turned away every Northern vote inclined toward the measure, and lost.

After a time the new presidential election sent to office James Polk, of Tennessee and North Carolina. A strong believer in expansion, Polk was to bring in not only Texas but other parts of old Mexican land, California, New Mexico, and a large stretch of Oregon up the Pacific. For the South, Polk's election marked a considerable gain. From then until the Confederate war, as Historian Clement Eaton has pointed out, the President was either a Southerner or a Northerner with Southern sympathies—in the ironic term, a "doughface."

Texas finally entered, with slaves and a provision that four other states might later be drawn from it. Conflict with Mexico promptly began, and the ensuing war, like other American wars, produced a hero who would go on to politics. This was the plain-faced, weather-worn General Zachary Taylor, born in Virginia, reared in Kentucky, and later a Louisiana plantation owner. "Old Rough and Ready's" battles were marked by many errors but also considerable bravery. Vera Cruz, Palo Alto, Matamoros, Monterrey, Buena Vista . . . The public back home learned to recognize these strange names, while its soldiers learned to cope with dysentery, fleas, and fever.

The South provided a large share of the fighting men, and regarded the war as peculiarly its own. For another clash, not far in the future, the hostilities of the late 1840's provided a training ground. Leading officers included Robert E. Lee, Jefferson Davis, Thomas Jonathan (Stonewall) Jackson, Pierre G. T. Beauregard, Ulysses S. Grant, George Meade. The foundations of many shining military careers were established in the Mexican encounters.

The war's end brought a sequel that many had expected; the impending entry of California and New Mexico bred new conflict. Would they be slave or free? Taking office, Zachary Taylor had to cope with the growing issue. It was sharpened when a Pennsylvania Congressman, David Wilmot, introduced a famous proviso forbidding slavery in the territory taken from Mexico. The matter might have appeared academic, for these lands were hardly fitted for staple Southern crops and the Negro bondage that accompanied them. John Calhoun himself had described them as "forbidden fruit" that "would subject our institutions to political death." But to both South and North the point became one of "honor," to be fought to the burning end.

Again Calhoun stepped forward, shifting his stand. He voiced the feeling of thousands of other Southerners in crying out that they, more than any others, had won the region from Mexico, and they would not be cheated of it! He advanced a new principle: Congress could not ban slavery from any territory, as it had done in the past. It must protect slaves there, as it protected any property. By this theory, territories did not belong to the United States, but to all the states, and only when a state was finally organized might slavery be barred by a vote. Going still further, Calhoun declared unconstitutional the Missouri Compromise line the country had accepted for thirty years, with slavery permitted below it, forbidden above.

Northerners countered by demanding the end of slavery in the District of Columbia. Pointing to bondsmen being marched past places that honored Jefferson and Washington, they called the sight a shame in the eyes of the Christian world. Southerners did not agree, but they had fresh complaints of their own. All

"Gone to Texas." The settlers kept on coming.

And Texas Was To Continue a Place of Many Men. They lived a simple and vigorous existence.

too many slaves were being encouraged to escape; all too many Northerners were giving them aid in passage. . . . Then the nation's attention was diverted briefly when diggers brought up bits of shining metal in the disputed territory of California, and the gold rush broke.

While men argued in Washington, California filled swiftly; lawlessness increased, and with it the need for a stable government. President Taylor urged that California enter the Union at once as a state, avoiding harassing dispute about territorial conditions. By an overwhelming vote the Californians of 1849 approved a constitution and asked admission.

But the Californians proposed to bar slavery, and Southerners were furious. The Union now had fifteen slave states, fifteen free ones. If California entered as free, and the North kept bondage from the rest of the old Mexican land, the South would be placed in shadow. A delegation visited Zachary Taylor to imply that, as a Southerner, he had betrayed the region. Robert Toombs exclaimed: "In the presence of the living God, if by your legislation you seek to drive us from the territories of California and New Mexico, I am for disunion!" To this view Old Rough and Ready answered much as Andrew Jackson, another Southerner, had before

Battle of San Jacinto. The Texans triumphed.

The Spanish Look Remained. The influence from Mexico remained strong.

Left: Presidential Expansionist. James K. Polk of Tennessee gave the signal for Texas' entry into the Union.

"Rehearsal" for Another War? In the war with Mexico new names were heard: Lee, Davis, Grant . . .

General With an Eye on the White House. Winfield Scott, who never made it.

him: Let them try that, and he himself would lead an army to string up their leaders, just as he had strung up spies and deserters in Mexico.

The hour was tense. John Calhoun, working on like the machine to which Harriet Martineau compared him, knew gloomy hours in which he foresaw an inevitable break between North and South. His region had one hope, he said, and that was to struggle with a new purpose against what he termed Northern "encroachment"; it must give up nothing, unite its people to "force an issue as soon as possible." Each year, Calhoun sensed, the other section became stronger. The "Cast-Iron Man" wanted the Union preserved (he never ceased to speak of himself as a Union man), but only if the South maintained "full equality" with the North. Otherwise it must peacefully separate from the other states, "dissolving the partnership."

In these last years of his life Calhoun became ever more absorbed in his efforts. "Relaxation is no longer in the power of his mind," Miss Martineau wrote; "I never saw anyone who so completely gave me the idea of possession." Now he introduced his theory of "concurrent majority," under which no measure involving the South could pass unless the South approved. To this end he urged a true novelty—two American Presidents, one representing the slave group, the other the free, each having a veto power over the other.

Then, in 1849, Calhoun took another tack and summoned all Southern Congressmen to a meeting at which he presented a strongly worded list of grievances, asking them to back him in a body, regardless of party, in offering an ultimatum to the North. Here was the germ of a third-party movement. It did not grow, because less than fifty of the eighty-eight in attendance would go along. A few

"Old Rough and Ready." General Zachary Taylor, of Louisiana and Kentucky, leaped from officer's saddle to Washington, not altogether happily.

months later Calhoun arranged a Nashville convention that pointed toward secession. By this time Mississippi, in the center of the cotton South, had joined South Carolina in the forefront of the Calhoun movement.

To many the project had an ominous sound; the Union seemed close to destruction. It might have ended soon afterward, except for a Southern border leader, Henry Clay of Kentucky, a tired man, wan and sunken-cheeked. Near him in this new national testing stood two other elderly figures, about to leave the American scene with Clay; but first they would take part in a symbolic three-sided duel. The others were Daniel Webster of Massachusetts, the nation's supreme orator, and John Calhoun himself, with the mark of death already upon him.

There was tragedy in Washington during those early months of 1850, and also high drama. At seventy-three, Clay came forward with a proposal of compromise. The country, Clay exclaimed, was about to take "a fearful and disastrous leap," and he begged his listeners to halt. If the nation were to be torn apart, he asked as a blessing from Heaven that he be dead before then.

Specifically Clay urged that California enter as a free state, while the territories of New Mexico and Utah would join the Union with or without slavery as their constitutions eventually decided. He asked that the domestic slave trade be ended in the District of Columbia, though bondage would continue there, and that Congress adopt a stronger fugitive-slave law and also recognize that it had no control over domestic slave trading. Thus each side, giving concessions, would gain others.

Solemnly Henry Clay told the South that membership in the Union meant a great deal to her and to her future existence. If she seceded, it would not be in peace, as Calhoun thought. From his boyhood Clay recalled the fury of Tennessee and his own Kentucky when Spain shut down the Mississippi River mouth. "My life upon it," he warned, the people of the river and its tributaries would never let the outlet at New Orleans be held "subject to the power of any foreign State."

Clay's words were powerful and impressive. In retort, John Calhoun made his appearance to declare that Clay's proposals did not do enough. Ill and unable to talk, Calhoun, swathed in flannels, sank into a chair, and had a friend read his remarks. One after another, said Calhoun, the "cords that bind the States together" were breaking and the Union could be saved only if the South received guarantees against oppression. The North, he insisted, must end all agitation against slavery, give full rights to slavery in new territories, and agree to a constitutional amendment to balance the sections so that the South would not be overshadowed. As always, his statements had a marked effect.

Yet it was Daniel Webster who made the most profound impression. A silence fell, and listeners felt a surge of emotion with his first sentences. "I speak today for the preservation of the Union. 'Hear me for my cause.' " In phrases that combined reason and tolerance, Webster hit at hotheads of both sections. No matter what some claimed, he declared, secession would mean war. He went on: The North should not demand a flat ban against slavery in the new areas, because nature itself opposed such an extension. In the United States hardly a foot of land remained in which slavery was not barred by "irrepealable law." Then, to the dismay of many Northerners, Daniel Webster approved laws aimed at the discouragement of runaway slaves. His own section, he said, could afford to give way on some points, for "the Union was worth temporary concessions."

An Easygoing Texas on the Shore. Galveston, settled early, was always fond of a good time.

In New England hundreds of one-time friends attacked Webster as a Benedict Arnold. Yet his appeals struck fire with people in all parts of the country. The issue hung in balance for months, but compromise won recruits. Stephen A. Douglas, speaking for the West, gave important support. President Zachary Taylor, who did not like Clay and stood against his proposals, died suddenly, and his successor, Millard Fillmore, backed them. The stresses lightened slowly.

Soon after he spoke, the grim John Calhoun also died, to receive one of the most striking demonstrations in Southern history. Carolinians came out by the uncounted thousands to mourn him; for a month the casket rested aboveground while they passed before it, and long afterward they stopped regularly at his grave to lay flowers. While Congress still argued, men who had followed Calhoun in life prepared for the Southern Convention he had recently arranged in Nashville. It heard resounding calls for hard action, burning references to the memory of the dead leader. But the convention failed, because most of the South was not ready to leave the Union.

Despite the stand of large elements of South Carolina and Mississippi, the Compromise of 1850 won the approval of the South as well as of the North. In state after state the Unionists defeated the Calhoun men. Jefferson Davis of Mississippi, who had made Calhoun his guide, lost in his opposition to the Compromise, and left public life, as did others who agreed with him.

"The United States Preserved," a newspaper declared. "Most Glorious News . . ." Over all the country, men and women gave thanks in their prayers. In effect, Henry Clay had called for time in which the country might make full adjustment of the differences that tormented it. It was to be granted a brief ten years.

Seagoing Mule. At Galveston on the Gulf, mule carts helped unload schooners.

Right: Texas' Capital Move. Austin acquired and kept the center of government. Left: Houston, Biggest in Texas. In time it would throb as the heart of a spreading empire.

Steamboat Captain to Cattle Rancher. Richard King, once a steamboat man of the Rio Grande, in 1854 began acquisition of one of the world's great cattle holdings, near Corpus Christi.

Crisis That Followed the Mexican War. South faced North in an epochal debate involving John Calhoun, left, soon to die, and the aging Daniel Webster.

Henry Clay Moved To Save the Union. The Kentuckian, ever inclined to a united nation, proposed the compromise that staved off conflict for a decade.

Playing Keno. Some parts of Texas did not calm with the years.

Rangers Started Early. In 1835 Texas had Rangers who could "ride like Mexicans, shoot like Tennesseans and fight like the very devil."

Busy Port, Gulf Capital. Mobile in Alabama along the Gulf of Mexico dominated a region with remaining hints of France.

North Carolina's Port. Entry point for a large area was Wilmington, seen in this Market Street view.

"Riding to Nashville." For Tennessee, the town with a windswept elevation above the water had a many-faceted appeal.

Grace at the Water's Edge. Louisville in Kentucky took on a settled ease, a quiet grace.

An Outlying Virginia. Wheeling was in Virginia, but with a character that would eventually lead its people to form a new state.

"Most Northerly of Southern Cities." At times Baltimore had felt certain it would outrank New York in American trade.

Quiet After Turbulence. Along the St. Johns River, which had seen many turbulences, Jacksonville knew a more peaceful Florida day.

Wheels and Spires. Such was Courthouse Square at Lexington.

Casual, Semi-Somnolent. High Street in Richmond was a familiar thoroughfare to hundreds of thousands of Southerners.

Late but Growing. Helena and Fort Smith, Arkansas, came after many other Southern cities, but they thrived as the 1800's went by.

Sails and Sawmills. Old Pensacola was a place of trade by the water, with Spanish overtones from its earlier days.

"Liberty" but Not "Equality," He Said. Yet the caustic John Randolph ordered his slaves freed and once declared that the greatest orator he had ever heard was a slave mother, making an appeal from the block.

# 14

# TWO IMAGES: "SLAVOCRACY" OR "BLESSING"?

". . . our patriarchal scheme awakens the higher and finer feelings of our nature." —THOMAS R. DEW

"Slavery will everywhere be abolished, or everywhere be reinstated." —GEORGE FITZHUGH

THE SOUTH had altered in its philosophy, and so, too, had other sections in their attitude toward the region. In a real sense, a contest was under way for the minds of Americans. Many of the events that followed grew out of two images of the South, its own and that of its opponents.

Two Views: the Happy, the Discontented. Singing, dancing in the servant quarters, left. A hopeless effort to escape bondage, right.

For generations there had been marked differences between North and South, in climate, geography, in economics, in mood and outlook, and yet the nation had survived. Now, from the 1850's onward, positions narrowed and the two sides faced each other in growing hostility: the tariff desired by the North, opposed by the South; an industrial-urban civilization against an agrarian one, states' rights as opposed to a steady gain in the concept of a national government. Above all, slavery cast an ever-longer shadow over the land.

Most Southerners, of course, did not possess a single slave, nor ever hoped to own one. Until the 1850's most Northerners had no profound feelings about slavery or emancipation, and wanted no share in name calling or other forms of hostility. Nevertheless new forces were at work, and stereotypes were fixing themselves in men's thoughts. "Slave power," "black abolitionist" . . . Each time opponents threw out such words they helped paint a picture of completely irreconcilable elements and involved men's basic emotions in the process.

At an earlier period slavery had embarrassed and disturbed thousands of Southerners as an obvious wrong. But with the retirement of Thomas Jefferson many had begun to turn against his antislavery views and his generally liberal philosophy. John Randolph of Roanoke ridiculed the Jeffersonians with a trenchant remark: "I am an aristocrat. I love liberty. I hate equality." The French Revolution appalled many Americans, who thought its excesses might be transferred to America, and one member after another of the later generation referred to Jefferson's beliefs as "glittering generalities." Slowly interest declined in emancipation laws, and few men talked of freedom, present or future, for the slaves.

Cotton's splurging new growth further intensified the trend agianst Jeffersonian liberalism. The younger, more violent Deep South had no time to concern itself with abstract questions of justice and human rights. "Rose-water philosophy," one critic called such considerations. . . . At the same time Northern feeling over slavery had risen. For years the North had nurtured political and social reform movements, such as woman suffrage and universal education, which had only limited reflection in the South, and were frequently based on religion. At first, efforts to restrict slavery were merely one phase of many humanitarian programs, but gradually abolitionism came strongly to the fore.

By 1831 William Lloyd Garrison of Boston had established his *Liberator*, first American journal to demand prompt freeing of the slaves. Garrison, scarcely a calm, judicious man, aimed blows in every direction. Flatly he declared: "I do not wish to think or speak or write with moderation. I will not retreat a single inch, and I will be heard." Garrison was to be heard, and often. Roaring at Southern Congressmen, he announced that he would sooner trust the country's welfare to convicted inmates of penitentiaries than to the slave representatives. That observation set the tone of his utterances. Others joined him in a New England Anti-Slavery society, an American Anti-Slavery society, and related organizations.

Under such banners there enlisted men and women of assorted interests—simple visionaries, furious zealots, devout churchgoers who saw slavery as an outrage before God. Some were wildly impractical individuals, others earnest businessmen; many members of old New England families joined. The English movement against slavery, which had ended the practice in the West Indies, stirred hundreds to action. The United States was the last civilized country in which the institution continued, they noted, and into the campaign came ministers like Henry Ward Beecher, Editor Horace Greeley, and elevated figures of American literature, Emerson, Lowell, Thoreau, Whittier.

By the 1840's, abolitionists increasingly operated the "Underground Rail-

Two Southern Partisans. The slavery advocate, William Lowndes Yancey of Alabama, left, became "the Orator of Secession." Hinton Rowan Helper of North Carolina, right, attacked bondage on behalf of non-slave-holding whites.

road," a system by which sympathetic hands aided bondsmen from "station" to "station," town cottage to rural cabin, in flight to the North or to Canada. Solemn congregations gathered to view Negroes who had thus left the South and to provide funds that would assist them on their way. Yet even in their home areas, abolitionists were often unpopular; they were beaten, their meetings broken up, their newspaper offices wrecked. These tactics frequently spurred the victims to new effort and helped the movement gather strength.

More and more the abolitionists oversimplified, indulged in strokes that were far too broad. Every Southerner became a slaveowner and probably an inhuman monster, master of a "harem" of assorted shades, and every slave a mass of welts and burns. More and more their listeners learned the word "slavocracy" and its connotations.

Already Southerners had gone to work in defense or counterattack. Steadily the South developed a new ideology. Slavery was no longer an unmitigated evil but a "necessary" one, and as some commented, the more "necessary" it seemed to be, the less evil it became. During the first thirty years or so of the 1800's, two slave rebellions stirred Southerners to strong fear and what they regarded as protective measures. The Denmark Vesey insurrection of 1822 in South Carolina and the Nat Turner uprising of 1831 in Virginia brought stringent laws against education, sometimes against even religious training. Through the years a number of Southerners defied such restrictions, among them "Stonewall" Jackson, the Pres-

Left: Owner and Agent. Two familiar figures in the Deep South, upper South and border slave states were the planter and his overseer.

Right: A Scene That Repelled Many. A slave coffle within sight of the United States Capitol raised many questions.

Left: The Intercontinental Slave Trade Went On. Until 1861 daring shippers slipped in cargoes of Negroes from Africa or the islands.

Right: Waiting for a Purchaser: Mothers and Children in Richmond

byterian schoolteacher whose illegal Sunday-school classes for Negroes brought him in conflict with several disapproving Virginia neighbors. Nonconformity was growing more and more unpopular.

A year after the Turner rebellion a young professor at the earliest of Southern colleges, William and Mary, began to advance a theory that would have sorely startled Jefferson. The man was Thomas R. Dew, back from studies at German universities, where he had absorbed an eminently practical philosophy, in keeping with Teutonic thought of the day. Slavery was not a thing for which the South should apologize, said Dew, but a beneficial system sanctioned by God and practiced by the classic republics. The professor pointed to Grecian bondage, which had been, he said, the true groundwork of that civilization. He quoted the words of Paul and Moses, and contradicted Jefferson's views on the equality of human beings: "It is as much in the order of nature and of God that men should enslave each other as that other animals should prey upon each other."

Thomas Dew's words were repeated, reprinted, proclaimed. Chancellor William Harper of the South Carolina Supreme Court came forth in behalf of a society of rigid classes, with slaves forever fixed at the base. In his opinion, "if there are sordid, servile and laborious offices to be performed, is it not better that there should be sordid, servile and laborious beings to perform them?" Senator James H. Hammond, also of South Carolina, continued from there. "God created Negroes for no other purpose than to be subordinate 'hewers of wood and drawers of water' . . . to be the slaves of the white race." And Senator Hammond described slavery, oratorically, as "the greatest of all the great blessings which a kind Providence bestowed upon our glorious region."

Few went so far as George Fitzhugh, the influential editor and writer, in attacking the system of free society of the North and of the Western world as well. Fitzhugh plainly advocated a return to feudalism, a regime of white-skinned slaves. He gave an idyllic picture of life among slaves: a guaranteed home, "security of employment," care in illness and age, no jealousy or envy of competition, such as existed among benighted wage earners who had to hunt jobs and quarrel with their employers over wages!

"Now Look Your Best." Before a New Orleans slave dealer's office, men and women were offered in borrowed regalia.

Repeatedly Fitzhugh and his partisans pointed out the undeniable suffering among Northern millworkers, slum conditions and privations. They extended their claims: Slavery was the "natural" state for poorer whites as well as for Negroes, and a wholesome condition as well. Capitalism was destroying itself around the world, in Fitzhugh's mind, because it lacked control and discipline; men must be better managed, given set places in keeping with their abilities. Seriously, boldly, the Southerner announced: "Slavery will everywhere be abolished, or everywhere be reinstated."

On the other hand some Southerners now made hard attacks on slavery from the economic viewpoint. Daniel R. Goodloe questioned the wisdom of investing billions of dollars in human property. If slaves were freed, the money could be spent to improve the land and make other, better investments. Slavery, Goodloe argued, was one of the great brakes upon Southern progress. Dr. Henry Ruffner, president of Washington College at Lexington, viewed slavery as a system which mined Virginia's soil, wasted wealth, and caused impoverished men to move increasingly to freer lands.

Hinton Helper of North Carolina, in his book *The Impending Crisis of the South,* struck at the planter class in behalf of other whites of the region. Slavery, Helper declared, injured the white man and kept the South hopelessly behind the rest of the country. Southern officials banned the book, and it was lumped with dozens of other publications that could not circulate in the area. Slowly the South was building up bulwarks against the opinions of the North.

More effective than any of these philosophic debaters was a trio of major "fire-eaters" of the day, who gave everything to attack rather than defense. Edmund Ruffin of Virginia was a sickly man, timid at the start, who first drew notice as a highly respected advocate of better care of the soil and broad agricultural reform. But his later fame was made as one of the most heated and fiery opponents of the North. Ruffin traveled, gave speeches, and worked to organize a separate South. His region was being degraded, forced to the ground, he said, and it could only secede. Through the years Edmund Ruffin gained a variety of recruits, and eventually he quit the Old Dominion in disgust, to join the warmer-spirited South Carolinians.

"The Orator of Secession" was William Lowndes Yancey. Born in Georgia, he spent a dozen years, interestingly enough, in New York State as the stepson of a schoolteacher-minister-abolitionist. Going back South, Yancey at first followed the Unionist path, taking a firm pro-Union stand at the time of Calhoun's nullification effort. Then he left his law practice and went to Alabama as a planter, only to see all his slaves die of accidental poisoning. Taking up law again, William Lowndes Yancey turned secessionist; year by year his views grew stronger and harsher. His years in the North made him only the more "Southern" in manner and costume. Highly sensitive about his honor, he had two or three duels to his credit.

Yancey served for a time in Congress, but resigned in anger; he wanted nothing further to do with Federal office. He ranged the South, delivering addresses at the crossroads, in city meetings, at the Virginia springs where crowds hailed him as the region's greatest speaker since Patrick Henry. He advocated a direct program—a new revolution like the one of '76, against a foe he considered as oppressive as the British.

It was William Yancey who demanded that the international slave trade be reopened. New Negroes were needed, he argued, to help the South regain its share in the nation's life, a share he felt it had lost. Negro prices had become higher and higher, and this, too, was a hardship, Yancey said. The South's people must be increased; only by bringing in tens of thousands of Negroes could the region match the growth of the North's larger population, and also offset the addition of white workers emigrating from Europe. (The latter would not go to the South, where slavery ruled.) Reinstitution of the slave trade, Yancey declared, would aid both the large Southern planter and the small Southern grower by lowering the cost of bondsmen and extending the benefits of slavery to poorer people. . . . Many others repeated his words.

Fieriest of the "fire-eaters" was Robert Barnwell Rhett of South Carolina,

To Tens of Thousands a Rare Sight. Both Northerners and Southerners stared at slave auctions like this one in Richmond.

whose family had come from New England. His name had been Smith, but he changed it eventually to one he considered more "Southern." Here was a down-Easterner turned cavalier, with differences. Well-to-do, owning nearly two hundred slaves, Rhett still had little of the easygoing Southerner in his manner. He was strongly religious and strongly opposed to dueling; he labored to teach religion to seamen in Charleston, and, most strangely of all in that high-living coastal city, he belonged to a temperance society.

Yet there was no hint of temperance in Rhett's attitude toward his native North. Earlier than most extremists, he insisted that the South bring its disputes to a head, and as soon as it could. It must expand, quickly, or quit the Union at the first possible moment. "To hate and persecute the South has become a high passport to honor and power in the North," said Rhett. Again: "Let it be that I am a Traitor. The word has no terrors for me. . . . I have been born of Traitors, but, thank God, they have been Traitors in the great cause of liberty. . . ." Friends saluted Robert Barnwell Rhett as the Father of Secession.

Each member of the trio worked assiduously to persuade others that the Southerner belonged to a breed apart from the Northerner; that he must have a separate government, unhampered and uncontaminated by Yankee influence. Between the two sides stood the Negro, unable to influence the decisions in the making. To the Northerner he seemed a mute sufferer under the blows of his masters. To the latter he was the smiling beneficiary of a happy system.

The truth, as always, lay somewhere between the two contentions. The South had generous owners, who repeatedly refused to break up Negro families to which they were bound by ties of association only half understood by white or black. It also had harsh, unfeeling men who became tyrants and sadists. And there were "average" owners, part good, part bad.

But the extremists were determining the shape of events to follow. In the North they saw all Southerners as grasping despots, trying to lord it over America. In the South, they looked on the Northerners as enemies of "gentility," of all stability in life. The tragedy was that both elements gradually persuaded those around them to accept the view they conjured up.

Curfew for the Blacks. At Charleston, all must be inside by dark.

VALUABLE GANG OF YOUNG

**NEGROES**

**By JOS. A. BEARD.**

**Will be sold at Auction,**

**ON WEDNESDAY, 25TH INST.**

At 12 o'clock, at Banks' Arcade,

**17 Valuable Young Negroes, Men and Women, Field Hands. Sold for no fault; with the best city guarantees.**

**Sale Positive and without reserve!**

**TERMS CASH.**

**New Orleans, March 24, 1840.**

"Sold for No Fault." Mr. Beard was one of New Orleans' most prosperous of slave auctioneers.

No. 1847

**THE UNITED STATES LIFE INSURANCE COMPANY**

IN THE CITY OF NEW YORK.

ANNUAL PREMIUM. $ 15.07

HOW PAYABLE. Annually

SUM INSURED. $ 550

THIS POLICY OF INSURANCE WITNESSETH THAT

**THE UNITED STATES LIFE INSURANCE COMPANY**

IN THE CITY OF NEW YORK,

**In Consideration** of the sum of Fifteen dollars and Seven cents, to them in hand paid by John G Tellmann

and of the annual premium of Fifteen dollars and Seven cents, to be paid In advance on or before the Third day of September in every year during the continuance of this Policy. **Do Assure** the Life of Charles a slave, the property of John G Tellmann of Lexington in the County of Fayette State of Kentucky in the amount of Five Hundred and Fifty dollars, for the term of One Year to commence on the Third day of September 1852 at noon, and expire on the Third day of September 1853 at noon.

And the said Company do hereby **Promise and Agree**, to and with the said assured, his executors, administrators, and assigns, well and truly to pay, or cause to be paid, the said sum insured, to the said assured, his executors, administrators, or assigns, within three months after due notice, and proof of the death of the said slave Charles

**Provided always**, and it is hereby declared to be the true intent and meaning of this Policy, and the same is accepted by the assured upon these express conditions, that in case the said slave Charles shall die upon the seas, or shall, without the consent of this Company previously obtained and entered upon this Policy, pass beyond the limits of Kentucky or in case the assured shall already have any other insurance on the slave hereby assured and not notified to this Company and mentioned or endorsed on this Policy, or shall hereafter effect any other insurance upon the said slave without the Consent of this Company first obtained and entered on this Policy, or in case the said slave shall die by means of any invasion, insurrection, riot, civil commotion, or of any military or usurped power, or in case the slave shall die by his own hand, or in consequence of a duel, or by the hands of justice, or in the violation of any law of any State or of the United States, or in consequence of any extra hazardous employment, this Policy shall be void, null, and of no effect.

**And it is also Understood and Agreed**, to be the true intent and meaning hereof, that if the declaration made by the said John G. Tellmann and bearing date the Third day of September 1852 and upon the faith of which this agreement is made, shall be found in any respect untrue, then, and in such case, this Policy shall be null and void; or in case the said John G Tellmann shall not pay the said premiums as above reserved, on or before the several days herein before mentioned for the payment thereof, then and in every such case, the said Company shall not be liable to the payment of the sum insured, or any part thereof: and this Policy shall cease and determine.

**And** it is further agreed, that in every case where this Policy shall cease, or become or be null or void, all previous payments made thereon shall be forfeited to the said Company.

**And it is hereby expressly Agreed**, between the said assured and the said Company, that the said assured, for and in consideration of the premises, has waived, and hereby waives and releases to the said Company, all right and title to any mutuality or participation in the profits of the said Company

**And it is further Understood and Agreed**, that the interest of the assured in this Policy is not assignable without the consent of the said Company, manifested in writing.

**In Witness whereof**, the said **United States Life Insurance Company in the City of New-York**, have, by their President and Secretary, signed and delivered this Contract, this Third day of September one thousand eight hundred and fifty two

John Eadie Secretary.

P. Sheldon President.

Countersigned at ........ the ........ day of ........ 185

........ Agent.

"Slave Insurance." A Kentuckian took out this one-year policy, with a New York firm, against death or escape.

Examination for Defects. A purchaser wanted to know the quality of the merchandise.

A Slave Escaped. "Resurrection" for Henry Brown, who went from Richmond to Philadelphia in a box three feet long, two and a half deep, two feet wide.

"Walks Slow, Laughs Loud." Payment promised for a runaway's return.

# $100 REWARD.

**Ran away from my farm, near Buena Vista P. O., Prince George's County, Maryland, on the first day of April, 1855, my servant MATHEW TURNER.**

**He is about five feet six or eight inches high; weighs from one hundred and sixty to one hundred and eighty pounds; he is very black, and has a remarkably thick upper lip and neck; looks as if his eyes are half closed; walks slow, and talks and laughs loud.**

**I will give One Hundred Dollars reward to whoever will secure him in jail, so that I get him again, no matter where taken.**

**MARCUS DU VAL.**

BUENA VISTA P. O., MD.,
MAY 10, 1855.

# RAFFLE

Mr. Joseph Jennings respectfully informs his friends and the public that, at the request of many acquaintances, he has been induced to purchase from Mr. Osborne, of Missouri, the celebrated

## DARK BAY HORSE, "STAR,"

Aged five years, square trotter and warranted sound; with a new light Trotting Buggy and Harness also, the dark, stout

## MULATTO GIRL, "SARAH,"

Aged about twenty years, general house servant, valued at *nine hundred dollars*, and guaranteed, and

## Will be Raffled for

At 4 o'clock P. M., February first, at the selection hotel of the subscribers. The above is as represented and those persons who may wish to engage in the usual practice of raffling, will, I assure them, be perfectly satisfied with their destiny in this affair.

The whole is valued at its just worth, fifteen hundred dollars; fifteen hundred

## CHANCES AT ONE DOLLAR EACH.

The Raffle will be conducted by gentlemen selected by the interested subscribers present. Five nights will be allowed to complete the Raffle. BOTH OF THE ABOVE DESCRIBED CAN BE SEEN AT MY STORE, No. 78 Common St., second door from Camp, at from 9 o'clock A. M. to 2 P. M.

Highest throw to take the first choice; the lowest throw the remaining prize, and the fortunate winners will pay twenty dollars each for the refreshments furnished on the occasion.

N. B. No chances recognized unless paid for previous to the commencement.

**JOSEPH JENNINGS.**

Highest Throw for a Horse and a Girl. A raffle at a dollar a chance.

Left: Southern Abolitionist. James G. Birney of Kentucky changed from a slaveholder to an opponent of bondage. A Cincinnati mob wrecked his newspaper and he suffered other losses.

Right: It Outlived Them All. The ancient slave block at New Orleans lasted longer than the institution itself.

Advertisement of the "Underground Railroad" for Slaves

The Earnest Grimké Sisters. Angelina and Sarah Grimké, of a well-placed South Carolina family, shocked friends by throwing in their lot with the abolitionists.

A Slave Recaptured

Meanwhile, Casual Southern Life. Negroes along a canal of the Dismal Swamp in Virginia.

They ran the rapids of New River, Virginia.

They hunted the popular raccoon at night in the forest.

Left: In the Quarters. The "hands" take their places for a photograph at the estate of James Hopkinson at Edisto Island, South Carolina.
Right: Florida Had Crackers, Too. In their semitropic setting, they shared the heritage of Southern plain folk.

"Georgia Crackers." They represented a large, often unseen element, far removed from the plantations.

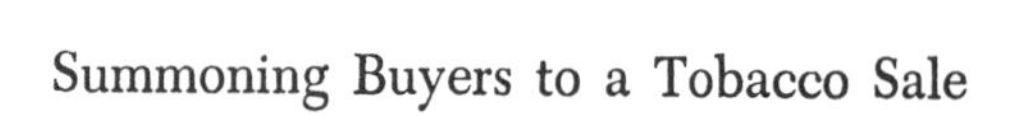

Summoning Buyers to a Tobacco Sale

Left: A Glory of Liveoaks at Pass Christian, Mississippi.
Right: Stemming Tobacco. Scene in a Richmond factory with all ages at work.

Indispensable, Favored Character—the Cook in the Kitchen

Kentucky Was the Capital. The Bluegrass country became the sporting capital of the South, and a major center was the Oakland House track, seen here at its height.

Hurrying to the Races

Rolling the Race Track

Racing à la New Orleans. In time the Metairie track became one of the nation's most resplendent courses.

Boys, Gentlemen, Men Not So Gentle. Everybody attended races at the fairs or wherever Southerners scheduled them. Greenville, South Carolina, provided this scene.

Plainer Folk Came on Foot

For the Ladies. Sidesaddle or by carriage, women went to the course for a lively afternoon.

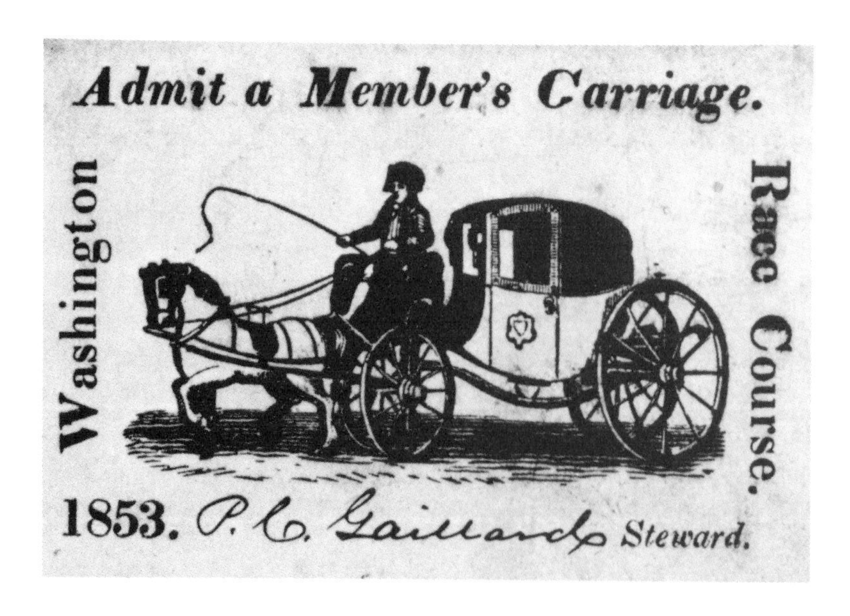

Left: He Began with Prospects of Peace. Franklin Pierce, President from New England, had a mild manner and Southern sympathies.

Right: His Mood Was Quiet. Jefferson Davis, once a warm Calhoun man, began as a conciliatory Secretary of War.

# 15

# FROM "UNCLE TOM" TO "JOHN BROWN'S BODY"

"I will write something. I will if I live."—Harriet Beecher Stowe

For a brief time after the Compromise of 1850 the country enjoyed a respite. Commercial men of the Atlantic seaboard and the bustling Midwest of Chicago beamed as peace settled about them; they had vital ties to the cotton market, to Southern trade in general, and as conservatives they favored an end to the harmful agitation and unrest. A fresh prosperity swept the South, to continue largely unchecked for a decade, and the merchants in Louisiana, Tennessee, Alabama, and other states below Mason and Dixon's line likewise favored an end to

Left: "Gray-Eyed Man of Destiny." William Walker struck repeatedly at Latin America, took Nicaragua for a time, and proposed to extend slavery there.

Right: The United States Indicted This Mississippi Governor. John Quitman, Southern fireater (from New York), was named for encouraging pro-slavery invasions of Cuba.

recriminations. One Southern diehard complained in a letter that even in the remote country districts the people refused to be "stirred."

With the presidential election of 1850 came developments that seemed to presage a further quieting of mood. The mild-mannered new executive, Franklin Pierce of New Hampshire, gave no indications of a wish to rake up controversies of any kind. He brought back to public life as his War Secretary an old associate, Jefferson Davis of Mississippi, and Colonel Davis' mood had altered. He spoke no longer like a fire-eating partisan of John Calhoun.

Nevertheless underlying stresses remained, and both South and North had men to play upon them. Each element watched for opportunity, and neither had long to wait. Pierce proved a weak, vacillating man, who soon pursued a course

No Novel Had Such an Impact. For many decades the world sighed and cried as Eliza crossed the ice on-stage.

that the North felt certain favored the South to a marked degree. In this dangerous decade great figures left the national scene, and a series of lesser ones, from the President downward, dominated the stage. When the new President announced that his government would not be halted by "timid forebodings of evil from expansion," many Southerners began to look about them. If slavery were to be halted to the northward by hostile forces or by nature, why not try the tropical lands of the nearby Caribbean and Central America?

Cuba was tempting. Its lands grew thickly with sugar cane, and perhaps it could be carved into several slave states. Then why not take it, invade the island, and let the theorists justify the step? In New Orleans, Memphis, Jackson, Mississippi, and other cities adventuresome youths marched, practiced shooting and joined filibustering expeditions headed for Cuba. More than six hundred launched an attack in one case, and John Quitman, fire-eating Governor of Mississippi (a former New Yorker!) was indicted by a Federal grand jury in New Orleans because of his connection with the venture. On Cuban soil the invaders issued ringing proclamations urging the people to join them. But few Latins rose up, and the American leaders died before the firing squads. One victim was the nephew of a United States senator.

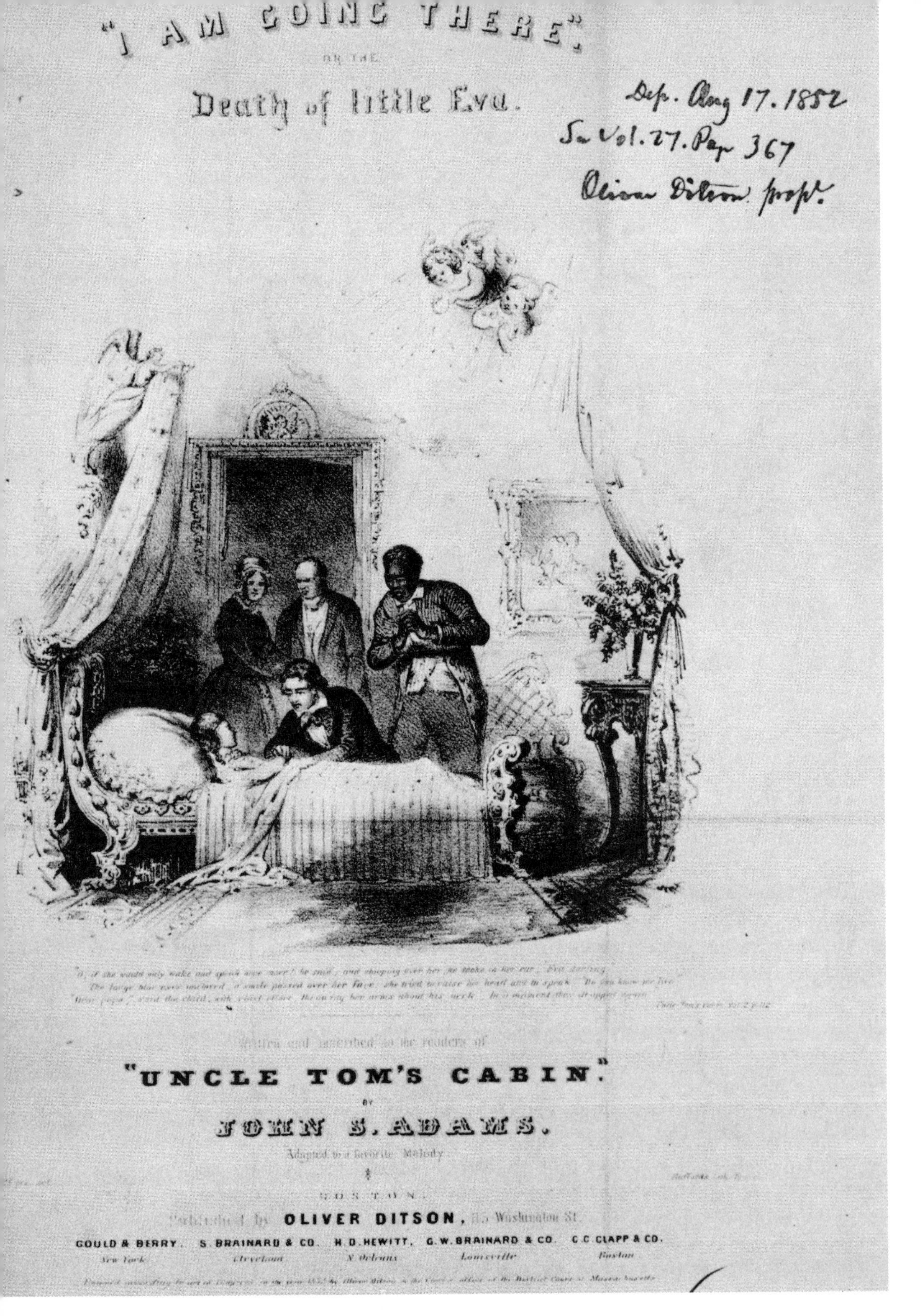


People Sang It, Too. From New York to Siam, they read *Uncle Tom's Cabin* and they hummed words such as these.

Not long afterward the Tennessee-born William Walker, a tiny, delicate-boned man (he weighed barely one hundred pounds), became the South's so-called "Gray-Eyed Man of Destiny" in bold attacks on western Mexico and later Nicaragua. There he took over the office of president-dictator, executing a general who had supported him, and made a play for general Southern backing by calling for a slavery regime in Nicaragua. When other Latin American republics joined in ejecting the "Man of Destiny" from power he escaped to New Orleans and launched one new invasion after another. In the end he was to die before a firing squad. Meanwhile he went about the South for years, an arresting and popular figure.

Cuba continued as a place of intrigue. Dozens of Southern officials proposed that the nation acquire it by purchase, but Spain declared firmly that it would not sell. Steadily President Pierce and his close associate, War Secretary Jefferson Davis, tried to persuade Spain to change its mind. At one point Pierce assigned his three most important European ministers to the delicate task of discovering a way to achieve a transfer. The result was a red-faced fiasco.

Pierre Soulé of Louisiana, John Mason of Virginia, and James Buchanan of Pennsylvania, sympathetic to the South, issued a crude manifesto: Every law "human and divine" declared that Cuba should belong to the United States, and Spain must accept an offer to buy the island for a sizable sum. If the Spaniards did not realize their "own interest," and were held back by "a stubborn pride and a false sense of honor," in the words of these three unwise men, the United States should seize the island. Finally, the trio advised Spain to use the millions of United States dollars it would receive to make herself a tourist center and to produce more wine! As Europeans guffawed at these gaucheries, the South winced in embarrassment, the North felt a new sense of shock, and the manifesto had to be repudiated. . . . Other Southerners did not give up their expansionist plans, but talked of obtaining all or most of Mexico by invasion or through the work of a mysterious band of "Knights of the Golden "Circle."

The South had no monopoly on provocative acts. From the time of its adoption, the Compromise of 1850 revealed a weakness in its provisions calling for the return of escaped slaves. It allowed Federal commissioners to pass on fugitive cases without jury trial in the North. A slaveowner or his agent could arrest a man or woman and bring him to a commissioner, who received $10 whenever he ruled against a Negro, $5 when he ruled for him. An alleged slave had no right to testify or call witnesses.

Charges arose repeatedly that callous "slave catchers" were snatching up Negroes at random, including some born free or emancipated in earlier years. In scores of incidents people with no previous convictions for or against slavery had its unhappier side brought graphically before them. In one case in Boston, an escaped slave, shivering in fear, was taken through the town by officials while fifty thousand men and women carried banners and wore bands of mourning along black-draped streets. Marines, artillery, and infantry were needed to make sure the slave would not be rescued on his way South. Churchbells rang mournfully, and bitter observers shouted, "Kidnapers, kidnapers!"

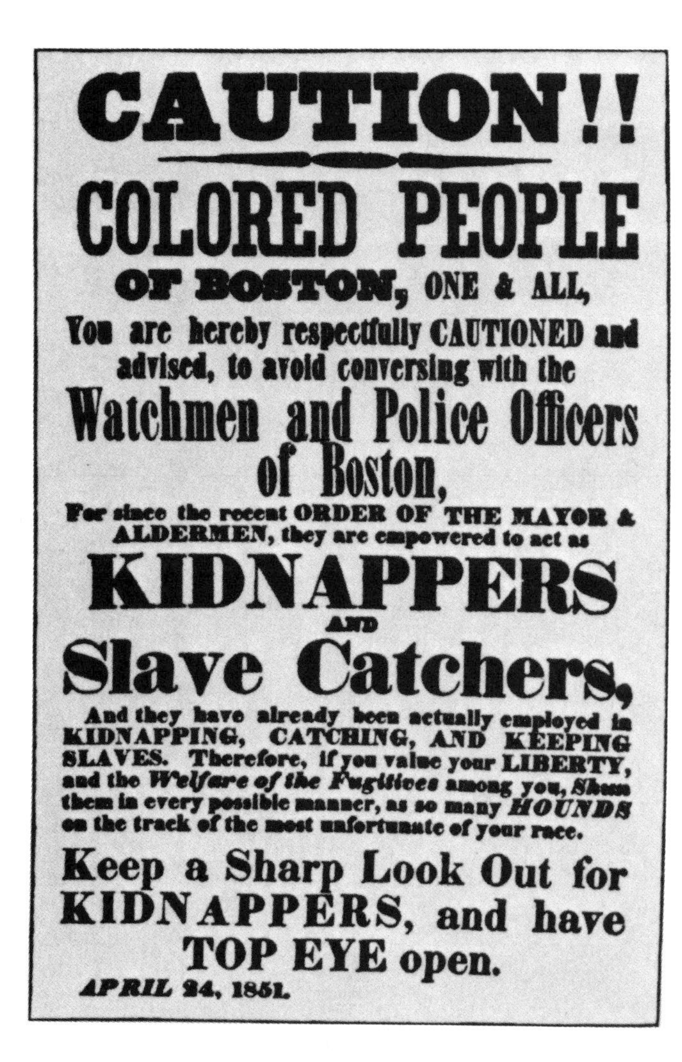

CAUTION!!

COLORED PEOPLE
OF BOSTON, ONE & ALL,
You are hereby respectfully CAUTIONED and advised, to avoid conversing with the
Watchmen and Police Officers of Boston,
For since the recent ORDER OF THE MAYOR & ALDERMEN, they are empowered to act as
KIDNAPPERS
AND
Slave Catchers,
And they have already been actually employed in KIDNAPPING, CATCHING, AND KEEPING SLAVES. Therefore, if you value your LIBERTY, and the *Welfare of the Fugitives* among you, *Shun* them in every possible manner, as so many *HOUNDS* on the track of the most unfortunate of your race.

Keep a Sharp Look Out for KIDNAPPERS, and have TOP EYE open.

*APRIL 24, 1851.*

The Issues Rose Again. The Fugitive Slave Law spurred feeling, then outbreaks in the North.

Each such episode led to new feeling against the South. Estimates are that hardly a thousand Negroes escaped annually through the Underground Railroad, while the fugitive-slave measure meant a large increase in hostility toward the region. Emerson, who had previously advocated a lessening of agitation over the matter of slavery, said of the law: "This filthy enactment was made in the nineteenth century, by people who could read and write. I will not obey it, by God." Others, by God or otherwise, felt the same way, and a number of Northern states adopted personal-liberty bills to protect escapees. To Southerners this was spite, to say nothing of outright violation of the law; to many Northerners it was a solemn and necessary expression of opposition.

In 1852, out of the fugitive-slave issue, came a book that probably influenced America and the world more than any novel ever written. Harriet Beecher Stowe, the high-strung wife of a Cincinnati theology teacher and sister of the minister Henry Ward Beecher, had received a note from a relative: "If I could use a pen as you can, I would write something which would make this whole nation feel what an accursed thing slavery is." To this, Mrs. Stowe answered, "I will write something. I will if I live."

Blood on the Senate Floor. After Charles Sumner of Massachusetts, left, spoke bitterly against a South Carolinian, the latter's relative, Preston Brooks, beat Sumner about the head with a stick until he collapsed.

What she wrote, *Uncle Tom's Cabin,* was an inartistic production, with passages of extreme bathos. To the South, Harriet Stowe's pages dealing with mistreatment of Negroes were a gross libel. Yet she presented her material out of a searing conviction, and its effect on the world was overpowering. In much of America, in Paris and London, in Rome and eventually the Orient, readers clenched their hands and wept, as Uncle Tom achieved a place as the most celebrated fictional figure of his age. Curiously, the author presented the Southern planter-prototype in a somewhat happy light, while the reeking villain Legree was a Yankee overseer.

Within a year the novel achieved a sale of three hundred thousand copies in America; it outsold every book in England except the Bible. *Uncle Tom's Cabin* went on steadily for a quarter-century afterward in American stage versions that ranged from cramped productions by hundreds of traveling troupes to spectacular versions with Eliza racing across the "ice" before the bloodhounds. To millions this was their first play, one of the compelling experiences of their lives. At the court of Siam a high-born figure made *Uncle Tom* the motif of her life, calling herself Harriet Beecher Stowe Son Klin. Abraham Lincoln supposedly stared in wonder at Mrs. Stowe, and said, "So you're the little woman who made the book that made this great war." While the words were exaggeration, *Uncle Tom* did more than its share to bring on the conflict.

Other Northerners and other Southerners performed their roles. In 1854 men on both sides co-operated in a curious power play that produced the Kansas-Nebraska Act. Senator Stephen A. Douglas of Illinois, sometimes hailed as a "Steam-Engine in Britches," was working energetically for a transcontinental railroad through the ever more prosperous Midwest. Ingeniously he proposed to help his purposes by creating two new territories through which the railroad might pass, Kansas and Nebraska. To win Southern votes, Douglas offered bait—repeal of the old Missouri Compromise that kept slavery out of the area. The matter of freedom or slavery would be decided in each territory by the inhabitants themselves. This change would "raise the hell of a storm," Douglas admitted, but he thought the result worth the risk. What he fashioned instead was a time bomb.

Although no one thought Nebraska would ever vote slavery, Kansas lay next to Missouri, which already had bondage, and some Southerners saw possibilities in the new project. The Kansas-Nebraska Act passed, to reap a harvest of hate and turmoil that few anticipated. While the South eventually received nothing, thousands of Northerners cried out: A great new area was to be opened to slavemongers, shut to free men!

Political lines cracked, and out of the ensuing turmoil and resentment there rose a new party, the Republicans. Many conservatives left the Whigs because that organization would not take a clear stand on slavery, while others quit the Democrats on the grounds that they favored slavery. And "bleeding Kansas" emerged as North and South fought for the territory in a squalid and degrading contest. Organizations were formed in both North and South to pack the territory, paying families to go there. Armed desperadoes, ambushes, guerrilla fighting, crude murder—Kansas knew them all.

Within a year slavery groups from Missouri dominated a Kansas territorial legislature, which put into effect a code sponsoring slavery. A rival antislavery government formed. An eight-hundred-man proslavery posse, led by a United States marshal, swept into the free town of Lawrenceville to sack it, smash newspaper offices, burn homes. In revenge, another mob, headed by an obscure fanatic named John Brown, rode into a proslavery settlement and killed five men. The unhappy Kansas issue was to hang on until January of 1861, after most of the Southerners had left Congress, when the territory finally entered the Union as a free state.

At the height of the agitation there occurred an ominous event in Congress. Charles Sumner, the caustic Massachusetts senator, delivered a violent antislavery address in which he attacked an elderly South Carolina member, Senator Andrew Butler. Representative Preston Brooks, Butler's nephew, discovered Sumner sitting at his desk and, using a gutta percha walking stick, beat the New Englander about the head until he fell unconscious. In North and South partisans shouted charges and countercharges, and each man became a hero. The injured Sumner stayed away from the Senate for three years, his empty chair a silent reproach.

In an atmosphere of high tension, the United States voted for President in 1856. The new Republicans nominated John C. Frémont, and drew an astonishingly large vote, but the Democrats won with the Pennsylvanian James Buchanan,

Scene of Historic, Hopeless Raid. At strategic Harpers Ferry, with its B.&O. railroad crossing, John Brown directed his wild attack.

"The Last Moments of John Brown." The old man died well.

Left: Uncertain President, Deteriorating Situation. James Buchanan faltered, and the country approached ever-grimmer trouble.

Right: His Ruling Infuriated the North. The Southern Chief Justice, Roger Brooke Taney, declared a slave an owner's "property," to be protected everywhere by law.

a kindly, unforceful man with Southern connections. Soon afterward the Southern Chief Justice of the Supreme Court, Roger Taney, handed down a decision that served as another landmark on the road to war. Dred Scott, slave of an Army man, sued for freedom in Missouri on the grounds that he had lived for two years in free Illinois and Minnesota Territory, north of the Missouri Compromise line.

The court ruled that Dred Scott was property and that the Constitution protected his master's ownership wherever he went. Going further, the judges declared that Congress had no power to prevent slavery in any of the territories; they would hereafter be open fully to owners with their slaves.

Few court decisions ever caused such fury. "The Triumph of Slavery Complete," a newspaper headline blazoned the word, and hundreds of thousands agreed. John Calhoun's stand had been supported completely by a court dominated by Southerners.

A new spark set off a thunderous explosion in 1859, when twenty men suddenly appeared under gray October skies at the strategic Virginia town of Harpers Ferry on the Potomac, in a fantastic venture designed to stir a slave rebellion.

One View of the Impending Acts of Separation

Their leader was the bearded John Brown, veteran of the Kansas fighting, a strange, almost insane man.

Brown's party captured the Federal arsenal, seized several Virginians, and went on to meet a prompt failure. No slaves rose up; the scheme had no chance of success. The state's governor mobilized the militia, and Colonel Robert E. Lee of the United States Army answered orders to take troops to the scene. Brown's meager forces quickly gave up, and after a trial he was ordered hanged for treason. The old man died with a dignity that he had not possessed in his lifetime, and with a warning: "You may dispose of me very easily . . . but this question is still to be settled. . . ."

For a short time nearly all elements had condemned Brown's wild act. Then came a second response. While many Northern moderates regretted Brown's example, others regarded him as a martyr, a symbol of righteous attack on a great wrong. Henry D. Thoreau called him an "angel of light." Southerners reacted bitterly, and when it was revealed that a number of Northern reformers had given money used in Brown's raid Southern fury spread. Rumors of great Negro rebellions spread through the South, and although they were without basis they contributed strongly to the tension on both sides.

Congressmen took to carrying guns to their meetings, as members yelled threat and insult, and government approached paralysis. Every question, every argument was touched with the taint of the slavery issue; long-time friends quarreled at congressional dinner parties, and snubbed one another on the streets. Back

Secession Banner. Fifteen slaveholding states were listed, but all did not join the Confederacy.

South Carolina leaves the United States.

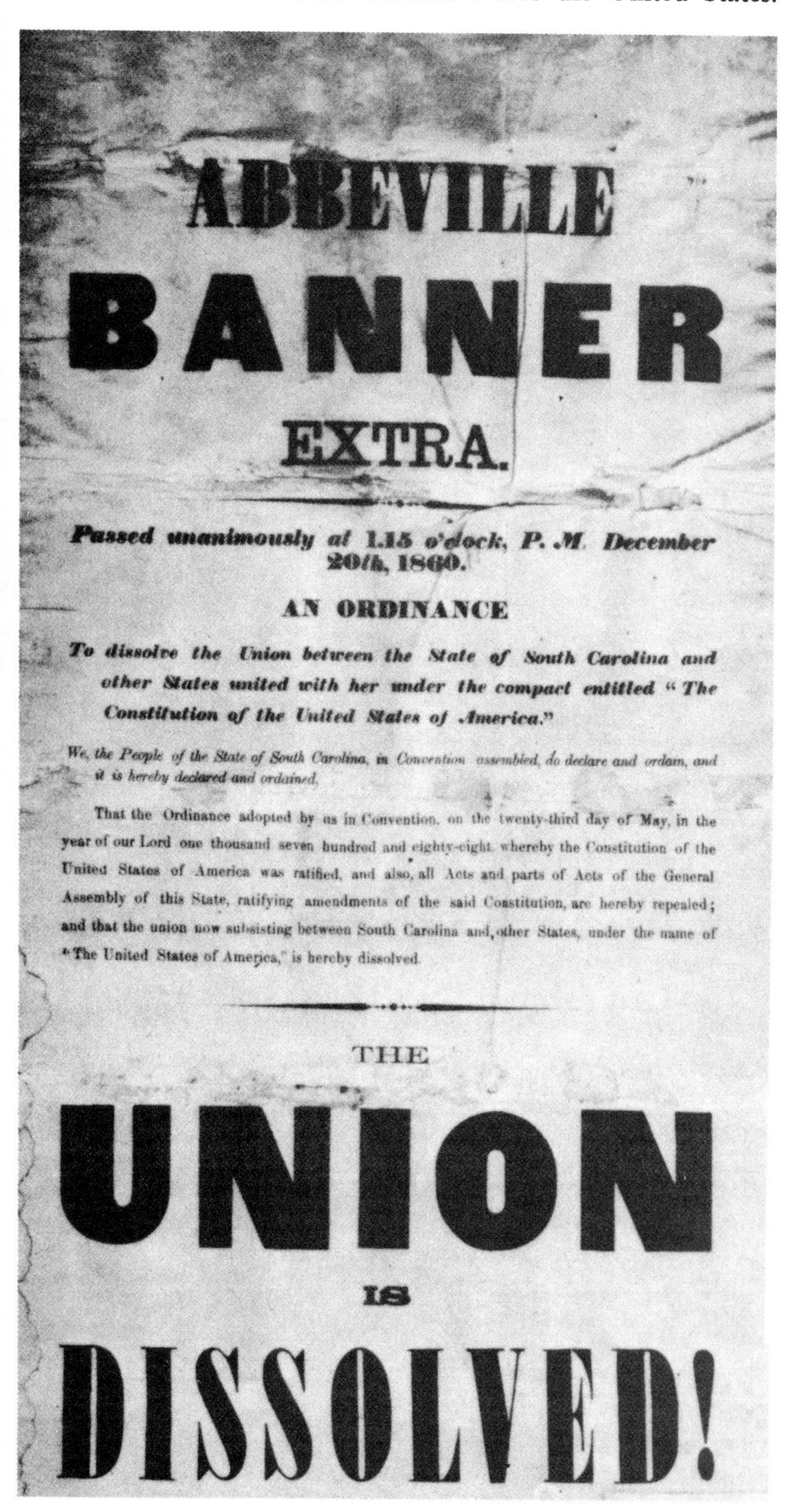

# ABBEVILLE BANNER

## EXTRA.

***Passed unanimously at 1.15 o'clock, P. M. December 20th, 1860.***

**AN ORDINANCE**

***To dissolve the Union between the State of South Carolina and other States united with her under the compact entitled "The Constitution of the United States of America."***

*We, the People of the State of South Carolina, in Convention assembled, do declare and ordain, and it is hereby declared and ordained,*

That the Ordinance adopted by us in Convention, on the twenty-third day of May, in the year of our Lord one thousand seven hundred and eighty-eight, whereby the Constitution of the United States of America was ratified, and also, all Acts and parts of Acts of the General Assembly of this State, ratifying amendments of the said Constitution, are hereby repealed; and that the union now subsisting between South Carolina and other States, under the name of "The United States of America," is hereby dissolved.

THE

# UNION

IS

# DISSOLVED!

The Cries Were Fervent. Mr. Davis pleased even some of those who had thought him too lukewarm.

The Vice President Had Doubts. "Little Aleck" Stephens of Georgia did not show complete enthusiasm.

in the Senate again, Jefferson Davis assumed something of the mantle of John Calhoun, although hotheads criticized him because he "did not go far enough."

A year later the Democratic party was wrenched into several pieces. In convention at Charleston the cotton South, led by the fire-eater William Lowndes Yancey of Alabama, pressed hard for a strong proslavery candidate and a platform calling for complete protection of slavery in the territories, nothing more, nothing less. Led by the Westerner Douglas, milder elements won the convention platform, and the cotton delegates stormed out. The gathering moved to Baltimore, and there a second angry rump movement took away more delegates, but Douglas received the nomination. The Yancey followers, convening in Richmond, launched a "Constitutional Democratic party" with John C. Breckinridge of Kentucky for President, and still a third, more moderate section formed a "Constitutional Union party" under John Bell of Tennessee.

Facing their second national campaign, the new Republicans nominated Abraham Lincoln, the rough-hewn, supposedly weak-willed yokel Illinois lawyer with a Kentucky background. To the free farmers of the West the Republicans offered land; to the businessmen they promised a tariff, and to workers they made a strong appeal as the party of democracy and liberty. As for slavery, the party (like Lincoln) declared that it would not touch the institution in the states but opposed its advance into the territories.

In the harsh, hard-driving campaign the South was torn by fears, by disturbing reports about Lincoln, and stirred by the fire-eaters. While Lincoln conducted a conciliatory campaign, the South saw him as the human culmination of all its fears, and also a front for more sinister figures. Lincoln won over the several other candidates, with 40 per cent of the vote, and received a majority of the electoral ballots. Even if the other three aspirants had combined, Lincoln would still have carried by 35 electoral votes.

Left: Children of the Confederacy. At the Confederate White House the younger Davises knew happy days, then sadder and sadder ones.

Right: Beneath Montgomery's High Columns. In Alabama, at the first capital, Jefferson Davis took his oath as dramatic changes impended.

Repeatedly Southerners had threatened to secede if Lincoln won. Now, promptly, one state acted. On December 20, 1860, after years of unsuccessful attempts to weld other parts of the South into a unified movement, South Carolina "dissolved the connection" between her and the Union. For a time other states held back; Jefferson Davis waited and so did Alexander Stephens, the sharp-minded "Little Aleck" of Georgia, who noted that if the South remained with the rest of the country the Democrats would yet have a majority in both House and Senate. Furthermore, as others pointed out, the South maintained its control of the Supreme Court.

Moderates on both sides still worked for compromise. Most of the Southern states had sizable elements opposed to immediate secession, men who favored a convention to thresh out their stand. Then, perhaps, after further solemn warning and a last effort, there might be joint action by the South. . . . In New Orleans, for instance, feeling for the Union continued strong, for war would halt the trade on which that world port lived, and in nearby Texas the doughty Sam Houston struggled to the end against those who wanted to break up the Union. Opponents of immediate secession pointed out that the North was not united against the South, which had many friends and economic allies in the section. Nor was the North fully committed against slavery per se; most abolitionists had declined to join the Republicans, claiming that they did not face the issue directly.

Nevertheless, as Alexander Stephens wrote, the people he saw "are run mad . . . wild with passion and frenzy." Particularly in the King Cotton region and most of the Gulf area, the fires burned high. For what happened, the gossipy wife of Senator Chesnut of South Carolina had her own explanation: "We separated from the North because . . . we have hated each other so!"

Over a period of several weeks Mississippi followed South Carolina in secession, then Florida, Alabama, Georgia, Louisiana, and, despite Sam Houston, Texas. Other states, notably Virginia, stood apart. The conservative Old Dominion had tradition, prestige, borders that lay close to Washington and also a lingering sympathy for the Union of the States that her sons had done so much to create. At Montgomery, Alabama, the first seven states established the Confederacy with Jefferson Davis of Mississippi as President and the long-reluctant Alexander Stephens of Georgia as Vice President, but certain hotheads found fault with both choices.

All over the South, local forces seized Union forts, until only Pensacola's Fort Pickens and Charleston's Fort Sumter remained in Federal hands. A stillness settled, and all of America turned its eyes toward a spot in the Carolina harbor. At Sumter a small Federal force approached the end of its supplies. Confederate guns pointed toward the fort, and the Southerners called for its surrender. Who would move first? In Washington final anxious conferences went on, and Lincoln, new to the office and his grim responsibilities, hesitated, wavered.

Jefferson Davis communicated with General Beauregard, commanding Charleston's Confederates. After further uncertainty Lincoln ordered a relief expedition to Charleston, with supplies, and the Confederates acted. At 4:30 A.M., on April 12, 1861, Confederate guns blasted at Fort Sumter. To the white-haired fire-eater Ruffin, who had marched and drilled, incongruously, with the young men of Charleston, went the honor of firing the first gun. It was on, the war for which he and the other hotheads, South and North, had labored so long.

Men raced to the Battery, and women took places on roofs to stare across the rippling waters, and cry out in delight or perhaps only to weep as the bombardment went on until the Unionists surrendered. The act electrified the nation, bringing a rush of Union sentiment; the South had fired on the American flag, and civilians pressed forward to enlist. Below Mason and Dixon's line a similar wave of feeling buoyed the Confederacy. So it had come at last!

Lincoln took his first step to defend the Union, appealing for 75,000 volunteers to put down "armed insurrection." At that, Virginia moved, throwing her weight to the side of the Confederacy. By Virginia's view, Lincoln had issued an illegal call, signal for a wrongful aggression against the Southerners. Yet many Virginians like Robert E. Lee concurred in their state's stand, without hard conviction but for simpler reasons of local loyalty.

Lee, whom many considered to be America's best soldier of the era, learned overnight that if he remained with the Union he would become commander in chief of its army. As a professional military man, he could not have hoped for higher rank. And still, suppose that army were trained upon his native Virginia?

Lee had written ironically that he was one of the "foolish souls" who could see no great good in secession. He did not regard it as a constitutional right, and he had remarked severely on the "selfish, dictatorial" steps taken by the cotton area. Although he disapproved of the abolitionists and their operations, he freed the slaves who had come under his control. To a son he wrote: "I can contemplate no greater calamity for the country than a dissolution of the Union. . . ."

Then, however, after hours of bleak self-searching, he said: "I have been unable to make up my mind to raise my hand against my native state, my relatives, my children and my home." And so, as central figure in one of the great personal tragedies of the war, Robert E. Lee left the Union army for that of Virginia.

Now Arkansas joined the Confederacy, and Tennessee and North Carolina. To the Union the sharply divided Maryland, most northerly of the Southern states, was indispensable. If it left the North, Washington might be cut off from the rest of the Union. As the saying went, Lincoln wanted God on his side, but he *had* to have Maryland, and so he used soldiers to help keep it with the nation. Although Kentucky sought neutrality for a time, it ultimately cast its lot with the Union, and Missouri took similar action, while suffering a smaller, continuing internal war of its own.

Some were to feel that by holding these states on the edges of the South, the Union saved itself. But no matter what official stand North Carolina and Tennessee took, vigorous Union feeling lasted in each state, and at one point East Tennessee threatened secession from the seceding government. And soon western Virginia broke away to become a new state, and a Union one. . . . For most of the South the decisions were made, and now the band played "Dixie."

The First Southern Hero. At Charleston, Beauregard of Louisiana won the Confederacy's acclaim.

From the Battery, They Saw It Start. At Charleston men and women cheered or wept over the bombardment of Fort Sumter.

Soldiers Against Civilians. Lincoln acted, and Maryland stayed in the Union.

# JEFF. DAVIS FOREVER!

Yankees may sing of their rank pork and beans,
Their dollars and cents are but fabulous dreams,
They ne'er sang a line,
Half so grand—so divine,
As the glorious toast
We Confederates boast—
"The Confederate States and Liberty forever!"

DAVIS! the man of our choice, guides the helm,
No tempest can harm us, no North overwhelm,
Our sheet anchor 's sure,
And our bark rides secure,
So here 's to the toast
We Confederates boast—
"The Confederate States and DAVIS forever."

A free navigation, commerce and trade,
We seek for no foe—of no foe be afraid,
Our frigates shall ride—
Our defence and our pride,
Our tars guard our coast
And huzza to our toast—
"The Confederate States and commerce forever."

Washington! Marion—still live in our songs,
Like them our young heroes shall spurn at our wrongs,
The world shall admire
The zeal and the fire,
Which blaze in the toast
We Confederates boasi—
"The Contederate States and its advocates forever."

Fame's trumpet shall swell in Davis' praise,
And time grant a furlough to lengthen his days,
May health weave the thread
Of delight round his head,
No nation can boast
Such a name—such a toast—
"The Confederate States and its President forever."

"The Zeal and the Fire." They were to last forever.

It Would Be the New Capital. A stately view of Richmond, seat of the Confederacy, with canal in the foreground.

Above, and opposite page: Two Views of England and the War. "John Bull" found himself between the warring sections.

The Ladies Pointed the Way. As they worked to clothe soldiers, they told their beaux to join the army.

TREASON IN VIRGINIA.

The Code of Virginia defines treason to be

"In levying war against the State, adhering to its enemies, or giving them aid and comfort."

Such treason, if proved by two witnesses, is punishable by death.

MAY 15, 1861.

Warning to All

# 16

# END OF A KINGDOM, END OF A ROAD

"Teach him to deny himself."—ROBERT E. LEE

OFTEN IT was literally a war of brothers, as families split apart in anger or in quiet resignation. Natives of every Northern state joined the Confederate armies, while each of the Southern ones provided soldiers for the Union. The first commander of all Northern soldiers was Winfield Scott, who came from an old Virginia family, while John Pemberton, who held the besieged Vicksburg for the South, was a Pennsylvanian. Like Lee, countless other Southerners had to stand alone, at the edge of their fields, or in their darkened rooms, arguing with

"Palmetto Battery." Members of the Charleston Artillery lined up for the camera along an inlet near the city.

Watch Along the Potomac. Virginians guarding the river crossing, looking toward Georgetown.

themselves. What was right, what was to be done? Friends, relatives, wives waited to applaud them or look away in doubtful silence. But each man had to make his own decision.

On the basis of cold statistics—census tables, population, production charts—the South was destined to lose. Eleven states faced twenty-three; 5,000,000 to 6,000,000 whites, with 3,500,000 slaves in the background, were ranged against 23,000,000 free men; property valued at less than $5,500,000,000 against $11,000,000,000. The South had half as many miles of railroads as the North, in a day when the movement of supplies would be of fundamental importance. The South had less than a sixth the number of workmen in manufacturing, and it confronted an industrial region growing at a rate the world had never beheld. In many respects geography opposed the South; the Mississippi, Tennessee, Cumberland, and other rivers opened pathways deep into its territory, and its 3,500 miles of coast line, Atlantic and Gulf, provided easy targets for attack or blockade. . . . Some might have written off the Confederacy from the start.

But there were imponderables. The South had a flaming spirit, a conviction that it must win, or lose everything: the independence it sought, its racial rule, a set of attitudes summed up in the phrase "a way of life." The North fought for the Union and for another set of values summed up in the word "democracy." The South had most of the finest officers of the American Army, and for months, many of them had been lining up men and plans. From West Point came 148 generals. Then, too, the South had always fostered a tradition of military service, while its men were frequently magnificent horsemen, trained in the hunt and the militia drill. And a certain advantage lay in the fact that the newly created government would be defending itself on home soil, against those it called invaders.

From the beginning of the war the North gave signs of deep divisions, with hundreds of thousands, including many in influential positions, unconvinced that the South should be opposed. Throughout most of the war, Lincoln and his subordinates had to handle forces in the North that used any large defeat as a signal for demands to end the fighting. In the early days Jefferson Davis seemed to unbiased observers better fitted to his office than was Lincoln to his. Davis, a graduate of West Point, an important officer in the Mexican War, former Secretary of War, had an informed understanding of the realities of combat, as well as of the capabilities of chief officers on both sides. By contrast, Lincoln appeared incompetent, a fumbler; his military experiences had been meager, and for a long time he floundered as he tried one general, then another, and struggled against pressures from rival Northern factions, only to find and support the North's major commanders comparatively late in the hostilities.

The North was an inept giant, and at several points might perhaps have succumbed to one daring foray of its trim, more single-minded opponent. Yet, despite setbacks, occasional loss of morale and demonstrations against its leadership, the North's will slowly strengthened, as did its military direction. And Lincoln himself matured and grew in office until he came to rank as the great figure of the war, the great American of his century, just as Lee, the aristocrat of Virginia, became the personification of the best in the South.

Shrewdly, persistently, Lincoln directed the creation of what one Southerner of today, Francis B. Simkins, termed a political isolation, a "moral blockade." While progressive groups all over the world labored for national development, the South favored a "national disintegration," and it stood for a system of slavery that global opinion considered feudal and doomed. The Frenchman De Tocqueville spoke for many, without ties to the North or South, when he declared: "I earnestly hope that the great experiment in self-government which is carried out in America will not fail. If it did, it would be the end of political liberty in our world."

For thousands of Southerners (though not, significantly, for the realist Lee) the conflict started as one of bright, gay adventure. Romantics saw it as a matter of swirling capes, plumed hats, and daring bands that swept out of a forest on quick lightning raids, then disappeared. A number of Southerners conceived of the conflict as something out of Sir Walter Scott (the South's favorite novelist): battle by the rule, between competing knights. But war quickly showed its uglier face, the fighting turned harsh and brutal, and over the land were heard the groans of dying men, the screams of wounded horses. It was the first of the modern wars, the first to use great armies of civilians.

The South did give the war a special romantic flavor in its use of spies, especially women like Belle Boyd and Rose Greenhow, who employed their sex to advantage in stealing secrets and gathering vital information. These ladies functioned with a daring, a naïve directness that would have no parallels in later conflicts.

Southern individualism extended to operations other than espionage. Thousands of men resisted discipline of almost any kind, objecting to taxes and other levies, quarreling with their military associates. No gentleman, sir, would let himself be talked to in that manner, even by a superior in uniform! In some cases an officer challenged another to a duel of honor, and let the war wait.

As the long months passed, however, the struggle became far less genteel. Well-born youths who came to war with Negro attendants took up shovels when Lee and his aides so directed them. Indeed, Lee was often referred to as "the King of Spades." The privileged elements may have lost their great homes and plantations, but worse suffering befell the small farmers, clerks and artisans. The latter might grumble, as they did, that it was "a rich man's war and a poor man's fight," and swear and sicken at wormy bread and rotting meat, and rebel at the stink and crawling maggots beneath the bandages. Still, they fought on.

The South clung stubbornly for most of the four years—years of sacrifice, steady loss, rearrangement of dwindling resources, sorrow and acceptance, and return to the fray. Repeatedly, the Southerners told themselves: If only they could hold out a little longer at a disputed point, bear up under the blast of guns and agonizing weariness of flesh, the dimming of sight in the twilight . . . the war might finish with them as victors.

The Union held firm to its several objectives. It would blockade Confederate ports, keep the South from bringing in supplies from Europe and exporting its cotton and other produce. It would strike against the Mississippi and the lower South, cutting off Texas and Louisiana and Arkansas, and prevent the Confed-

To Keep Them From Federal Hands. The Confederates dismantled many a locomotive in the disputed area of Martinsburg, Virginia.

Overnight, "Stonewall." The odd professor, Thomas Jonathan Jackson, suddenly won his nickname and his fame.

eracy from getting food and goods from that fertile area. Meanwhile in both East and West it would labor to thrust back the Southerners in their own territories, town to town, valley to valley, point to point. With all that, the Union would marshal every available effort against Richmond, capital and symbol of the government.

Each spring the North stepped up its movements against Southern strongholds. It experienced major successes, and sat so close to Richmond that cannon fire echoed through the streets; still the Confederate capital stood fast. In its struggles the South acquired its special heroes: Lee, the grave, the compassionate man, but also the man of determination, who came to personify the Confederacy to tens of thousands of soldiers; Stonewall, the eccentric professor, dour Calvinist, victim of jokes of the more worldly, who changed overnight into one of the great military leaders of modern times; the flamboyant, feather-hatted "Jeb" Stuart; the brooding Louisianian Beauregard, high hero for an hour.

Nevertheless many have thought that the war's verdict was settled as much off the battlefield as on it—specifically in the South's policy toward cotton. From the first days the Confederacy felt that cotton would win her the war. Senator James Hamilton had told Congress: "Without the firing of a gun, without drawing a sword, should they make war on us, we could bring the whole world to our feet. . . . England would topple headlong and carry the whole civilized world with her. No, you dare not make war on cotton. . . . Cotton is King." After all, didn't English mills get five-sixths of their supplies of the staple from the South, and weren't

On the Way to Manassas. Confederate "Bull Battery," sketched by an officer at the scene.

the jobs of a million or more British workers dependent on cotton? Europe *had* to have cotton, the Southerners argued, and would break the Union blockade to get it.

As a matter of fact, ruling elements in England and France sympathized with the South in what they considered a war for "aristocratic principle" against dangerous democracy. Confederates saw evidence of an inclination on the part of Old World leaders to wound, if possible, the young and expanding American nation. Important English journals sided with the South, and hailed its victories with delight. William Gladstone, the Chancellor of England's Exchequer, felt that the Confederacy had made itself independent and merited rank as a nation. When Lee won at Second Manassas and prepared to move into the North, recognition appeared close.

None could deny that the English suffered as a result of the Union blockade. While Britain's trade with the North flourished, her mills were closing, and in 1862 and 1863 at least a half-million British workmen lost their jobs. If any class might have been expected to favor the South because of its economic interests, it was this one. Nevertheless, the English workers used their growing power to discourage government action in favor of the Confederacy. To them it was a contest between slavery and freedom, and they stood with the American Union.

Guarding a Vital Port in North Carolina. The broad Fort Fisher earthworks protected Cape Fear River, entrance to Wilmington, through most of the war.

Then, in midwar, Abraham Lincoln added a new dimension to the war with his proclamation freeing slaves in territory held by the Confederacy. For many months Lincoln had resisted pressure on all sides to take such a step. "My paramount object . . . is not either to save or destroy slavery. If I could save the Union without freeing any slave, I would do it; and if I could save it by freeing all the slaves, I would do it; and if I could save it by freeing some and leaving others alone, I would also do that." No matter how unfair and how sinister the South considered the measure, the war took on the aspect of a crusade for liberty. As Henry Adams declared in London: "The Emancipation Proclamation has done more for us here than all our former victories and all our diplomacy." English workers held mass meetings that shouted approval of the Northern cause; for millions of people in the Union lines a milestone had been passed in the history of the world.

Gradually English mills began to get their cotton elsewhere; at the same time the American North and West survived without it, and new channels of industry and national development were opened, with incalculable future effects. Bit by bit the South sensed that not only had its cotton policy failed, but that the policy had hurt it grievously.

Some in both sections had predicted Negro uprisings as a result of the Emancipation Proclamation. Nothing of the sort occurred. Throughout the war the large body of the slaves stayed on the farms and plantations. There were, of course,

Danger Was Everywhere. Here, on a Charleston street.

thousands who followed the Union armies. But the majority of Negroes endured the war as little more than pawns.

Month by month the Union gained. Southern officers could summon their men to great efforts in crucial battles. But each such encounter left the Confederacy further depleted, while the North was left with enormous reserves of power and supplies.

After Lee's unsuccessful invasion of the North, the Union forces pushed steadily south, winning parts of Virginia, portions of the coasts, large sections of Tennessee and vital points on the Mississippi. With each loss the South was further crippled. The Confederacy was broken in half, the Mississippi artery cut, and now the pressure would be fiercer still.

For the civilians life grew more and more cramped. The South, because it had no choice, "did without," using corn and sweet potatoes to make coffee, fashioning suits and dresses out of ancient curtains, printing newspapers on wallpaper. Nearly everything was a substitute, and then there were substitutes for substitutes. The war became one of pinched stomachs, of messages from home: the crop is gone and the children are crying for food; ". . . unless you come home, we must die." Inevitably desertions multiplied.

Before then, Jefferson Davis also had political problems to grapple with on the homefront. Governors like Joseph E. Brown of Georgia and Zebulon B. Vance of North Carolina believed so strongly in states' rights that they refused to give up supplies to the Confederacy, and insisted that their men be assigned only in their vicinity. They defied agents trying to collect Confederate taxes. Because Davis

Its People Burned It Down. Residents of old Hampton, Virginia, set it afire to keep the Federals from taking it. Hardly five buildings remained.

First Great Battle at Manassas. Both sides bungled, but the South made fewer errors and won a resounding victory.

sought to direct a nation, they attacked him as a despot reaching out to "control" the sovereign states. Even Alexander Stephens, the Vice President, declared that the executive aimed at "absolute power." In later years a distinguished interpreter would suggest an epitaph for the Confederacy: dead of states' rights.

New Southern discontent sprang from other sources. While most of the Southern ports were ringed by blockaders, bold operators used small, swift steamers to make runs to the West Indies that brought the South vital supplies and also luxuries. This trade established new fortunes and new, overbearingly rich men. Corruption flourished as profiteers traded cotton and other supplies with the enemy in defiance of official orders. While prices soared fantastically, speculators cornered markets at strategic points. Heartbreak, acrid bitterness, grasping opportunism . . . the war spawned them all.

For Jefferson Davis the months were ever more agonizing. In all likelihood he did as well as any Southerner might have done in a situation with more than its share of handicaps. But he was frequently ill, and tight-nerved; he tended to antagonize others, to "freeze up" when his opinion was questioned, and he failed to understand many of the human factors that confronted his government. Nevertheless he was blamed for failures in enterprises no man could have turned into success.

In the later stages of the war some Southerners suggested that the South free and use its Negro slaves as troops. Faced with this decision, Jefferson Davis hesitated. A great many Southerners were violently opposed. As one said: "Liberate them? Then what have we been fighting for?" In this bleak hour the Confederacy made a desperate, last-minute offer: If England would grant recognition, the South would free the slaves. The offer came too late.

Ulysses S. Grant, the strongest general in the Union armies, was tightening his grip upon Virginia while William T. Sherman moved in from the southeast. For years Georgians would remember the smoke of burning houses, large and small, the rotting of animal carcasses, and the cries of displaced families as Sherman marched through that state. Then he swept into South Carolina for yet more determined destruction. Hadn't the Carolinians started everything? his soldiers asked. In Sherman's words, the state "deserves all that is in store for her," and soon he and his men were wrecking Columbia, the capital. And in Virginia, Phil

Burning Cotton. In this vivid, unfinished drawing Frank Vizetelly pictured Confederates burning cotton to keep it from Federals.

Sheridan destroyed so much that he could say "a crow flying over the country would need to carry his rations."

By March of 1865 Lee had to give up Richmond. Soon afterward his soldiers found their only way of escape cut off by Union troops. His officers asked: Would Lee approve a scheme to carry on with guerrilla fighting—no quarter given—as long as they could survive? In a fresh torment, Robert E. Lee debated his course. If he would only ride slowly forward a little way, his struggles would end in a moment. "But it is our duty to live," he declared, "for what will become of the women and children of the South, if we are not here to support and protect them?"

In April, Lee went calmly to U. S. Grant at Appomattox Court House, to make a simple pact. His soldiers would lay down their arms; generously the Union victor, who had fought with Lee in Mexico, allowed the Southerners to retain their mounts, taking them home "to work their little farms." Grant also permitted the men who had been his enemies to keep their guns, and provided food for the half-famished Southern army. Then, with kindly consideration, he ordered victory salutes halted out of respect for the solemn Lee. The Virginian, his hair now white, walked to the doorway and his eye went over the banner, the stars and stripes, that rose among the Union troops before him. It had once been his flag; now it would be his flag again. As he moved toward his horse, Northern soldiers gazed at him in wonder and admiration. Like Stonewall Jackson and Jeb Stuart, Lee had become a great man in the eyes of the men who had been his enemies.

From Richmond, Jefferson Davis and his cabinet had fled southward. One, Judah Benjamin of Louisiana, had an adventure-laden escape down the Florida coast and found his way to England and a new, distinguished career as a jurist. Jefferson Davis got as far as Georgia, where he was seized and made to serve as a scapegoat for his defeated nation. Then, on a windy morning, the grave-faced Abraham Lincoln rode into a broken Richmond, to survey the rubble of that dimmed, still beautiful city.

In Atlanta and New Orleans, in Savannah and St. Augustine, Nashville and Memphis, Charlotte and Mobile, and in Jackson, Mississippi, the old flag was flying once more. They were in the Union again. . . . Back in Washington, Abraham Lincoln went to the theater for an evening's relaxation, and a Southern fanatic inflicted a mortal wound on Lincoln and a grave one on the nation.

Another bullet rang out in the South when Edmund Ruffin, the long-haired fire-eater of fire-eaters, killed himself. He had no wish to live under the flag that he had come to despise. But most Southern leaders thought as did Lee: it was their "duty to live." The future was uncertain, but it must be faced with as much courage as a man could summon to his support.

With calm resolution Lee, as president of Washington College, later Washington and Lee, gave his energies to the education of Southern youth. A father

Left: "If You Want a Good Time . . ." Just join the cavalry, said the refrain. But the soldier, punished in camp, hardly agreed.

Right: "I Wish I Was in Dixie." As a Southerner drew it, Abe Lincoln sang the plaintive words through all the conflict.

once asked him what he would suggest for his boy, and Lee answered, "Teach him to deny himself." The words summed up a lifetime that honored the man and the South.

For the South, endless denials lay ahead. In the months immediately after the war there was little bitterness between the soldiers who had done the fighting. With Lincoln's death, most literate Southerners agreed that they had lost the one man who could have prevented many of the agonies of the Reconstruction. Then, as men of smaller vision, and less humanity, rose to control, the hatred began to grow. . . .

It had ended, the day of the Old South, and with it much of its physical grandeur. One after another of the big houses fell apart, the prey of torch or cannon or of simple, long-continued neglect. Others survived, graying yet keeping more or less intact. Gone were most of the great landholdings, the spreading acres of cotton in Alabama and Mississippi, the thick stalks of cane near New Orleans, the damp rice plantings of South Carolina, and with them the hordes of field and house servants who attended them.

For a long time much lay in decay—broken levees, neglected canals, empty fields. Thousands who had known more profitable days laid bricks, dug ditches, or

"Worn Out!" This is the artist's own title for his "Chickahomene Swamp Scene" of 1864. Artist was Alexander Meinung of the 26th North Carolina Regiment Band.

In the Field. Edwin Forbes sketched the infantryman, artilleryman, and cavalryman of the war.

Left: On the Homefront. The Virginia Reel lived on at a soldiers' dance at Huntsville, Alabama.

Right: War in the Home. Unionists found arms in a Maryland residence. Some ladies also used their bustles to carry drugs and information for the South.

Soldiers Will Be Soldiers. An operator took a portable peep show from camp to camp, charging each for a look.

"Captain Sally" Tompkins. Nurse Tompkins became the only female officer commissioned by the Confederacy.

Top left: "The Soldiers' Friend." Emily Mason won the title for her remarkable record of hospital service.

Top right: "La Belle Rebelle." The spy Belle Boyd flirted, filched secrets, rode through the lines, got arrested, and eventually married.

Lower left: The Rose of Washington. Mrs. Rose Greenhow, mature beauty and Southern agent, was liked by men old and young, and made use of both varieties.

Lower right: Confederates Hailed Her, but . . . Actress Pauline Cushman was "removed" from Union-held Nashville as an ardent Confederate, then proved to be a Northern spy. Nearly everyone had admired her, especially the boys.

"Crazy Bet" Was Grant's Spy in Richmond. Seen in later years beside her pillared home, Elizabeth Van Lew was dismissed by Richmonders as only an eccentric. Yet she sent important information through the lines.

Lee and His Generals: John B. Hood, Braxton Bragg, Richard S. Ewell, Albert Sidney Johnston, Wade Hampton, E. Kirby Smith, Jubal A. Early, A. P. Hill, Stephen D. Lee, Richard H. Anderson, John B. Gordon, Theophilus H. Holmes, William J. Hardee, Joseph E. Johnston, Simon B. Buckner, James Longstreet, Leonidas Polk, Robert E. Lee, N. B. Forrest, Pierre G. T. Beauregard, Thomas J. Jackson, Samuel Cooper, J. E. B. Stuart, Richard Taylor, J. C. Pemberton, and D. H. Hill.

Davis and Cabinet. With Lee in the center, after his rise as Davis' adviser, were Stephen Mallory, Judah Benjamin, Leroy Pope Walker in back; Davis, Lee, John H. Reagan, seated in front; Vice President Alexander Stephens, seated in back; Christopher G. Memminger and Robert Toombs, both standing.

One Aspect Unchanged. Despite new technology, foraging remained the same, as in Louisiana.

Left: Ripping Out Railroad Tracks. This modern war saw new touches.

Right: Carnage at Fredericksburg. In mid-December, 1862, Marye's Heights witnessed some of the bloodiest fighting of the war.

A New Era in the Making. The armored *Merrimac* (or *Virginia*) and the *Monitor* met at Hampton Roads, signaling a naval revolution.

Score a Hit for the South. The Monitor *Tecumseh* was wrecked by a Southern torpedo at Mobile Bay.

Benjamin Butler, a Furious View. A strong Southern sympathizer used imagination in depicting the effects of Butler's "Woman Order" in New Orleans.

An Emotional Northern View of Emancipation. The millennium had arrived.

**Whereas,** On the Twenty-Second day of September, in the year of our Lord One Thousand Eight Hundred and Sixty-Two, a Proclamation was issued by the President of the United States, containing, among other things, the following, to wit:

"That on the First day of January, in the year of our Lord One Thousand Eight Hundred and Sixty-Three, all persons held as Slaves within any State, or designated part of a State, the people whereof shall then be in rebellion against the United States, shall be then, thenceforth, and **FOREVER FREE,** and the *Executive Government of the United States,* including the Military and Naval Authorities thereof, *will recognise and maintain the freedom of such persons,* and will do no act or acts to repress such persons, or any of them, in any efforts they may make for their actual freedom.

"That the Executive will, on the First day of January aforesaid, by proclamation, designate the States and parts of States, if any, in which the people thereof respectively shall then be in rebellion against the United States, and the fact that any State, or the people thereof, shall on that day be in good faith represented in the Congress of the United States by members chosen thereto at elections wherein a majority of the qualified voters of such State shall have participated, shall, in the absence of strong countervailing testimony, be deemed conclusive evidence that such State and the people thereof are not then in rebellion against the United States."

**Now, therefore, I, ABRAHAM LINCOLN,** PRESIDENT OF THE UNITED STATES, by virtue of the power in me vested as **Commander-in-Chief of the Army and Navy of the United States** in time of actual armed rebellion against the authority and government of the United States, and as a fit and necessary war measure for suppressing said rebellion, do, on this First day of January, in the year of our Lord One Thousand Eight Hundred and Sixty-Three, and in accordance with my purpose so to do, publicly proclaim for the full period of one hundred days from the day of the first above-mentioned order, and designate, as the States and parts of States wherein the people thereof respectively are this day in rebellion against the United States, the following, to wit:— **Arkansas, Texas, Louisiana,** (except the Parishes of St. Bernard, Plaquemines, Jefferson, St. John, St. Charles, St. James, Ascension, Assumption, Terre Bonne, La Fourche, St. Mary, St. Martin, and Orleans, including the City of Orleans,) **Mississippi, Alabama, Florida, Georgia, South Carolina, North Carolina, and Virginia,** (except the forty-eight counties designated as West Virginia, and also the counties of Berkeley, Accomac, Northampton, Elizabeth City, York, Princess Ann, and Norfolk, including the cities of Norfolk and Portsmouth,) and which excepted parts are for the present left precisely as if this Proclamation were not issued.

And by virtue of the power and for the purpose aforesaid, I do order and declare that **ALL PERSONS HELD AS SLAVES** within said designated States and parts of States ARE, AND HENCEFORWARD **SHALL BE FREE!** and that the Executive Government of the United States, including the Military and Naval Authorities thereof, will recognize and maintain the freedom of said persons.

And I hereby enjoin upon the people so declared to be free to abstain from all violence, UNLESS IN NECESSARY SELF-DEFENCE; and I recommend to them that in all cases, when allowed, they LABOR FAITHFULLY FOR REASONABLE WAGES.

And I further declare and make known that such persons of suitable condition will be received into the armed service of the United States, to garrison forts, positions, stations, and other places, and to man vessels of all sorts in said service.

And upon this act, sincerely believed to be AN ACT OF JUSTICE, warranted by the Constitution, upon military necessity, I invoke the considerate judgment of mankind and the gracious favor of ALMIGHTY GOD!

*In Testimony Whereof, I have hereunto set my name, and caused the seal of the United States to be affixed.*

[L. S.] *Done at the* CITY OF WASHINGTON, *this First day of January, in the Year of our Lord One Thousand Eight Hundred and Sixty-Three, and of the Independence of the United States the Eighty Seventh.*

*By the President,*

A. Lincoln

*Secretary of State.*

J. MAYER & CO. LITH 4 STATE ST. BOSTON.

It changed a war and a nation.

Jubilee Seemed Near. Edwin Forbes sketched former slaves, now "contraband of war," as they approached Union territory.

An Emotional Southern View of Emancipation. A devil held an inkpot.

One Effect. Freed Negroes thronged to the Union lines at New Bern.

New Freedmen and Free Children. A strange new day awaited.

Yet Many Stayed on the Spot. Slaves concealing the master from a searching party.

"From the Free Schools of Louisiana." As the war continued, a new regime began in Union-held Louisiana.

Education Would Now Be Open. While many Southerners had quietly taught their slaves, the process would become more general, as eventually at Vicksburg.

"Prisoners from the Front." Winslow Homer saw the pathos in a situation involving tens of thousands on both sides.

Vicksburg. To capture the long-beleaguered town, U. S. Grant dug trenches and experimented with canals while people huddled in caves and ate horses and rats.

Army Life Sketched by C. W. Chapman. Left, a half-frozen sentry; right, one of the guns of Charleston's White Point Battery.

Lice, Hope, and a Coffin. A contemporary view of Richmond's Libby Prison, which had a sinister fame among Northerners.

From Prison for Unionists to Prison for Confederates. After Richmond's fall, Southerners waited to replace Northern men at Libby.

Andersonville, Georgia, a Synonym for Suffering. More than 32,000 prisoners were crowded here at one time, and 13,000 died. Foods and medicines were scarce, as they were throughout the South, and on a single day nearly 100 succumbed. In a bitterly disputed postwar action Commandant Henry Wirz was hanged on Federal charges of conspiracy to kill and torture.

Happier Prison Scene. Union captives at Salisbury, North Carolina, enjoy a ball game while a crowd watches.

They Brought the Finish Nearer. Generals U. S. Grant and William T. Sherman concentrated Union forces for the climactic hours.

Southerners fled South from Atlanta as Sherman pressed on.

Sherman left behind a shattered Atlanta.

Several Years Later. Robert E. Lee at White Sulphur Springs with George Peabody on right; W. W. Corcoran, John S. Wise, and General John B. Magruder; General Pierre G. T. Beauregard, back row, fifth from left.

Charleston Bombarded. Hundreds clogged the roads of escape.

For Richmond, a Curtain. Its people set flames to large parts of the Confederate capital.

A New Southern President of the United States. The Unionist, Andrew Johnson of Tennessee, took Lincoln's place as a bitter day began.

tended small stores in order to feed their families. The smaller farmers, those who had made up the bulk of Southern growers, survived best, though, like the sons of the major planters, they had to work out the new, not always easy relations with men now free. The difficult systems of hired labor or tenancy for the Negroes were not simple to achieve. Regardless of the resistance of many Southerners, the South would now have to cope with the demands of citizenship for a race which had long been debarred from liberty.

In the main the shape of a future America had been established. It would be a centralized, expanding commercial and industrial civilization, not the agricultural one that the South had upheld, and for the most part a town and city culture rather than a country one. It was also to be an economy of wages, of contractual relationships between employer and employee.

As the years went by, the South was to receive the industry, the mills and factories, which had been slow to enter under the former regime. The great staples of cotton, sugar, and rice continued, but they no longer dominated so much of the region.

Some of the lovelier aspects of the earlier life survived: majestic double lines of oak that outlived a crumbled Greek temple along the Mississippi; Atlantic coastal gardens of azaleas, restored by a woman's deft hands and her will to achieve something of a former glory; the river landings of Memphis and Vicksburg, the Spanish balconies of Florida and Texas, the Creole patios and fountains behind the brick façades of New Orleans.

They are symbols of a lasting Southern "style," though one that varies from place to place: a quality of speech, conversation that lifts sometimes to the level of an art; a cuisine that may occasionally be among the worst, again perhaps the most satisfying in America; not least the inherited habit of casual but generous hospitality, even if the house is of the plainest and the porch rickety at the corners.

There have been less pleasant survivals: here and there an excessive preoccupation with past family achievement, a lack of concern with the world beyond the county line. Some have taken flight in fantasy. Too many dead Southerners have been transformed into plantation owners: "My grandfather had five thousand slaves, at the least." "Our house was the biggest in the whole valley, acres of magnolia trees, sure 'nough." For others the South has become a land of rankling memories. "Right there the soldier smashed his fist into my old uncle's face." "Near where you're sitting, they buried thousands of pieces of the finest silver, yes, indeed they did—and never found it again."

On the better side there remains a set of intangibles: a capacity for a certain serenity that is not out of touch with the world and its events; a gift of humor, a sharp wit that may also be a kindly one; an ability to enjoy life's offerings, savoring them without the strain that marks much of modern American existence. There is a tradition of full appreciation of leisure, the silent hours of a summer afternoon, a picnic along the lake, a soft-voiced exchange in the twilight. . . . The South still has its demagogues, its mellifluous, vapid senators and clown-governors. But in spite of them, and the frequent turmoils and outbursts of today, the modern South advances, to the quiet echoes of the older one.

A Tribute from His Enemies. With Colonel Charles Marshall, Robert E. Lee rides away from the McLean House at Appomatox after the surrender. An on-the-scene sketch.

# PICTURE CREDITS

**New York Public Library:** 11, 12, 30B, 43, 45, 50TL, 51TR, 52TR, 52BR, 52TL, 53, 56TR, 77, 82TL, 98TL, 106L, 110, 120TL, 121, 130T, 136T, 136M, 137M, 141L, 146, 147BL, 158B, 162B, 164, 165, 166T, 199, 200B, 200R, 204B, 229M, 234BR, 236T, 236B, 237BL, 245M, 252T, 258BR, 266B, 267T, 267M, 269T, 270, 272L, 280T, 295L, 298L, 298R, 300TR, 306T, 314, 318L, 328BR, 329T, 341B. **Florida State Library:** 13, 16B, 22, 26B. **Howard Tilton Memorial Library, Tulane University:** 9, 16T, 17M, 20B, 20T, 24, 37L, 79R, 79L, 80B, 130B, 131L, 132B, 137B, 147BR, 171R, 172L, 187, 189, 218T, 218B, 224L, 224R, 225, 229B, 229T, 230BR, 232BR, 232BL, 233B, 233L, 234TR, 234BL, 235T, 237BR, 238T, 238B, 239T, 239B, 241T, 242T, 242B, 243B, 248B, 249R. **Collections of the Library of Congress:** 26T, 31T, 31B, 32, 44, 48M, 67L, 68B, 68T, 72B, 78, 98M, 100T, 101, 108, 112, 120B, 124LM, 132TR, 137T, 138, 148L, 152T, 152B, 156T, 156B, 161, 162T, 168L, 182B, 184T, 191, 194, 198L, 206, 207, 210, 210B, 213BL, 214T, 214BL, 215TL, 215TR, 221L, 221R, 222T, 222B, 223, 230BL, 231, 246T, 248T, 249L, 250R, 254T, 258BR, 261, 263TL, 264TR, 267B, 269M, 271R, 274L, 277, 278B, 279B, 280B, 281TL, 282M, 282B, 283T, 283B, 284BR, 284TR, 287B, 288B, 289R, 291, 292, 294, 297T, 299, 300BR, 308BR, 308B, 309B, 312B, 316, 318R, 322BL, 322T, 322BR, 324T, 330B, 331, 332T, 333T, 334T, 334B, 335T, 336, 338T, 345. **Hall of History, State Department of Archives and History, Raleigh, N. C.:** 34, 35L, 36, 38B, 41, 42, 51T, 71, 76, 98TR, 111, 113, 115, 124TR, 124BR, 124BL, 124UM, 127, 139R, 167, 168R, 170B, 170T, 215TL, 266M, 272R, 313, 326. **New York Historical Society:** 48T, 83, 109, 158T, 159, 174, 184B, 212T, 216BL, 234TL, 244TL, 247, 284TL, 338B, 342B. **Colonial Williamsburg:** 51BL, 54BR, 56TL, 59, 80T, 81, 82BL, 82BR, 84B, 84T, 85, 91, 144. **Metropolitan Museum of Art:** 52BL, 70, 88, 142, 143T, 143B, 155, 157BR, 157BL, 160, 175B, 213BR, 216TL, 259, 297B, 332B, 335B. **National Gallery of Art:** 57. **Enoch Pratt Free Library, Baltimore, Md.:** 64TL, 64TR. **Cook Collection, Valentine Museum, Richmond, Va.:** 72T, 151R, 193, 245T, 285TR, 309T, 323B, 324TL, 341T. **Baltimore Museum of Art:** 74. **James Servies Library, William and Mary College, Williamsburg:** 92T. **Chicago Historical Society:** 96, 312T. **Frick Art Reference Library, N. Y.:** 98B, 102. **Collection of Carolina Art Association, Gibbes Art Gallery, Charleston, S. C.:** 100B, 103, 106R. **Charleston Library Society:** 107T. **Hugh Lefler Collection, University of North Carolina Library:** 117, 118L, 118R, 122R, 123R, 157T. **Museum of the City of New York:** 340B, 342T. **Museum of Fine Arts, Boston:** 337B. **Old Salem Restoration, Winston-Salem, N. C.:** 122L, 124TL, 135. **Archives, Ursuline Convent, New Orleans, La.:** 128. **Collection of Caldwell Delaney, Mobile, Ala.:** 132L. **Old Print Shop, New York:** 134, 150, 235B, 264B, 302R, 327, 339T. **Virginia State Library, Richmond:** 140, 141R, 276, 284BL, 300L. **Historical Society of Pennsylvania:** 147T. **Cooper Union:** 149L, 212M, 214BR, 306B, 307, 311, 315, 329B. **Yale University Art Gallery:** 154. **Louisiana State Museum:** 175T. **Southern Historical Collection, University of North Carolina Library:** 196L, 258TL, 264TL, 295R, 304. **Pennsylvania Academy of Fine Arts:** 200L. **North Carolina Collection, University of North Carolina Library:** 202L, 209, 211T, 343. **Transportation Museum, University of Michigan, Ann Arbor:** 215B. **Old Court House Museum, Vicksburg, Miss.:** 233R. **Grover C. Henley, Jacksonville, Fla.:** 237T. **National Park Service:** 237BL. **University of Texas Library:** 250L, 251L, 253R, 257, 263TR, 263B, 265B. **Virginia Historical Society, Richmond:** 260. **Abby Aldrich Rockefeller Folk Art Collection, Williamsburg:** 271L. **Speed Art Museum, Louisville, Kentucky:** 286T. **Confederate Museum, Richmond:** 301, 302L, 305R. **Houghton Library,** 317. **Moravian Music Foundation, Winston-Salem, N. C.:** 319. **Maryland Historical Society:** 330T. **Valentine Museum, Richmond:** 325T, 333B, 337TL, 337TR.

***All illustrations not otherwise listed are from the author's collection.***

# BIBLIOGRAPHY

In addition to several hundred other books, monographs, special studies and related sources, the following have proved especially helpful:


ABERNETHY, T. P., *Three Virginia Frontiers,* University, La., Louisiana State University Press, 1940

ANDREWS, CHARLES M., *The Colonial Period of American History,* 4 vols., New Haven, Yale University Press, 1934-1938. *History of Maryland: Province and State,* New York, Doubleday, 1929

ANDREWS, M. P., *Virginia, The Old Dominion,* New York, Doubleday, 1927

BAIRD, C. W., *History of Huguenot Emigration to America,* 2 vols., New York, Dodd Mead, 1885

BARCK, OSCAR T., JR., and LEFLER, HUGH T., *Colonial America,* New York, Macmillan Co., 1958

BEATTY, R. C., *William Byrd of Westover,* Boston, Houghton Mifflin Co., 1932

BECKER, CARL L., *The Declaration of Independence*, New York, Harcourt, Brace & Co., 1922

BEVERLEY, ROBERT, *The History and Present State of Virginia*, Chapel Hill, North Carolina, University of North Carolina Press, 1947

BILLINGTON, R. A., with HEDGES, JAMES B., *Westward Expansion, A History of the American Frontier*, New York, Macmillan Co., 1949

BRIDENBAUGH, CARL, *Myths and Realities: Societies of the Colonial South*, Baton Rouge, Louisiana State University Press, 1952

BROOKS, CLEANTH, "The English Language in the South" in *A Vanderbilt Miscellany*, ed. by R. C. Beatty, Nashville, Vanderbilt University Press, 1944

BROWN, WILLIAM G., *The Lower South in American History*, New York, Macmillan Co., 1902

BRUCE, PHILLIP A., *Economic History of Virginia in the Seventeenth Century*, 2 vols., New York, Macmillan Co., 1896. *Social Life of Virginia in the Seventeenth Century*, Richmond, Virginia, privately printed, 1907

CHITWOOD, OLIVER P., *A History of Colonial America*, New York, Harper & Bros., 1931

CLARK, THOMAS D., *Frontier America: The Story of the Westward Movement*, New York, Scribner's, 1959. *A History of Kentucky*, New York, Prentice-Hall Inc., 1937

COIT, MARGARET L., *John C. Calhoun, American Portrait*, Boston, Houghton Mifflin Co., 1950

CONNELLEY, W. E., and COULTER, E. M., *History of Kentucky*, 5 vols., New York, American Historical Society, 1922

COULTER, E. M., *Georgia, A Short History*, Chapel Hill, University of North Carolina Press, 1947

CRANE, VERNER M., *The Southern Frontier, 1670-1732*, Durham, North Carolina, Duke University Press, 1928

DODD, WILLIAM E., *The Cotton Kingdom, A Chronicle of the Old South*, New Haven, Yale University Press, 1921. *The Old South: Struggles for Democracy*, New York, Macmillan Co., 1937

EATON, CLEMENT, *A History of the Old South*, New York, Macmillan Co., 1949

FITHIAN, PHILLIP VICKERS, *Journals and Letters*, Williamsburg, Virginia, Colonial Williamsburg Inc., 1943

FOREMAN, H. C., *The Architecture of the Old South*, Cambridge, Harvard University Press, 1948

FREEMAN, DOUGLAS SOUTHALL, *R. E. Lee*, 4 vols., New York, Scribner's, 1934-37. *George Washington*, 6 vols., New York, Scribner's, 1948-54

FRIES, ADELAIDE L., editor, *Records of the Moravians in North Carolina*, 7 vols., Raleigh, North Carolina, Edwards & Broughton Printing Co., 1922-1947. *The Road to Salem*, Chapel Hill, The University of North Carolina Press, 1944

HAMILTON, P. J., *Colonial Mobile*, Boston, Houghton Mifflin Co., 1897

HANSEN, MARCUS L., *The Atlantic Migration 1607-1860*, Cambridge, Harvard University Press, 1940

HESSELTINE, WILLIAM B., *The South in American History*, New York, Prentice-Hall Inc., 1943

JESTER, ANNIE L., *Domestic Life in Virginia in the Seventeenth Century*, Williamsburg, Virginia, 350th Anniversary Celebration Corp., 1957

KENDRICK, BENJAMIN B., and ARNETT, ALEX M., *The South Looks at Its Past*, Chapel Hill, University of North Carolina Press, 1935

KIMBALL, S. F., *Domestic Architecture of the American Colonies and of the Early Republic*, New York, Scribner's, 1922

LEFLER, HUGH T., and NEWSOME, ALBERT R., *North Carolina: The History of a Southern State*, Chapel Hill, University of North Carolina Press, 1954

MERENESS, NEWTON D., *Maryland as a Proprietary Province*, New York, Macmillan, 1901

NICHOLS, ROY F., *The Disruption of American Democracy*, New York, Macmillan, 1948

OSTERWEIS, R. G., *Romanticism and Nationalism in the Old South*, New Haven, Yale University Press, 1949

OWSLEY, FRANK L., *King Cotton Diplomacy*, Chicago, University of Chicago Press, 1959

PHILLIPS, U. B., *American Negro Slavery*, New York, D. Appleton & Co., 1918. *Life and Labor in the Old South*, Boston, Little Brown & Co., 1929

RANDALL, J. G., *The Civil War and Reconstruction*, New York, D. C. Heath & Co., 1937

SCHACHNER, NATHAN, *Thomas Jefferson*, 2 vols., New York, Appleton-Century-Crofts, Inc., 1951

SCHLESINGER, ARTHUR M., JR., *The Age of Jackson*, Boston, Little Brown & Co., 1945

SIMKINS, F. B., *The South, Old and New: A History, 1820-1947*, New York, Alfred A. Knopf, Inc., 1947

TURNER, FREDERICK JACKSON, *The United States, 1830-1850*, New York, Henry Holt & Co., Inc., 1935

WALLACE, DAVID D., *The History of South Carolina*, 4 vols., New York, American Historical Society, 1934

WERTENBAKER, THOMAS J., *The Shaping of Colonial Virginia*, New York, Russell & Russell, 1958. *The Old South: The Founding of American Civilization*, New York, Scribner's, 1942. *The Golden Age of Colonial Culture*, New York, New York University Press, 1942

WHIFFEN, MARCUS, *The Public Buildings of Williamsburg*, Williamsburg, Virginia, Colonial Williamsburg, 1958

WHITE, LAURA, *Robert Barnwell Rhett: Father of Secession*, New York, The Century Co., 1931

WINSOR, JUSTIN, *The Mississippi Basin*, Boston, Houghton, Mifflin & Co., 1895

WRIGHT, LOUIS B., *The Atlantic Frontier: Colonial American Civilization, 1607-1763*, New York, Alfred A. Knopf, Inc., 1947. *The First Gentlemen of Virginia*, San Marino, California, The Huntington Library, 1940

## ACKNOWLEDGMENTS

About twenty years ago I began to gather factual data and illustrations of life in the Old South, in the course of research and other trips about the area. Then, three and a half years ago, I intensified the process in a series of journeys to each of the Southern states and adjoining ones, visiting and revisiting many friends, and spending weeks or months of study in some of the nation's great repositories of documentary material, prints, photographs, and other illustrative data. Scores of people in libraries and other organizations, as well as writers and acquaintances, assisted me by going through their own collections or by suggesting dozens of other sources. Some of the material in these pages appears, I believe, for the first time between book covers.

During visits to Paris and London I took the opportunity to study data relating to American colonial periods, including broadsides and descriptive matter, prints and related material at the Bibliothèque Nationale, the British Museum, and other collections.

For whatever reason, no heavily illustrated book on the Old South has previously been published. That fact proved, in a fashion, a help to me in enlisting the aid of many institutions and many persons, professional and nonprofessional.

My particular thanks are due to Scott Bartlett, Robert Amussen, and Gabrielle Wunderlich of New York, who counseled with me in the arrangement of the illustrations and in the harassing problems of semifinal and final eliminations. Betsy Swanson of the Newcomb Art School was of special aid in the developing—sometimes several times in troublesome cases—of several hundred picture prints.

Robert D. Meade of Randolph-Macon College, Lynchburg, Virginia, the major authority on Patrick Henry, advised me on disputed points in that individual's life. Samuel Gaillard Stoney and Robert Molloy, the distinguished South Carolina authorities, gave counsel in my work in Charleston. Caldwell Delaney, author of many studies of Mobile, gave swift replies to my appeals, as did Vergil Bedsole, Archivist of Louisiana State University; Mrs. Dorothy Whittemore, head of the Reference Department of the Howard-Tilton Library of Tulane University; Roy Kidman, Acting Librarian; Mrs. Clayre Barr of the staff, and Robert Greenwood, Circulation Librarian.

Dr. Hugh Lefler, of the University of North Carolina history faculty, gave me time and sound advice in appraising data on his state, as did William S. Powell, Director, North Carolina Collection, University of North Carolina; James W. Patton, Director, Southern Historical Collection of the university library; Dr. Christopher Crittenden, Director of the State Department of Archives and History at Raleigh; Mrs. Joye E. Jordan, Museum Administrator; Samuel M. Boone, head of photo reproduction at the University of North Carolina Library, and Lambert Davis of the University of North Carolina Press.

During visits to Charleston, South Carolina, I was the beneficiary of guidance by Helen McCormack of the Gibbs Museum; Milby Burton, Director of the Charleston Museum; Virginia Rugheimer of the Charleston Library Society; Mrs. Granville Prior of the Charleston Historical Society Library; Emily Sanders of the Charleston County Free Library, Elizabeth Allen, and others of the same city.

Thomas D. Clark, author and historian of Lexington, Kentucky, was uniformly helpful in his various suggestions. Paul Harris of the J. B. Speed Art Museum, Louisville, provided illustrations and referred me to other sources. Richard H. Hill of the Filson Club, Winston Coleman of Winburn Farm, and Mrs. Isabelle McMeekin, all of Louisville, gave leads, and loaned books and monographs.

Karl Bickel, of Sarasota, authority on Florida's West Coast, responded to many inquiries, as did Ralph Newman of the Abraham Lincoln Bookshop in Chicago; and India Thomas and Eleanor S. Brockenbrough of the Confederate Museum at Richmond, Virginia.

Mrs. Marion Harris of the Harris Bookshop located out-of-print items, with the help of Mrs. Zelda Soignier of her staff. Albert Lieutaud, long-time authority on old prints and drawings, counseled many times, lent me materials, and gave expert advice.

Elizabeth E. Roth, First Assistant in the Print Room of the New York Public Library, suggested many collections and related data in her city and elsewhere. In Washington, Virginia Daiker, Reference Librarian, Library of Congress, and Milton Kaplan of the Maps Division, directed my search for Washington prints and other illustrations.

Others who gave consistent assistance were Mrs. Merrill Parrish Hudson, Memphis, Tennessee; Cameron Plummer, Mobile, Alabama; Marian Murray, Sarasota, Florida; John G. Baker, New York, of the National Audubon Society; Ruel McDaniel, Port La Vaca, Texas; Frank H. Wardlaw, Austin, Director of the University of Texas Press; T. T. Wentworth, Pensacola, Florida, historian; Robert Meyer, Jr., of Festival Information Service of New York; Congressman Charles E. Bennett of Jacksonville, Florida.

Harry Shaw Newman of the Old Print Shop, New York City, and Robert L. Harley of his staff, made many suggestions during the days of my inspection of their collection. Peter A. Brannon of Montgomery, Alabama; Anthony Ragusin of Biloxi, Mississippi; Bill Sharpe of *The State* magazine, Raleigh, North Carolina; M. Albert Krebs of the staff of the Bibliothèque Nationale, Paris; and Charles W. Porter, III, Herbert Evison, Roy M. Stubbs, C. R. Vinten, and others of the National Park Service were of help.

Jonathan Daniels of Raleigh aided me during my North Carolina visits. In Winston-Salem, Mrs. Kate Pyron, Librarian of Salem College; Mrs. Grace Siewers, Archivist of the Moravian Archives, and Mrs. Lloyd T. Presley of Old Salem, Inc., contributed much material. Lamar Wallis, Jesse Cunningham, and Carey Moore of the Memphis Public Library outlined data in their area. Essae M. Culver, Executive of the Louisiana State Library, and Charlotte Capers, Director of the Mississippi Department of Archives and History, called my attention to Southern collections.

David J. Mays, chairman of the Virginia Library Board; Randolph Church, State Librarian, Virginia; Milton Russell, head of the Reference Department; and W. Edwin Hemphill of the library's *Cavalcade* magazine, assisted in numerous inquiries. Lovick Pierce, publisher, and Leland D. Case, editor of *Together*, publication of the Methodist Publishing House, sent data on earlier Southern religious work.

Florence Kane Reynolds, my sister, assisted in all phases of my research, manuscript and copy reading. Mrs. W. J. Kane and Anna Kane also gave steady aid. Charles E. Frampton of the Louisiana State Museum came to my assistance on several occasions, as did Francis Haber, of the Department of Social Sciences, University of Florida, at Gainesville.

In Baltimore I benefited by the counsel of Senator George Radcliffe, President of the Maryland Historical Society; James W. Foster, Director; Mrs. Ferdinand Latrobe, Frederick Stieff, and Louis Azrael.

In Williamsburg, Virginia, during several of my visits, many of the staff members gave time and advice, including George B. Eager, Thad Tate, Jr., Rose Belt, Van McNair, Lucius Battle, Donald J. Gonzales, and others.

John Jennings, Director of the Virginia Historical Society; Miriam Babb, of the North Carolina Department of Conservation and Development; David J. Harkness, of the University of Tennessee Division of University Extension, and Colonel Allen Julian, answered a series of questions.

In Richmond Mrs. Ralph Catterall of the Valentine Museum, and her assistant, Elizabeth J. Dance, worked steadily and resourcefully in helping me to identify earlier photographs and drawings of Virginia. Joe Templeton, Director of the Mobile Public

Library, and Arless Nixon, Librarian, of the Fort Worth Public Library, gave similar aid.

In New Orleans I was the beneficiary of advice by John Hall Jacobs, City Librarian, and members of his staff, including George King Logan, Ruth Renaud, Margaret Ruckert, Gladys Peyronnin, Mrs. Alice V. Westfeldt, Mrs. Ellen Tilger, Ruth Scheuermann, Mrs. Bernice Zibilich, Frederick Low, Marion Mason, Adelaide Schmidt, Mrs. Susan Baughman, Mrs. Marion Borchers and Mrs. Elizabeth Buchanan.

At the Howard Tilton Library of Tulane University I was helped over a long period by Betty Mailhes, Mrs. Martha Robertson, Mrs. Beverly Peery, Mrs. Camille Jones, Mrs. Laura Hope, Mrs. Molly Eustis, Mrs. Margery Ohlsen, Mrs. Fay Swanson, Mrs. Elizabeth Beelman, Anna Wood, Mrs. Eunice Van Kirk, Mrs. Connie Griffith, Mrs. Berthe Baker, and Mrs. Aline Richter Stevens. James W. Dyson, Librarian of Loyola University at New Orleans, advised me regarding his collections. In Baltimore Miss Elizabeth Litsinger, of the Enoch Pratt Library, and Miss Martha Ann Peters, her assistant in the Maryland Room, helped me to trace many involved references.

James Meeks, Librarian of the Dallas Public Library; Mrs. Margaret Pratt, head of the Texas Local History and Genealogy Department; and Marie Stanley, her assistant, made special loans of books and photographs. James Record of the Fort Worth *Star-Telegram* made available one or two historic Texas pictures. Others to whom I feel indebted are: Angela Gregory, Captain Robert Estachy, Joseph M. Shields, Jr., Dan S. Leyrer, Mrs. William C. Wharton, Roger Baudier, James Bezou, Mrs. Robert G. Robinson, Alistair Maitland, Consul General of Great Britain; Robert Turner, Mother M. Claire Rivet, O.S.U., Archivist of the Ursuline Convent, all of New Orleans.

Ruby Parker and Mary Herbert, Pensacola, Florida; Mrs. Kay Bynum and Mrs. Dever Woods, Corpus Christi, Texas; Lon Tinkle, Decherd Turner, and Evelyn Oppenheimer, Dallas, Texas; Roy Bird Cook, Charleston, West Virginia; Mrs. E. Randolph Preston, Winston-Salem, North Carolina; Richard Walser, Raleigh, North Carolina; Chip Chafetz, New York City; Gertie Espenan, Baton Rouge, Louisiana; Kate Savage, Baltimore, Maryland; Dr. N. Philip Norman, New York City; Mrs. Marie Eggleston Thompson, Charleston, South Carolina; Boyd Stutler, Charleston, West Virginia;

Jay W. Johns, Charlottesville, Virginia; Mrs.Mary Eleanor Clark, Chattanooga, Tennessee; Grover C. Henley and Walter A. Anderson, Jacksonville, Florida; William S. Lacy, Jr., and Clifford Dowdey, Richmond, Virginia; Dr. Fred Hanna and Mrs. Kathryn A. Hanna, Winter Park, and Lile Chew, St. Petersburg, Florida;

Dr. Alfred Leland Crabb and Stanley Horn, Chattanooga, Tennessee; Stanley P. Deas, New Orleans; Mrs. Powers McElveen, Sumter, and Mrs. St. Julien R. Childs, Mrs. Cambridge M. Trott, Jr., the Reverend S. Grayson Clary, and Joseph E. Jenkins, Charleston, South Carolina;

Curtis Carroll Davis, Baltimore, Maryland; J. McHenry Jones and J. Holliday Veal, Pensacola, and Mr. and Mrs. Tod Swalm, Sarasota, Florida; Reber Henderson and Mrs. Edith Wyatt Moore, Natchez, Mississippi; Admiral Whittaker Riggs and Walter Hoover, New Orleans, Louisiana;

Mr. James Bailey, Baton Rouge, Louisiana; Howard Gwaltney, Smithfield, Virginia; Franklin M. Garrett, Atlanta, Georgia; Robert Armstrong Andrews, Edisto Island, South Carolina; Pollard White, Cadiz, Kentucky; S. J. ("Stonewall Jackson") Birshtein, Clarksburg, West Virginia;

Mrs. R. C. Haynes, Ennis, Texas; Gordon L. Atwater, New Orleans; Robert H. North, Washington, D. C.; Ivy W. Duggan, Atlanta, Georgia; Caroline S. Coleman, Fountain Inn, South Carolina; Glendy Culligan and Hudson Grunewald, Washington, D. C.; North Callahan, Bronxville, New York; Mrs. Paula Coad, Savannah, Georgia; Mrs. Wallace Westfieldt and Mrs. Frances Bryson Moore, New Orleans;

Mrs. Celestine Sibley and Mr. Frank Daniell, Atlanta, Georgia; the late Jean Selby, Vicksburg; Mrs. Earle Rowe Glenn, Natchez, Mississippi; David Westheimer, Houston,

Texas; the late Martha Rivers Adams, Lynchburg, Virginia; Mrs. Edythe Capreol, Beaumont, and Vernol Mayers, Houston, Texas;

Mrs. Margaret Dixon, Baton Rouge, Louisiana; William Fountaine, Columbus, Ohio; Mrs. Gertrude Carruth, Beaumont, Texas; Edith Dupre, Lafayette, Louisiana; Fred Dobie, Austin, Texas; John Temple Graves and Sallie Hill, Birmingham, Alabama; Mrs. Anna Clyde Plunkett, Waco, Texas; Louise Guyol and Flo Field, New Orleans, Louisiana; S. Sanford Levy, Judge Anna Veters Levy, Daisy Poole, and Dolly Veters, New Orleans;

Mrs. David Terry, Little Rock, Arkansas; and Mrs. Percy Leahmon McGeehee, Chicago; Mrs. Esther de Vasques, San Antonio, and Mrs. H. Welge Lewis, Fredericksburg, Texas; H. C. Nixon, Nashville, Tennessee; Mrs. Fay Profilet, St. Louis; Mrs. George Coleman, Williamsburg, Virginia; Mrs. Gay White and Pressly Phillips, St. Petersburg, Florida; Mrs. Edith Amsler, Houston, Texas;

Julien Martin, Wilmington, North Carolina; Mrs. Elmer Deiss, Lexington, Kentucky; James Murfin, Hagerstown, Maryland; Julia Estill, Fredericksburg, Texas; James Ricau, New York; Mrs. Yvon du Quesnay and Yvonne du Quesnay, New Orleans; Edna H. Fowler, Los Angeles; Mrs. Walter C. White, Gates Mills, Ohio; Mrs. F. M. Robinson, McAllen, Texas;

Jane Buchanan, Caney Creek Community Center, Pippa Passes, Kentucky; Sidney S. Field, New York; Mrs. Jessie Smith Young, Cartersville, Georgia; Mrs. John D. Britton, Kingstree, South Carolina; Mrs. Shackelford Miller, Louisville, Kentucky; Mrs. Ruby Donahey, St. Petersburg, Florida; Louis Engelke, San Antonio, Texas;

Dr. W. G. Bean, Lexington, Virginia; Mrs. Marie Jackson Arnold Pifer, Buckhannon, West Virginia; Patricia O'Driscoll, London; Monroe F. Cockrell, Evanston, Illinois; Margaret Preston, Atlanta, Georgia; Professor Chalmers Davidson, of Davidson, North Carolina; Junius R. Fishburne and Miss Anna Barringer, Charlottesville, Virginia;

E. B. (Pete) Long, Oak Park, Illinois; Elizabeth Jarrett, Chattanooga, Tennessee; Mrs. Ed Vandergriff, Blacksburg, and V. C. Barringer and John Barringer, and Dr. J. Morrison Hutcheson, Richmond, Virginia; J. Walker Caldwell, Roanoke, North Carolina; Mrs. W. F. McFarland, Florence, Alabama; Mrs. B. Morrison Sales, Lexington, Virginia; Sylvester Vigilante, Ossining, New York; John K. Bettersworth, State College, Mississippi;

Milton Edward Lord, Director of the Boston Public Library; Richard G. Hensley, Chief of Reference and Research, and Mrs. Marjorie Bouquet, Deputy Supervisor; David C. Mearns, Chief of the Manuscript Division, Library of Congress;

Floyd Shoemaker, Secretary, and Sarah Guitar, Reference Librarian, State Historical Society of Missouri, Columbia; Clarence E. Miller, Librarian, and Elizabeth Tindall, Reference Librarian, St. Louis Mercantile Library Association; Charles Ravenswaay, Director, and Mrs. Eileen J. Cox, Reference Librarian, Missouri Historical Society, St. Louis;

J. Paul Hudson, Museum Specialist, National Park Service, Richmond, Virginia; Eleanor Norton, Librarian, Front Royal, Virginia; Lucia M. Tryon, Librarian, Pensacola, Florida, Public Library; Sarah E. Maret, Librarian, Athens Regional Library, Athens, Georgia; Mrs. Josephine Johnson, Reference Librarian, Louisville Free Public Library; Doris C. Wailes, Administrative Assistant, St. Augustine Historical Society, Florida; Fant H. Thornley, Director, Birmingham, Alabama, Public Library, and Helen Stamps, Assistant;

Edith Overbey, Pittsylvania County Public Library, Chatham, Virginia; Helen C. Frick, Director, and Mrs. Henry W. Howell, Jr., Librarian, Frick Art Reference Library, New York City; Mrs. Bettie Giles, History Department, Roanoke Public Library, Roanoke, Virginia; Virginia Ebeling, Librarian, Ohio County Public Library, Wheeling, West Virginia;

Stanley Pargellis, Librarian, Newberry Library, Chicago; Janice S. Brown, Chief of

Reference and Circulation, Smithsonian Institution, Washington, D. C.; Annie Lou Flesher, Librarian, Free Public Library of St. Augustine, Florida; Mrs. Phyllis S. Burson, Librarian, La Retama Public Library, Corpus Christi, Texas; Mrs. Alice Hook, Picture Division of the Special Libraries Association, Cincinnati;

Josephine Cobb, Archivist in Charge, Still Picture Branch, General Services Administration, National Archives, Washington, D. C.; Kenneth K. McCormick, Historian and Archivist, State Department of History, and Frances L. Gerard, head, Reference Department, Kanawha County Public Library, Charleston, West Virginia; Ted R. Worley, Executive Secretary, Arkansas Department of Archives and History, and Orville W. Taylor of the staff, Little Rock, Arkansas;

Norma B. Cass, Reference Librarian, University of Kentucky, Lexington; J. H. Easterby, Director, South Carolina Archives Department, Columbia, South Carolina; Arthur M. Kirkby, Librarian, and Mary C. Brown, Sergeant Memorial Room, Norfolk Public Library, Norfolk, Virginia; Norah Albanell, Chief of Public Services, Columbus Memorial Library, Pan American Union, Washington, D. C.;

C. Percy Powell, Research Director, Lincoln Sesquicentennial Commission, Washington, D. C.; Mrs. Forman Hawes, Librarian of the Georgia Historical Society, Savannah; Géraldine Le May, Library Director, and Joy Trulock, Assistant in Reference Department, Savannah Public Library; Walter Stillwell, Sr., President of the Savannah Historical Research Association; Margaret F. Willis and Jessie Orgain, Reference Librarians, State Library Extension Division, Frankfort, Kentucky;

Cornelia Davis, Librarian, Public Library, Chestertown, Maryland; Erin Humphrey, Librarian, El Paso Public Library, Texas; Mrs. Elizabeth Edwards, Librarian, and Mrs. Kathryn P. Arnold, Historical Collection, Chattanooga Public Library, Tennessee; Betty W. Service, Sarasota Public Library, Florida; Mrs. Mildred B. Turnbull, Librarian, Warder Public Library, Springfield, Ohio;

James H. Renz, Librarian, Florida Collection, Miami Public Library, Florida; Mrs. Virginia H. Taylor, State Archivist, Texas State Library, Archives Division, Austin, Texas; Marie Berry, Reference Librarian, San Antonio Public Library, Texas;

Mrs. Margaret Armstrong, Librarian, Palmetto Public Library, Florida; Foster L. Barnes, Director, Stephen Foster Memorial Commission, White Springs, Florida; Ella May Thornton, State Librarian, and Vera Jameson, Associate, Georgia State Library, Atlanta, Georgia;

Mrs. Grace Carnahan, Librarian, Pulaski County Free Library, Pulaski, Virginia; Mrs. W. W. Griffith, Librarian, Public Library, Fredericksburg, Virginia; Francis R. Berkeley, Jr., Curator of Manuscripts, and William H. Runge, Assistant, Alderman Library, University of Virginia, Charlottesville; Mrs. Adrian Belt, Librarian, Morgantown Public Library, West Virginia;

Dorothy Dodd, State Librarian, Tallahassee, Florida; Louise Crawford, Librarian, and May H. Edwards of the City-County Memorial Library, Bay St. Louis, Mississippi; Mrs. Miriam G. Reeves, Librarian, Louisiana State Department of Education; Emerson Greenaway, Director, Free Public Library of Philadelphia; Llerena Friend, Librarian, Texas Collection, University of Texas, Austin;

Maria Person, Librarian, Gulfport Carnegie-Harrison County Library, Mississippi; Mildred Stevenson, Reference Librarian, Rosenberg Library, Galveston, Texas; May Sherard, Librarian of the Vicksburg Public Library, Mississippi; Gratia A. Meyers, Librarian of the Carnegie Library of Bradenton, Florida; Eleanor Norton, Librarian, Samuels Library, Front Royal, Virginia.

# INDEX

*Illustrations are in italic; text references are in ordinary type.*